I0093375

DISRESPECTFUL DEMOCRACY

EMILY SYDNOR

DISRESPECTFUL DEMOCRACY

The Psychology of Political Incivility

Columbia University Press / New York

Columbia University Press
Publishers Since 1893
New York   Chichester, West Sussex
cup.columbia.edu
Copyright © 2019 Columbia University Press
All rights reserved

Library of Congress Cataloging-in-Publication Data
A complete CIP record is available from the Library of Congress.
ISBN 978-0-231-18924-8 (cloth)
ISBN 978-0-231-54825-0 (e-book)
LCCN: 2019021844

Cover design: Lisa Hamm

CONTENTS

CONTENTS

5. MIMICRY AND TEMPER TANTRUMS:
Political Discussion and Engagement

110

6. A MORE DISRESPECTFUL DEMOCRACY?

141

ACKNOWLEDGMENTS

W RITING A BOOK is no easy feat, yet it pales in comparison to the challenge of articulating my gratitude for the individuals and institutions that have helped me through this process. First and foremost, I have to thank Columbia University Press and Stephen Wesley, who championed this project from the moment I showed up at APSA thinking it could be a book. Even when he was buried under piles of acquisitions and managing dozens of authors, he read drafts, offered insightful comments, and helped me navigate the challenging waters of the dissertation-turned-book process.

It is rare in academia that you find a university and a department that are well suited to your strengths and preferences, and even more so to find that home as an ABD grad student. But from the first thirty-minute interview I had with Alisa Gaunder and Shannon Mariotti, I knew Southwestern was one of those places. Since I started at Southwestern, Alisa Gaunder has carved time out of her busy schedule as dean to be my department colleague, offering advice about the publication process and strategies for effective project management. Shannon Mariotti and Eric Selbin have helped me navigate drafts and reviewer responses and talked ideas out over lunches and in the spare moments between classes. Bob Snyder helped me keep the project relevant to contemporary politics as we struggled with current events over 600 Degrees pizza. To the four of you: thank you for being incredible mentors, respectful colleagues, and valuable friends throughout this process. And to Samuel Kim, now an SU alum, my profound gratitude for your willingness to join forces with a brand new professor to work on the experiment in chapter 4.

Of course, the journey did not start at Southwestern. This book started as dissertation work at the University of Virginia, where I had the fortune to work with top scholars in both political science and psychology. Nick Winter, Paul Freedman, and Lynn Sanders taught me how to be a scholar of political behavior and offered the support and resources necessary to become an independent member of the academic community. Brian Nosek invited me into his lab and introduced me to a community of scholars who taught me psychological principles, debated political policies, and exemplified the collegiality we strive for in academia. Edward Smith showed up in the first discussion I ever taught, struggling to understand the concepts underlying racial politics in the United States. Two years later, he graduated with honors from UVA, having conducted independent research on the effects of voter ID laws. It was my first "proud teacher" moment, and our work on the presence of incivility in television news cemented my love for collaborative research with undergraduates. I am pleased to include our research together in chapter 4 of this book. Finally, I would not have ended up at UVA without Kim Gross's support (and University of Michigan connections) and Jerry Manheim's prodding during my time at George Washington University's School of Media and Public Affairs. The thrill of designing and conducting experimental research started with my SMPA honors thesis and has never left.

None of the empirical work included here would have been possible without generous assistance from several sources. Many thanks to the University of Virginia's Department of Politics and to Southwestern University for their research support. The Political Psychology Working Group at the University of Virginia and UVA's Bankard Predoctoral Fellowship funded the experiments in chapters 3 and 4. And the experiment in chapter 5 would not have been possible without the generous sample size afforded by the TESS Young Investigators competition.

The project has also benefited from feedback from a variety of groups along the way. Many thanks to attendees of the Political Communication workshop series at the University of Texas at Austin's Moody College of Communication, especially Talia Stroud, Sharon Jarvis, and Bethany Albertson. I am also grateful to Robert Boatright and other faculty affiliated with the National Institute for Civil Discourse for their discussion of a part of this work at their national research convening in 2017.

No one deserves more thanks than Emily Pears. A scholar of the Founding and a natural skeptic of empirical research, Emily has nonetheless read every element of this manuscript, much of it multiple times. She has helped me focus on the big picture, interrogated my theory, and pushed me to think about the broader implications and complications inherent in studying something as contested as the nature of civility. She also cut words, clarified my writing, and generally held me accountable to self-imposed deadlines and writing goals.

Many other individuals have made this book possible by keeping me sane outside of the office. I am thankful to have so many supporters in my academic network and beyond who were happy to talk about the book, but also to go to a movie, play softball, or grab dinner. Andrew Clarke, Justin Peck, Boris Heersink, Joel Voss, Lauren Santoro, and Kylee Britzman have become important collaborators and conference buddies, trading research ideas and teaching strategies. Mike Gesinski, Ron Geibel, and Jess and Joe Hower have helped make Texas feel like home, and I cannot thank John and Lauren Ross enough for their sense of adventure and excellent vacation planning. All the foot fives in the world could not capture my love and respect for Elizabeth Kaknes, Sarah Andrews, and Heidi Schramm. As scholars and as friends, they have been there to celebrate every success and provide support through every struggle.

Of course, I cannot forget my many cheerleaders and supporters outside of the academic world. Allie, Alan, George, Heather, Lyle, Alice, Andre, Crystal, Alister, Alex, Casey, Amalfi, LaMarre, Lauren, Matt, Kate, Jeff, and Lizzie were always available if I needed a sounding board. Emory, Theo, Henry, Abigail, Adah, Alex, and Alex proved to be perfect, adorable distractions from academia. Catherine, Hannah, and Cadence showed up when I wanted company, encouraged me through my frustrations, and remind me that writing this book counts as a "major life event." Katie encouraged me to watch *The Bold Type*, ultimately helping me identify the scene that would open the book. I have been blessed with these and so many other friends who supported this manuscript by supporting my life outside of my job—by being travel buddies, teammates, dining companions, cat sitters, and dance partners. I am so grateful for each and every one of you.

Mom and Dad: words fail to capture my thanks and love for the role you have played in where I am today. Your encouragement made it possible for me to take risks, challenge myself, and pursue a love of reading and writing, whether it was elementary school stories about cats or this book. Barrett, thanks for playing along, even when it results in your getting pushed off the sheep. You force me to strengthen my arguments and reflect on my political ideals in the best ways possible. I love you all, and everyone else that I have inevitably, accidentally left off this list.

DISRESPECTFUL DEMOCRACY

1

INTEGRATING THE POLITICAL
AND THE PSYCHOLOGICAL

THE TELEVISION SERIES *The Bold Type* tells the fictional story of three young adult women, Jane, Kat, and Sutton, navigating challenges in their professional and personal lives while working at a fashion magazine in New York City. In the third episode, Kat, the social-media director for the magazine, is trolled online for publishing an article about how virtual reality (VR) technology is more likely to make women experience motion sickness than men (Weyr 2017). As the nasty tweets, rape threats, and harassment escalate, the viewers watch Kat and her friends arrive at different strategies for handling the trolls.

JANE: Maybe you should stop looking.

KAT: Oh, jeez. Oh, yeah, I'm a slut because I took a topless photo of myself in the south of France. What is wrong with these people?

SUTTON: Okay, hey, look. It's not all bad. The CEO of a VR company tweeted at you. Emily Ramos says "Sorry for what you're going through. I support you and have your back."

KAT: Oh, wow. Followed immediately by someone who thinks my boobs aren't that great. [Starts typing a response] "He says as he takes a break from masturbating in his parents' basement."

JANE: Come on. Don't engage.

KAT: I'm not engaging, Jane. I'm fixing this.

Kat's fictional story reflects a contemporary reality: incivility is increasingly a part of our online experience. While incivility comprises a relatively small part of the total text in Internet comments sections (Coe, Kenski, and Rains 2014; Muddiman and Stroud 2016, 14), it has nonetheless become a creeping presence on social media. And it has become even more central to political discourse in the past few years as Americans elected a president who is particularly prolific on Twitter. The *New York Times* keeps a running list of the "People, Places and Things Donald Trump Has Insulted on Twitter" since he declared his candidacy in 2015. The list started with 199 items; as of February 2019, it had grown to 567 entries, many of which had been insulted multiple times (Lee and Quealy 2019). As incivility becomes more prominent in online political discourse, those who are active on social media—whether for fun or as part of their job—must figure out how they are going to respond when things get nasty.

Kat's experience is emblematic of that of many female journalists who regularly face online incivility and harassment as part of their job. In a series of interviews with women in journalism around the world, Gina Chen and her colleagues (2018) found that many journalists have specific strategies—blocking users, filtering out comments that include specific words—for combatting trolls; others shift how they cover the news, focusing on positive stories or showing multiple sides of issues to avoid abuse. The approach an individual journalist takes is to some extent dictated by the institutional norms and practices of her own media outlet, but it is also a matter of personal preference and comfort when faced with conflict.

Ultimately, Kat decides that the solution to handling the trolls is to engage with civil comments online, while simultaneously giving Emily Ramos, the VR CEO, the first shot at working with the magazine to develop VR fashion tools. Before she arrives at this decision, however, we see different reactions to targeted online incivility. Kat's gut reaction is to respond to the trolls, matching their incivility and aggression with her own insults and outrage. Jane, on the other hand, encourages her "not to engage," to step away from Twitter and, in doing so, protect herself from the barrage of hate.

Why do Jane and Kat have these divergent reactions to incivility? And what are the consequences? In this book, I explore how a personal predisposition—conflict orientation, or one's innate reaction to conflict—shapes how the American public reacts to incivility. Political thinkers and democratic theorists worry that incivility threatens the survival of American democracy. Without mutual respect and tolerance, we are incapable of arriving at compromises in public policy or agreement about national identity and values (Mill [1859] 1989; Gutmann and Thompson 1996). Yet modern critiques of civility's democratic role point to its power to silence dissent and maintain an unequal status quo (Chafe 1980; Zerilli 2014).

The ideal tone of discourse falls somewhere in the balance: a politics grounded in mutual recognition and respect, where incivility is only employed strategically to call attention to cases where that respect is absent. In the absence of this ideal, I argue that we must pay greater attention to individuals' reactions to routine incivility—the incivility experienced when you turn on the television or open your social-media apps—while recognizing that those reactions will differ among people.

Individuals experience conflict in different ways. Some people enjoy arguments and are perfectly comfortable entering a shouting match in public; others are uncomfortable at the sight of an argument and avoid face-to-face confrontation. I expect that people on the polar ends of this spectrum of "conflict orientation" will have different emotional and behavioral reactions to contemporary in-your-face politics, regardless of their gender, partisan identity, or ideological commitments.

Kat, for instance, finds arguments exciting. She is quick to jump into the fray, whether to fight back on Twitter or argue with a man on the street when he insults her Muslim friend for wearing a headscarf. Jane, on the other hand, is naturally inclined to avoid conflict. She shies away from confrontation in most situations and worries about how to deal with conflicts with her boss, her boyfriend, or the subject of her latest news piece. It is no surprise, then, that when faced with uncivil comments, the two women have very different responses. You can sense Jane's anxiety about engaging with the Twitter trolls, and her response—"don't engage"—demonstrates her desire to step away from the conflict. Kat, on the other hand, is angry with her attackers, and one senses an underlying enthusiasm for the fight. These two women have a lot in common—age, occupation, education, political perspectives—yet their reactions to incivility lead them to very different behaviors. This book focuses on those reactions: the interaction between conflict orientation and incivility in political media. How does the presence or absence of incivility in television coverage of politics and in entertainment differentially affect us?

The media cover political issues ranging from economic deficits to immigration policy to appropriation of funds to Planned Parenthood as civil or uncivil, sometimes all within the same sixty-second television package. Those who are uncomfortable with conflict, whom I call "conflict-avoidant," are anxious and disgusted in the face of incivility. But the "conflict-approaching" react with enthusiasm or amusement to the same coverage. Besides this store of positive feelings toward political coverage, the conflict-approaching will go on to participate in more political activities, particularly those in which they might face conflict and incivility themselves.

Incivility causes a set of Americans to engage in politics, but it can also alter the quality of that engagement. Incivility breeds incivility. As citizens see name-calling and vitriol as part and parcel of elite political communication, they are more likely to use it themselves. The conflict-approaching, however, are equipped with more armor in the battle for civil discourse. They react more positively toward incivility than their conflict-avoidant peers, but they are less likely to search it out in their media diet and no more or less likely to use it in their own political discussions. In the meantime, they are more engaged in political activities beyond voting—they protest, they call their representatives, and they attempt to persuade their peers. Just as time, money, and skills act as resources for citizen engagement in politics (Brady, Verba, and Schlozman 1995), so too does one's psychological response to conflict.

Our reactions to incivility are, of course, not only a reflection of our orientation toward conflict. Incivility is strategically deployed by politicians, journalists, and citizens alike (Herbst 2010), and our response is contingent on our relationship to those using the language and our own preferences and identities. It should be no surprise, then, that our partisanship colors our identification of and reaction to incivility. When incivility comes from their own party or affiliated media (e.g., MSNBC for Democrats or Fox for Republicans), people are more likely to use incivility themselves, but they are also likely to depolarize, becoming more ambivalent about the two political parties. When incivility is used in attacks against their party, however, people are not only more likely to use incivility in their own responses, they are also more likely to react by moving to the extremes (Gervais 2015; Druckman et al. 2019).

To the dismay of some theorists and practitioners, democratic politics will never be exclusively civil. People will disagree, and they will disagree with strong emotions and in emotional language that reflects their identities and values. The goal of this book is to demonstrate that some— those who are more likely to approach conflict—continue to learn about and participate in politics even when it gets ugly. While there is constant tension between participatory and deliberative approaches to democracy, the conflict-approaching are better equipped to walk that tightrope. Meanwhile, the conflict-avoidant stand just outside the ring, discouraged and disillusioned by the toxicity of uncivil politics.

AMERICA'S "CIVILITY PROBLEM"

If the first step to overcoming a problem is to acknowledge you have one, American democracy should be well on its way to rehabilitation. Americans are not afraid to admit that they have a "civility problem"—that our political leaders and the mass public struggle to be polite or respectful to those with whom they disagree. Americans also prefer elected officials who stand their ground to those who choose compromise. In 2010, Lanny Davis, founder of the Civility Project and former White House counsel to President Clinton, commented that the level of vitriol was the worst he'd seen in his forty years in Washington (Karl and Simmons 2010). In a June 2017 PBS/NPR/Marist poll, 70 percent of respondents said they believe the overall tone and level of civility in Washington has gotten worse since Donald J. Trump was elected president (Taylor 2017). When pressed to allocate blame for increasing incivility, individuals point to both the politicians and the media (Weber Shandwick, KRC Research, and Powell Tate 2013).

Americans are quick to acknowledge that incivility is a nationwide problem, but most report that it has little effect on their own behavior. Public relations firm Weber Shandwick reports that Americans encounter some form of incivility about 10.6 times in an average week, or one to two times per day. Half of these experiences are offline, in "real life," while the other half are online (Weber Shandwick, KRC Research, and Powell Tate 2018). While citizens acknowledge that incivility has become a daily part of their lives and are quick to point fingers at politicians and the media as the cause, only a quarter of respondents report that they have taken any action in response.

Incivility shapes Americans' political behavior. But incivility does not affect everyone equally or in the same direction. Instead, its power depends on how an individual is predisposed to react to conflict—whether the person finds it exciting, uncomfortable, or so anxiety-inducing as to be avoided it at all costs. Psychological conflict orientation and political incivility shape our emotional reactions to media content and, ultimately, our decisions about political news consumption and engagement in political discussion and activities. From this perspective, the rise of incivility in political media—critical institutions that inform and motivate citizens—has transformed the nature of who gets involved by changing the resources needed to successfully engage with the style and structure of political discourse. Specifically, citizens must now regularly tolerate or even welcome incivility in the political sphere. Citizens with a conflict-approaching orientation, who enjoy conflict, can navigate political media and certain political activities in a way that their conflict-avoidant counterparts do not.

It has been well established that incivility, whether on television, in the comments section of a newspaper article, or over social media, has a range of good and ill effects on political behavior. Scholars have emphasized television's unique visual perspective on politics, our tendency to react to what we see on screen as though we are experiencing it face to face, and the ease with which camera angles can be used to violate social norms for personal space (Mutz 2015; Reeves and Nass 1996). Each of these makes it easier for televised incivility to affect those watching—reducing their trust

6

in government, their perceptions of its legitimacy, and their participation in it (Brooks and Geer 2007; Geer and Lau 2006; Kahn and Kenney 1999; Mutz and Reeves 2005).

The rise of the Internet made incivility's presence even more explicit. The web offers a cloak of anonymity and limited constraints on citizens' ability to express their opinions. These structural components of online discourse facilitate uncivil behavior to the point that scholars find considerably more uncivil behavior online than in face-to-face interactions (although not quite as much as on television or talk radio) (Chen 2017; Coe, Kenski, and Rains 2014; Papacharissi 2004; Sobeiraj and Berry 2011). Consequently, online incivility begets incivility—exposure to uncivil comments makes people more likely to critique the original poster or engage in flaming[1]—as well as polarization, closed-mindedness, and lower credibility for political news sites (Borah 2014; Gervais 2015; Hmielowski, Hutchens, and Cicchirillo 2014; Thorson, Vraga, and Ekdale 2010).

CONFLICT COMMUNICATION IN POLITICS

Political science is an inherently interdisciplinary field, and the subfields of political communication and political psychology are unabashedly so. Both disciplines are interested in the roots and results of political behavior, but with different antecedents. Political psychologists turn to cognitive and social patterns to explain behavior; political communication examines the causes and effects of media and interpersonal communication within the political sphere.

While political-communication scholars have been investigating the political effects of incivility, political psychologists have grown more interested in the role of individual differences and personality traits in influencing political behavior. These traits are "internal psychological structures that are relatively fixed and enduring, that are susceptible to observation, and that predict behavior" (Mondak et al. 2010, 85). Psychologists believe personality develops and crystalizes in youth, remaining relatively fixed throughout life. Research on personality and politics has focused on the core dispositional traits commonly referred to as the Big Five (e.g., Gerber et al. 2010; Mondak 2010) and midlevel individual differences that are thought to be products of dispositional traits and the environment, such as altruism (Fowler 2006; Jankowski 2015), racial resentment (Feldman and Huddy 2005; Kinder and Sanders 1996), and right-wing authoritarianism (e.g., Hetherington and Weiler 2009; Stenner 2005). Findings about the relationships between personality and political participation have been mixed, however, particularly for the Big Five traits. For example, in one sample, Mondak and Halperin (2008) found that agreeableness, a prosocial or communal orientation that can include traits like altruism, has a negative effect on voter turnout. However, this finding was not replicated in their second sample. They also found that agreeableness can lead to greater participation in certain types of local political participation, but not participation at the national level.

How can we reconcile these divergent findings? Mondak and his colleagues (2010) argue for a more complex framework for the relationship between personality, environment, and behavior. On the one hand, they argue, much media-effects research has focused on isolated homogeneous effects, such as the assumption that the media's agenda-setting power influences the prioritization of political issues irrespective of the attributes of the citizens watching the news.[2] On the other hand, political scientists can investigate situational, heterogeneous effects in which variations in people's psychological predispositions lead them to respond differently to the same environmental stimuli. As Mondak et al. explain, "For both personality traits and environmental factors, we must detail in clear terms how and why effects on political behavior are expected to operate, and ultimately in what circumstances" (2010, 91). This book applies this framework to individual traits operating within a specific media environment. The uncivil political environment influences political behavior, but how and to what extent differs depending on the individual's predisposition toward conflict. Put another way, conflict orientation can shape political behavior, but the expression of these effects differs across civil and uncivil media environments.

CONFLICT COMMUNICATION IN POLITICS

Harold Lasswell (1936) states that communication is about "who says what, to whom, in what channel, with what effect" and that "politics is who gets what, when, and how." If both of these statements are true, then political communication is rife with conflict, as people seek to use an increasing range of interpersonal and mediated platforms to persuade others that resources should be distributed in their favor. Policy arguments are still made in the op-ed pages of newspapers, but they are also found in citizens' tweets at congressional representatives and the back-and-forth discussion of guests and journalists on cable news channels. It is easier than ever for citizens to connect to political elites directly through social media and express their opinions about the allocation of political resources. The news media also make it easier for political elites to go head to head in making their public case for policies, programs, and political decisions. Political communication is frequently the communication of disagreement, of competing perspectives, and of conflict.

Yet we should not think of communication of political conflict on a one-dimensional scale. Political-conflict communication more accurately contains two dimensions: the degree of disagreement over substance, and the degree of incivility. As Brooks and Geer note, "some comments can, in fact, be quite critical of an opponent and still not earn a classification as 'uncivil.' Incivility requires going an extra step; that is, adding inflammatory comments that add little in the way of substance to the discussion" (2007, 5). While incivility can take many forms and definitions, I use it throughout this work to emphasize a particular tone—a continuum that ranges from the polite to insults to racial slurs and obscenities.

Political communication can vary in substantive disagreement and incivility simultaneously. For example, imagine that NBC's *Meet the Press* invites Democrat Nancy Pelosi and Republican Mitch McConnell to discuss the government's response to increased militarization in the Middle East. The two could agree on the substantive issue and solutions to the problem at hand (unlikely, in this case) or disagree. They could also convey their agreement or disagreement in more or less civil ways. It is one thing to say, "I do not think that sending troops is the most effective strategy," and another to say, "You're insane to think sending troops is a remotely effective strategy!" There is clear disagreement in both statements, but only the second approach is uncivil.

Figure 1.1 displays the two dimensions of conflict communication along a continuum demonstrating that individuals can be exposed to high or low levels of incivility and high or low levels of disagreement. Although the two components are portrayed here as orthogonal to one another, it is more likely that there is a relationship between them. As more contrasting perspectives are added, the conversation could take on a more uncivil tone[3]—these types of conversations would be clustered in the top right side of the figure. As figure 1.1 shows, contemporary cable news programming could be seen as high-incivility/high-disagreement communication. Similarly, those familiar with high school debate competitions or Robert's Rules of Order that govern many legislative bodies can envision conversations in which there is a wide range of competing perspectives but minimal incivility. These examples of political communication would fall in the lower right quadrant. The more challenging types of conflict communication to imagine are those that minimize disagreement, only showing one

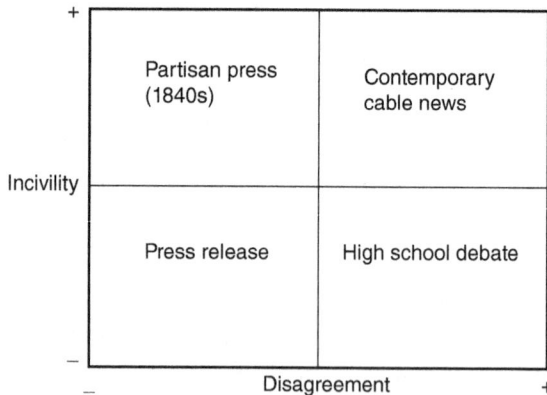

FIGURE 1.1 Dimensions and examples of communication conflict.

perspective on an issue. However, a document like a press release is often written from a single point of view and in civil, respectful terms. We can turn to history for an example of communication that was high in incivility but low in disagreement. The partisan newspapers of the early 1800s presented only their own perspective on the day's issues but did not hold back in their vehement expression of disgust and disdain for the other side (Ladd 2011; Schudson 1981). It's not that these papers didn't challenge the "other side"—they did, and vehemently. But unlike contemporary papers that emphasize "balance" between two or more sides, the partisan papers of yore presented only one perspective, much like a press release.

Conflict communication can be interpersonal, as in a high school debate or conversation with a friend, where two or more individuals express their personal opinions face to face. It can be mediated, when a viewer watches, reads, or listens to the disagreement and incivility of others. Considering all the ways in which discussion varies across dimensions of communication and conflict could fill volumes. Therefore, while I recognize the importance of substantive disagreement in shaping political behavior, my focus here is on a single dimension of communication conflict, incivility, as expressed in a single communication sphere, the mass media.

I emphasize incivility in the media for three primary reasons. First, the media are our primary source for learning about politics. Downs (1957) notes that the rational voter does not have the time to learn about every facet of government, and subsequent research on voting behavior demonstrates that, regardless of the cognitive processes by which people arrive at political decisions, the media are a well-worn path to political information (Campbell et al. 1980; Lau and Redlawsk 2006; Lupia 1994). Delli Carpini and Keeter add that "much of one's observed knowledge about politics must come, at least initially, from the mass media" (1996, 185). People turn to the media to learn the details and tenor of the political climate, so it is important to understand how the media's tone might influence citizens' perceptions and decisions.

Second, research by Mutz and Martin (2001) suggests that citizens are exposed to the greatest amount of cross-cutting exposure—what I have been calling substantive disagreement—by watching and reading media.

Disagreement is a given in the contemporary media environment. Americans expect political debate on important issues to include disagreement, and they expect to encounter this disagreement when they turn on the television or read an article. Disagreement, then, remains a constant in my empirical investigation, and we consider communication conflict in the form in which citizens are most likely to encounter it. When disagreement is constant across all of the experimental treatments, any media effects must be coming from the presence or absence of incivility, rather than from some interaction between incivility and disagreement.

Third, the media's role as a source of disagreement opens it up as a likely source of uncivil messages. Indeed, we see that as general negativity increases in political ads and news coverage, so too does incivility. Sobieraj and Berry (2011) found that cable news programs, blog posts, and talk radio shows all had at least one "outrage incident"—the presence of one of thirteen different types of rude or uncivil behavior, such as mockery, misrepresentative exaggeration, insulting language, and name-calling. These types of language are manifestations of incivility that I argue are shaping citizens' reactions to media across different media formats.

WHAT COUNTS AS UNCIVIL POLITICAL COMMUNICATION?

Political scientists typically view civil discourse as a normatively desirable characteristic of democratic government. Though they agree it is a normative good, they do not agree on what counts as civility. Civility has been defined in so many ways that it becomes difficult to parse out what it really means to be civil or uncivil. George Washington carried with him a list of "Rules of Civility and Decent Behavior" that included maxims such as "use no reproachful language against anyone neither curse nor revile" (Washington 1988, 18). Washington's rules are the mirror image of a more modern definition of incivility: "gratuitous asides that show a lack of respect and/or frustration with the opposition" (Mutz and Reeves 2005).

Others see incivility as tied much more closely to democratic values and disregard for community, elected officials, and the truth (Jamieson and Hardy 2012; Maisel 2012). Still others see it as a function of those in power. The labeling of particular language or actions as civil or uncivil is a tool that can keep certain ideas and groups at the margins of society (Chafe 1980; Zerilli 2014). Washington's definition facilitates the arrangement of discourse from completely civil—no reproachful language, to borrow his words—to completely uncivil: curses, revulsion, and more. The second definition conflates the tone and substance of the message, suggesting that someone who is polite but still derogatory toward a group or individual is being uncivil. The third conception emphasizes the extent to which incivility is a societal construct used to achieve strategic ends.

Each of these components—power dynamics, democratic commitment, and norms of etiquette or politeness—is integral to the architecture of incivility's three-legged stool, and each has its benefits and its shortcomings for capturing the relationship between the concept and political behavior. Ignore that African Americans were accused of incivility by virtue of showing up and claiming rights, and the stool collapses. That being said, considering each component of incivility is too great an endeavor for a single book. Following the path laid out by many empirical scholars of incivility, I characterize the concept primarily as a function of the tone of communication.

Many definitions of incivility go beyond understanding it as simply impolite tone and language, tying the concept to more substantive articulations of disagreement and value-laden content that reflects shared civic and social norms. Communications scholar Zizi Papacharissi accepts this definition in her work, arguing that incivility requires "disrespect for the collective traditions of democracy" (2004, 267). She lists three ways for people to be labeled uncivil in their online commentary: verbalizing threats to democracy, assigning stereotypes, and threatening others' rights. This definition effectively separates the concept from impoliteness but also complicates it. Now civility and incivility have a substantive component; they are not solely dependent on tone, and one can be uncivil while also remaining polite. In creating examples of this conception of incivility, one can imagine the "polite racist" who denies African Americans service in a restaurant or admission to a theater while using techniques of politeness—optimism, apology, reciprocity: "I'm really sorry, sir, but you understand that while we would like to help you, we cannot serve you here." Polite expression can convey an antidemocratic, exclusionary message that denies civil and political rights.

Incivility can encompass substantive violation of democratic norms, but our ability to identify these violations also depends to some extent on the power dynamics in play. Chafe (1980) draws on the experience of African Americans in the Jim Crow South as an example of antidemocratic civility:

> Blacks also understood the other side of civility—the deferential poses they had to strike in order to keep jobs, the chilling power of consensus to crush efforts to raise issues of racial justice. As victims of civility, blacks had long been forced to operate within an etiquette of race relationships that offered almost no room for collective self-assertion and independence. (8–9)

This portrait of race relations suggests that white citizens of Greensboro, North Carolina, were polite to their African American counterparts, but used that politeness to prevent them from gaining equal rights and access to services. If the discourse shifted toward increasingly vulgar language, however—racial epithets, insults to their intelligence—then the scenario would become uncivil as defined here.

I use the previous excerpt from Chafe to specify the confines of this book's research enterprise. Many examples of specific language that ordinary observers deem civil or uncivil are politically important. Polite-sounding words can be deployed in politically oppressive ways. But because the expression is polite, such a message—as offensive and antidemocratic as it is—does not produce the same behavioral responses because it does not violate the norm of politeness in public discourse. Its rude, off-putting content is not matched in its tone, which, to the contrary, is perfectly polite. Citizens' responses to uncivil political discourse are not driven primarily by this type of substantive incivility (Sydnor 2019), but by the tone and word choice.

For these reasons, I limit this book's understanding of incivility to conceptual equivalence with impoliteness.[4] I am interested in the effects of incivility independent from substance. This way, we might understand responses to discourse as occurring not because the conversation is negative, partisan, or demeaning toward an individual or group, but because it violates acceptable social norms for the tone of communication. Incivility manifests in the tone and style with which a speaker attacks someone's "face," or public self-image. Uncivil or impolite communication, therefore, is any statement that is not respectful of individuals' desire to maintain their self-image, while polite and civil discourse suggests respect for others and their desires or needs (Brown and Levinson 1987; Culpeper 2011). For example, one could say it is either uncivil or impolite to use obscenities or character aspersions in conversation.

This focus on tone and word choice in identifying incivility aligns with our own perceptions of what constitutes uncivil communication and behavior. Two recent surveys asked Americans what constitutes incivility; more than three-quarters of respondents emphasized cursing, belittling, personal attacks, shouting, and interruption (Shea and Steadman 2010; Weber Shandwick, KRC Research, and Powell Tate 2013; "Allegheny Survey" 2016). Research by Huckfeldt and Sprague (1995) demonstrated that objective identification of conflict—in this case, substantive disagreement or cross-cutting exposure—matters less for behavioral outcomes than individuals' perceptions of that conflict and its existence. By extension, any definition of incivility that helps us understand political responses should take into account what Americans think incivility is.

Incivility includes language that is consistently viewed as outside social norms—racial slurs and obscenity—but also less obvious aggressions, such as sarcasm and finger-pointing. These less dramatic discourteous gestures should also be considered an important part of conflict communication. These sorts of low-drama gestures are more socially acceptable—Joe Wilson would likely have received less press coverage if he had rolled his eyes or sighed during Barack Obama's 2009 address to Congress instead of yelling, "You lie!" While the media's tendency toward entertainment and sensationalism favors the more dramatic shouting, reactions like an eye roll, finger-pointing, or sarcastic comebacks are more likely to be included in everyday coverage and conversation. Citizens react to these minimal cues in much the same way they react to highly demeaning language, obscenity, and name-calling. We can therefore think of incivility as a continuum, with civil language on one end; moderately uncivil language and tone, such as sarcasm or eye-rolling, somewhere in the middle; and highly uncivil language, such racial slurs and obscenity, toward the other end.

The following list includes several examples of the types of language scholars have identified as uncivil. Many empirical tests of the effects of incivility on political behavior emphasize these elements of impolite tone in their operationalization of uncivil language.

MEASURES OF UNCIVIL TONE IN PREVIOUS STUDIES

Investigators	Measures That Capture Incivility
Mutz and Reeves (2005)	Hyperbole, insults, exaggerated emotions, physical proximity, eye-rolling, finger-pointing
Brooks and Geer (2007)	Inflammatory and superfluous language
Disbrow and Prentice (2009)	Foul language, impoliteness, belittlement, nasty or derogatory comments
Thorson, Vraga, and Ekdale (2010)	Derogatory terms and insulting language
Sobieraj and Berry (2011); Berry and Sobieraj (2014)	Mockery, misrepresentative exaggeration, insulting language, name-calling, character assassination, slippery slope, emotional language, emotional display, obscenity, verbal fighting or sparring, conflagration, mockery/sarcasm, ideologically extremizing language
Coe, Kenski, and Rains (2014)	Name-calling, aspersion, lying, vulgarity, pejoratives
Gervais (2014)	Name-calling, mockery and character assassination, spin and misrepresentative exaggeration, histrionics
Hwang, Kim, and Huh (2014)	Name-calling, contempt, and derision
Mutz (2015)	Intolerance, impoliteness, physical closeness

INCIVILITY'S PERSISTENT PRESENCE

Citizens are quick to spot conflict and incivility at the extremes of politics and in the midst of upheaval. Shea and Sproveri (2012) use the prevalence of references to "mean" and "nasty" politics in American history to suggest that writing about uncivil politics has varied greatly over the past two hundred years and that the peaks in these references occur in tandem with the "critical elections" proposed by many historians and political scientists (see, for example, Burnham 1970; Key 1955; Sundquist 1983). Geer (2012) notes that incivility in television news has increased in tandem with the use of negative advertisements by political campaigns. These historical observations raise the possibility that incivility is at its most prevalent when a fundamental economic or social issue is forcing the political parties to reconsider their platforms and make substantial changes to their policy stances. Beyond these critical elections, which have occurred relatively infrequently throughout American history, other forms of political upheaval and extremism facilitate the use of uncivil communication. History suggests we should not be surprised by shouting, character assassination, and other fighting words during times of political upheaval.

But citizens do not hear shouting and fighting words only during political turmoil. There are dozens of examples of politicians engaging in uncivil discourse in routine interactions with one another, from Alexander Hamilton describing John Adams as having "great and intrinsic defects in his character" (character assassination) to Representative Joe Wilson's shout of "You lie!" during President Obama's address to a joint session of Congress (shouting, accusations of lying; Grim 2009; Hamilton 1800). As with most political exchanges throughout history, Americans did not witness either of these comments or actions firsthand, but instead learned of them over the radio, in a newspaper, or through some other form of mass media. Incivility and impoliteness are most likely to arise from disagreement over substantive issues, and much media coverage of politics is focused on these disputes (Bennett 2002; Graber 2001; Patterson 2011). The focus on the horse race, the desire to get a catchy sound bite, and the need to pit opposing perspectives against one another ensure that the media serve as mirror and magnifying glass, reflecting the tenor of political discourse and augmenting the incivility that is already present.

Throughout American history, media coverage of politics has compounded political incivility. The partisan newspapers of the early 1800s were unabashed in their mockery and disdain for the opposition. These papers stuck to the party line, minimized the diversity of perspectives and disagreement present in their pages, and were quick to dismiss perspectives that did not align with their own in rude and confrontational ways. For example, one Civil War–era Wisconsin newspaper reported that "Mr. Lincoln is fungus from the corrupt womb of bigotry and fanaticism" (Clayton 2012). The goal was to undermine the opponent by whatever means necessary, leading to media that were willing to privilege particular perspectives while denigrating their opponent through uncivil dialogue.

At the turn of the twentieth century, the press adopted a norm of journalistic independence and objectivity, advocating "principles and ideas rather than prejudices and partisanship" (Emery, Emery, and Roberts 2000). Different perspectives were encouraged, often in the same articles, but politicians and journalists still managed to interject the sensational and uncivil into the daily paper, particularly in the editorial section. Early media mogul William Randolph Hearst focused on the principles behind what he called the "Raw Deal" and wrote to his editors, "President [Roosevelt]'s taxation program is essentially Communism. It is, to be sure, a bastard product of Communism and demagogic democracy, a mongrel creation . . . evolved by a composite personality which might be labeled Stalin Delano Roosevelt" (Proctor 2007, 192). In the everyday discussion of policy and politics, incivility became a way to express dissatisfaction and disagreement with the establishment and the status quo.

The era of broadcast television and radio was the most likely of these three historical periods (early 1800s, early 1900s, and mid-1900s) to minimize incivility and maximize viewers' exposure to diverse viewpoints, in part because of the Federal Communication Commission's Fairness Doctrine, which was operative from 1949 to 2011. The doctrine was designed to ensure that all political discussion over the airwaves—so, all programming on network television and radio—did not exclude any particular point of view. Broadcasters were also required to alert individuals of personal attacks against them and give them a chance to respond (Federal Communications Commission 1949; Matthews 2011). Not only were media outlets trying to incorporate as many perspectives as they deemed necessary, they were also presenting that information in a relatively polite manner. As one writer for *Fortune* magazine noted in 1960, "American political debate is increasingly conducted in a bland, even-tempered atmosphere and extremists of any kind are becoming rare" (Seligman 1960). Incivility as a component of everyday media coverage has ebbed and flowed throughout history as norms and resources have changed.

The advent of cable news channels and the Internet has fragmented the media environment and encouraged a subset of outlets to return to the partisan perspectives common in the 1800s. The increasing number of news sources and the ease with which citizens can access them only reinforce the perception that incivility is increasing and the media are to blame. In the 2010 Allegheny College Survey of Civility and Compromise in American Politics, 48 percent of those surveyed said they believed civility had declined in contemporary politics, and more than half of these respondents pointed to radio talk shows and television news programs as playing a major role in the decline (Shea and Steadman 2010).[5] Content analysis of "outrage incidents"—a set of characteristics that overlap with my understanding of incivility—in newspaper columns, talk radio, cable news, and Internet blogs, found that this type of discourse is more common in radio talk shows and cable television than in newspapers and blogs, with an average of twenty-three to twenty-four incidents per radio or television show compared to six per blog or newspaper column (Sobeiraj and Berry 2011). As the examples sprinkled throughout this chapter suggest, modern political coverage is rife with incivility in day-to-day political communication.

So, modern incivility is less distinctive than we might think. This variation in incivility across history shows that uncivil discourse can be an effective way to reach specific groups of followers (as was the case in the era of the partisan press) or to garner increased media coverage (as cable shows and Internet sites hurry to replay outrageous messages). No matter the era, certain types of media could be considered more disposed to publish incivility than others. In addition, each of these historical examples highlights the presence of "everyday" or "routine" incivility that is a part of political communication. None of the speakers referenced above are considered extremists presenting views outside the "acceptable" range of their time. Several of them, like Alexander Hamilton and William Randolph Hearst, were members of a core group of political elites using incivility not in an environment of protest and revolutionary action but in the course of regular political exchange with their peers.

The contemporary use of political incivility is not new, nor should we treat it as such. What is new is our ability to investigate American citizens' responses to this "everyday" use of incivility in standard political communication. While it is impossible to go back and assess the personal characteristics of readers of the partisan press or muckraking journalism, enduring psychological constructs like the response to conflict likely led certain individuals to seek out those information sources in the same manner that people's media choices today are shaped by their predispositions. Despite the enduring nature of these traits, little research has been done into how and why individuals respond to incivility. Incivility provokes different responses across individuals, and these differences can be attributed to one's willingness to engage in confrontational or argumentative communication.

INDIVIDUALIZED INCIVILITY

Conflict communication is not expressed in a vacuum. When political elites debate one another on cable news shows or express their dissatisfaction with a policy decision on their Facebook accounts, citizens react. Some people will be drawn into the fray, while others will change the channel or scroll over a nasty post. In short, incivility in political media interacts with individuals' predispositions toward conflict.

As individuals, we experience and respond to conflict in different ways. This conflict orientation, defined as one's psychological experience of argument, confrontation, and disagreement, is a reaction to both dimensions of conflict. A person's conflict orientation shapes how he or she feels when faced with someone who disagrees—regardless of whether the disagreement is expressed in a civil or uncivil manner. But, more important for this project, it also shapes how one feels in an environment with low disagreement but high or low incivility. The studies in the following chapters attempt to separate content from tone, varying incivility but not disagreement, to tease out the ways in which conflict orientation is a response to the tone of disagreement, rather than to disagreement itself.

For example, let's return to the hypothetical discussion between Nancy Pelosi and Mitch McConnell on *Meet the Press*. Both of the statements— "I do not think that sending troops is the most effective strategy" and "You're insane to think sending troops is a remotely effective strategy!"— express disagreement, but the first does so in a civil manner while the other invokes uncivil language. We react differently to the first statement than to the second. However, while the political science literature suggests that citizens will have uniformly more negative responses to the uncivil statement, I argue that their responses will differ on the basis of their conflict orientation. Those people who have a negative reaction to conflict—who dislike argument and are uncomfortable when they witness fighting—will respond poorly to the uncivil version of the comment. They will feel anxious or disgusted by what they have just heard. However, those who enjoy conflict—who find argument exciting and are entertained by the couple across the restaurant who are shouting at one another—will feel amused and entertained by the same uncivil statement.

Incivility is an enduring component of political communication with implications for citizen behavior, affecting trust in government, perceptions of legitimacy, and participation. Previous research has predominantly assumed that incivility has homogeneous effects across individuals, but there are some indications that its impact depends on characteristics of the individual. Specifically, Mutz and Reeves (2005) found that the relationship between incivility and trust in government is moderated by an individual's conflict orientation—one's comfort when experiencing conflict in social settings. Mutz and Reeves experimentally manipulated the expression of incivility in a televised debate while attempting to hold the political content of the debate constant. In other words, they conceived of incivility in the same way that I do here: as a tone distinct from the political messages being conveyed. When they looked at the interaction of this experimental condition with individuals' conflict avoidance, they found that people who have moderate to high levels of avoidance trust the government much less when exposed to incivility. However, those who are low in conflict avoidance report slightly higher levels of political trust in the uncivil condition than in the civil condition.

In her book *In-Your-Face Politics*, Mutz (2015) argues that incivility is particularly detrimental not only to Americans' trust in government, but also to their respect for oppositional political viewpoints. This work touches on conflict orientation at several points, but the characteristic is not integrated into her theoretical argument. There are thus two primary differences between Mutz's work and my own: my more rigorous exploration of conflict orientation as a psychological characteristic that influences political behavior, and my focus on engagement rather than attitudes. I argue that the interaction between incivility and conflict orientation extends to behavior beyond trust in government, influencing decisions about where to get one's political news and how to get involved in political activities.

Why would conflict orientation shape our reactions to incivility? Conflict orientation is a stable personality trait that determines how one experiences and reacts to conflict (Bresnahan et al. 2009; Goldstein 1999; Testa, Hibbing, and Ritchie 2014). I will elaborate further on conflict orientation and the strategy for measuring it across individuals in the next chapter, but I stress here that it is about a person's feelings when faced with conflict, rather than the explicit strategies he or she uses to resolve that conflict. When people are exposed to conflict in the form of incivility, their reactions will be colored by their conflict orientation.

As with incivility, we can think of conflict orientation as arrayed along a continuum. Some people have a very strong avoidance reaction to conflict; others are very willing to approach conflict; most fall somewhere in the middle, with a "conflict-ambivalent" response. When these individuals are placed in a high-conflict environment, they will react in different ways.

Because people try to minimize their experience of negative emotions while repeating events that produce positive emotions, conflict will produce divergent responses across the range of conflict orientations (Cacioppo, Priester, and Berntson 1993; Fredrickson 2002). The conflict-avoidant will try to minimize the presence of incivility in their lives because it elicits negative emotions and reactions, while the conflict-approaching will create positive, enjoyable associations with conflict. In politics, attempts to minimize or emphasize exposure to incivility will manifest in behavioral choices—decisions about from which media to seek political information and in which political activities to participate.

Besides determining that emotional responses to stimuli affect behavior, psychologists have found that people want congruence between their personal predispositions and their environment and will take action to increase that congruence (Deutsch 1985). In the context of political participation, both affective response and the need for congruence serve as mechanisms by which the interaction between conflict orientation and incivility translate into different participatory habits for avoidant and approaching citizens. Those individuals who are conflict-avoidant will avoid activities in which they are more likely to be exposed to incivility or open themselves up to criticism from others: participating in protests, commenting on blogs, persuading others to vote, or working for a campaign, for example. Those who enjoy and embrace conflict—the conflict-approaching—will be more likely to participate in these sorts of activities. They will employ similar strategies when choosing which media they use to collect political information and how frequently they do so. The conflict-avoidant will turn to forms of media that citizens perceive as more civil, while the conflict-approaching will look to shows and sites that are willing to take a more impolite tone.

I expect these initial affective reactions to translate into differences in political behavior. Substantial research in political psychology has explored the connections between affect and political decisions, from vote choice to media attention to candidate evaluation (Brader 2006; Huddy, Feldman, and Cassese 2007; MacKuen et al. 2007). The buildup of these affective links—both positive and negative—between particular political activities, media platforms, and incivility leads conflict orientation to have an impact on individuals' decisions to participate in certain political activities and to consume particular types of political media. Specifically, individuals who like conflict are more likely to participate in political activities in which they might have to express or defend their own opinions and to report greater preference for high-incivility media like blogs and cable television.

The current literature misses interesting and important heterogeneity in the affective and behavioral effects of political incivility, as these effects vary with the conflict orientation of the individual experiencing uncivil communication. These heterogeneous effects are important to the extent that incivility has the potential to mobilize those individuals who enjoy argument and disagreement—the conflict-approaching—while discouraging those who have a negative association with conflict from pursuing certain information sources or political activities. The fact that the conflict-approaching are more involved in certain elements of politics raises concerns about democratic equality—specifically given that the conflict-approaching are more likely to have additional political resources because of their demographic and social characteristics. Ultimately, the results presented in the following chapters demonstrate not only the ways in which individual psychological differences can affect people's choices, but also an awareness of the broader political patterns that emerge from these individual reactions.

* * *

In our ideal political world, everyone speaks kindly to one another, even when they disagree. In reality, you don't have to go very far to find incivility in American political discourse these days—just open your web browser or tune in to cable news. While we work to move from the contemporary political experience toward that ideal, we also need to understand and reflect on the impact that incivility has on political discourse. Most importantly, we need to keep in mind that incivility is not all bad. For some people, the presence of incivility diminishes their democratic capacity: they react with more negative emotions, turn to entertainment over political news, and participate less in political discussions and activities. But for others, incivility provokes more positive emotional reactions, less biased information-search strategies, and more engagement in high-conflict political activities, whether offering their own opinions on political issues or persuading others to vote.

These two groups are divided by their conflict orientation, a psychological reaction to conflict in politics, sports, and daily life. Ultimately, conflict orientation can be considered a resource that—just like time, money, or facility speaking in public—facilitates our engagement with the political system. Those citizens who are comfortable with conflict have access to a wider range of sources of political information and means of political engagement because they are not turned off by the incivility that is a ubiquitous presence across many media outlets.

What is more, civility may not be the balm for mass democratic politics that some scholars might hope. While incivility brings the conflict-approaching into the political sphere, civility does not do the same for the conflict-avoidant. They experience negative emotions in the face of incivility, but they do not experience positive emotions when reading or watching a civil news story about the same topic. Civility is less entertaining and less memorable—key components in keeping Americans engaged with the political world.

This is not to say that politics should devolve into shouting, cruelty, and a resistance to compromise. A basic level of human kindness is essential to shared governance and collective decision-making. But incivility can be a necessary force of democratic accountability. While not universally and normatively positive, nasty language has a place in American politics. It can call attention to inequalities, discrimination, and opinions that are not heard in mainstream political discussion. It can draw in a set of people who enjoy and can engage with conflict, who then offer their own opinions and engage in democratic discussion of controversial issues. We need to practice civility while also helping conflict-avoidant citizens develop skills in and strategies for making their voices heard in the presence of uncivil political discourse.

2

THE POLITICAL PSYCHOLOGY OF
CONFLICT COMMUNICATION

*I hate conflict so much that I find myself agreeing with pretty much
everything that everyone says.*

—ANONYMOUS INTERVIEWEE, *HUMANS OF NEW YORK* BLOG

N 2010, BRANDON Stanton set out to photograph ten thousand New York
City residents, capturing glimpses of strangers' daily lives. Along the
way, he started interviewing his subjects and including quotes and short
stories from their lives alongside their portraits. The photos and interviews
turned into a popular blog, *Humans of New York* (HONY), and Stanton's
reach has extended to other geographic locations and to series of interviews
with specific populations, such as inmates and pediatric cancer patients
(Stanton 2018). The quote used in this chapter's epigraph is the only glimpse
we have into the life of that particular HONY interviewee; all we know is
that he avoids conflict. As he acknowledges, he is so turned off by conflict
in his social life that he has become a yes-man, agreeing with everyone else's
opinions because he wants to avoid confrontation.

Given this information, it is not hard to imagine his behavior as a
democratic citizen. Committed to avoiding confrontation, he does not
share his opinions with anyone—not his close friends, who he worries
might become upset or think less of him if they disagree, nor his elected
officials, because his views would then be open to public commentary and
ridicule. He does not attend protests or city council meetings because
they always result in a fight: people on one side of the issue trying to
shout down their opponents. And he steers clear of the news, because it

seems as though all anyone ever does in politics is argue. In other words, his ability to participate in democratic life is severely restricted; he has few outlets through which to articulate his preferences and priorities to those who represent him.

Conflict orientation exists along a continuum, with some individuals, like our HONY interviewee, having a very strong avoidance reaction to conflict, others being very willing to approach conflict, and most falling somewhere in the middle with a conflict-ambivalent response. When these individuals are placed in a high-conflict environment, they will react in different ways. Psychologists have found that people want congruence between their personal predispositions and their environment and will take action to increase that congruence (Deutsch 1985). Therefore, while those of us who enjoy conflict will be content in a highly uncivil or argumentative environment, our conflict-avoidant counterparts will adapt their behavior and environment to minimize incivility. People also try to minimize their experience of negative emotions and repeat events that produce positive emotions. Therefore, the conflict-avoidant will try to minimize the presence of incivility in their lives, because it produces negative emotions and reactions, while the conflict-approaching will create positive, enjoyable associations with conflict. In politics, attempts to minimize or emphasize incivility will manifest in behavioral choices—decisions about from which media to seek political information and in which political activities to participate.

In this chapter, I draw on research in cultural, organizational, and social psychology to offer a definition of conflict orientation: the way one experiences and reacts to a conflict situation, particularly conflict communication. I then review approaches used to measure conflict orientation and explain the Conflict Communication Scale used in the studies presented in this book. Using longitudinal data from the Qualtrics Panels study,[1] I demonstrate that conflict orientation is relatively fixed for individuals across time. Finally, I explore the relationships between conflict orientation and several demographic and political characteristics that also influence political behavior—relationships that may moderate or exacerbate the effects of these characteristics on political engagement.

PSYCHOLOGICAL PERSPECTIVES ON RESPONSES TO CONFLICT COMMUNICATION

Following from Kurt Lewin's (1935) work on positive and negative valence in personality, scholars have emphasized the importance of approach/avoidance motivations in ensuring that living organisms—from the single-cell amoebas to human beings—adapt and survive in their environment. Elliott (2006) defines the terms as follows: "Approach motivation is the energization of behavior by, or the direction of behavior toward, positive stimuli (objects, events, possibilities), whereas avoidance motivation may be defined as the energization of behavior by, or the direction of behavior away from, negative stimuli (objects, events, possibilities)." Zajonc (1998) argues that the ability to make these sorts of approach/avoid discriminations is hardwired; we make these judgments unconsciously in response to sets of stimuli.

Inherent in the conceptualization of approach and avoidance motivations is an emphasis on movement. It can suggest movement toward (in the case of approach) or away from (avoidance) a particular experience or object that is currently being experienced—for example, fleeing a bear in the woods or leaning into a hug from your best friend. It can also reflect the decision to keep one's distance from a negative stimulus—avoid walking in the woods when bears are most likely to be out—or to remain in the presence of something positive, as by sitting in a coffee shop catching up with your friend for hours.

Research in health communication and psychology has shown that messages framed to be congruent with individuals' approach/avoidance motivations are more effective in changing behavior. Specifically, in the congruent conditions, participants who were categorized as more approach-oriented were shown gain-framed messages promoting dental flossing, while those who were more avoidance-oriented were shown similar messages with a loss frame. In the incongruent conditions, the match of motivational orientation and message frame were reversed. Participants who had read congruent messages were more likely to floss and were more efficacious in their flossing than those who had read incongruent messages (Sherman, Mann, and Updegraff 2006). These findings suggest that individual differences (in this case, approach or avoidance motivations) and situational factors (message framing) interact in communication to influence individuals' feelings of efficacy, their intentions, and behavior change. This individual-differences framework can also be applied to our understanding of the effects of uncivil political messages on political behavior.

Psychologists' understanding of approach and avoidance motivation as a framework for understanding individual differences lays the groundwork for my argument that individual responses to conflict shape people's reactions to uncivil political messages. Conflict orientation can be seen as a specific type of approach/avoidance motivation; it is a stable personality trait centered around how people experience and react to conflict—whether they are excited by arguments, uncomfortable when others fight in public, or happy to handle a disagreement face to face (Bresnahan et al. 2009; Goldstein 1999; Testa, Hibbing, and Ritchie 2014). At one extreme, an individual can be highly conflict-avoidant, finding disagreement and argument uncomfortable and anxiety-inducing. Like avoidance motivations more generally, conflict avoidance produces behavior that drives individuals away from the negative stimulus: the expression or manifestation of conflict. These people dislike confrontation and face-to-face resolution of conflict and will ultimately institute strategies in their personal and political lives to minimize their exposure to potential conflict situations. At the other extreme are the conflict-approaching people, who have no problem expressing disagreement, are excited by the prospect of a debate, and are happy to air their arguments face to face in any environment. These people are not disturbed by the presence of conflict around them, and even thrive in a high-conflict environment. Therefore, they will not shy away from disagreements in their personal social networks, nor from environments that will expose them to conflict between other people. Most people, as I will show below, fall somewhere in the middle—leaning slightly toward conflict avoidance.

This book measures individuals' motivation to approach or avoid conflict in communication using the Conflict Communication Scale (CCS;

Goldstein 1999). The CCS is constructed to measure variability in the experience of conflict rather than strategies for reducing it. It is designed to provide measures that are relevant for conflict intervention such as mediation, but also broad enough to assess both cultural and individual differences in communication style in conflict situations. The CCS is designed around five subscales drawn from cultural research on the dimensions of conflict response: confrontation, public/private behavior, self-disclosure, emotional expression, and conflict approach/avoidance; the adapted scales used throughout this work draw from one to four of these subscales. Following is a list of the statements used across all of the studies in this book. While not widely cited in social- or organizational-psychology literature, this scale has previously been adapted to political questions (Mutz and Reeves 2005; Mutz 2015).[2]

ADAPTED CONFLICT COMMUNICATION SCALE

Please indicate your level of agreement with the following statements. (Strongly Agree, Agree, Neutral, Disagree, Strongly Disagree)

APPROACH/AVOIDANCE SCALE

I enjoy challenging the opinions of others.
I find conflicts exciting.
I hate arguments.
Arguments don't bother me.
I feel upset after an argument.

PUBLIC/PRIVATE BEHAVIOR

I avoid arguing in public.
I feel uncomfortable seeing others argue in public.
It wouldn't bother me to have an argument in a restaurant.
I don't want anyone besides those involved to know about an argument
    I've had.

I would be embarrassed if neighbors heard me argue with a family member.

CONFRONTATION

I feel more comfortable having an argument in person than over the phone.

I prefer to express points of disagreement with others by speaking with them directly rather than by writing them notes.

When I have a conflict with someone I try to resolve it by being extra nice to him or her.

After a dispute with a neighbor, I would feel uncomfortable seeing him or her again, even if the conflict had been resolved.

I prefer to solve disputes through face-to-face discussion.

EMOTIONAL EXPRESSION

Getting emotional only makes conflicts worse.

Everything should be out in the open in an argument, including emotions.

It makes me uncomfortable watching other people express their emotions in front of me.

I feel like running away when other people start showing their emotions in an argument.

It shows strength to express emotions openly.

Showing your feelings in a dispute is a sign of weakness.

Note: The entire set of questions was only asked as part of the Qualtrics Panel study (2016). To see which questions were included in each survey, see appendix A.

As Goldstein found in her assessment of the 75-item scale, the adapted 21-item scale used here displays strong enough correlations between items and Cronbach's alpha statistics to conclude that the items cohere into a relatively strong measure of a single dimension, conflict orientation.[3] When we combine these items into a single scale, participants fall across the entire range of possible values, from extremely conflict-avoidant (a score of –40 in the Qualtrics Panel) to extremely conflict-approaching (a score of 40). In each scale, zero indicates the neutral midpoint; people scoring here could be classified as conflict-ambivalent. Each subscale has a range from –10 to 10, with –10 indicating high avoidance, high preference for private conflict resolution, and high distaste for confrontation.

While the use of online samples prevents me from drawing conclusions about the distribution of conflict orientation across the U.S. population more generally, it is still helpful to get a sense of the range of orientations found in the participants. Figure 2.1 displays the distribution of participants on the Conflict Communication Scale across each of the seven times the scale was administered. As you can see from the figure, conflict orientation tends to be relatively normally distributed in each sample, although it can skew slightly right, as we see in the Project Implicit, Mechanical Turk Study 2, and GfK samples. It is also clear that individuals can vary widely on these same measures, as everyone does not find it equally easy to have a face-to-face conversation about uncomfortable arguments or to openly express their emotions.

Figure 2.1 demonstrates that at a single point in time, there is substantial variation across individuals in conflict orientation. But what about within an individual over time? If conflict orientation is malleable and susceptible to environmental influences over the course of an individual's life, then the relationships I am studying throughout this book could be endogenous. Individuals' conflict orientation could shape media exposure, but media exposure could also affect an individual's conflict orientation.

Psychological research suggests that this is not the case. Conflict orientation is a relatively entrenched component of our personalities by a young age, although it is shaped by cultural and social factors. For example, people raised in East Asian cultures tend to be more conflict-avoidant overall, specifically preferring private and nonconfrontational airing of disagreements. Americans are more willing to approach and handle conflict through face-to-face discussion (Gudykunst and Ting-Toomey 1988).

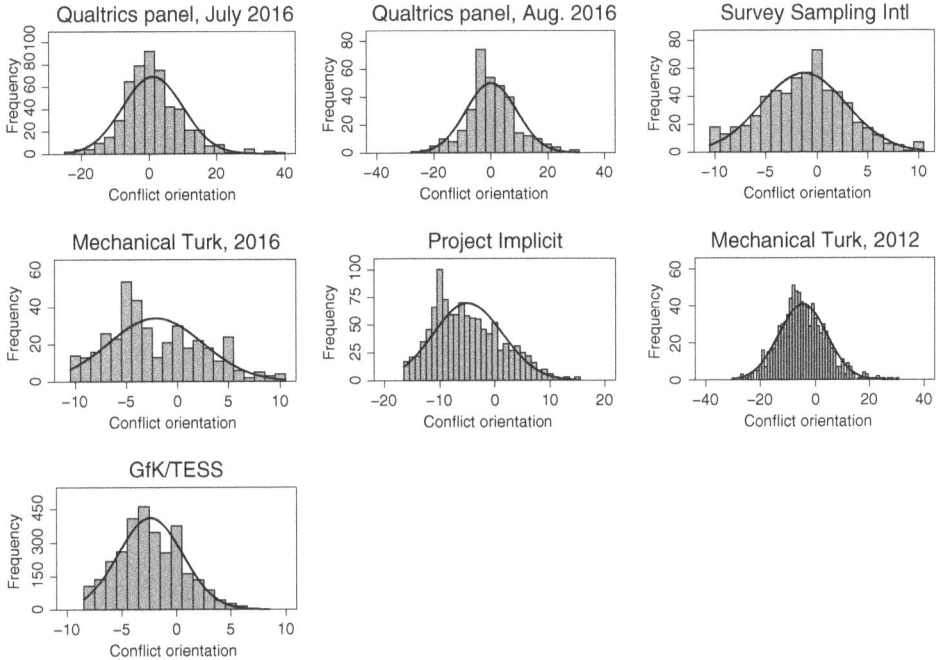

FIGURE 2.1 Distributions of participants on the conflict communication scale, by study.

Note: Lower numbers indicate greater conflict avoidance, higher numbers indicate greater conflict-approaching scores on the Conflict Communication Scale. Different numbers of questions from the full CCS scale were used across experiments, given sampling and timing constraints.

As we age or become more educated, we can become more comfortable and accepting of conflict (Birditt, Fingerman, and Almeida 2005; Eliasoph 1998). However, these changes are small fluctuations around an initial stable point; someone who is predisposed to be highly conflict-avoidant is not going to become highly conflict-approaching simply by growing older and becoming highly educated.

The stability of conflict orientation over a short period of time is apparent in the Qualtrics Panels survey. A sample of 333 participants completed an adapted 15-question version of the Conflict Communication Scale

(CCS; Goldstein 1999). The full scale is an additive measure of participants' responses to the 15 questions that ranges from a value of -40, indicating extreme conflict avoidance, to 40, signaling extreme conflict-approaching orientation. Participants' conflict orientation was measured for the first time between July 27 and August 3, 2016. They were then recontacted on August 15, 2016, and asked to complete a second battery of psychological measures that included the same set of CCS questions. The distribution of individual conflict-orientation scores changed minimally over the three-week span. The average conflict orientation score in the first survey was 0.11 (sd = 0.53), or just barely above the neutral zero point. The average score in the August survey was -0.64 (sd = 0.51), just below the neutral point. A paired t-test of conflict orientation across the two surveys is statistically significant ($p = 0.04$, two-tailed), but the difference between the two averages is just 0.74—less than one point on an 80-point scale. While some individuals did report dramatic changes in their conflict orientation from July to August, the majority of the participants' scores changed by four points or less. While these data cannot demonstrate that conflict orientation is immovable in the face of environmental shocks, it does suggest that it is a relatively stable trait that is unlikely to be affected by any single political event. Instead, conflict orientation influences the way that humans respond to politics.

I want to make an additional distinction: one's conflict orientation is not the same as one's strategies for conflict resolution. Conflict orientation is a psychological characteristic of an individual; it is entrenched in an individual's personality and only differs marginally across environments. Conflict-resolution strategies are situation-dependent. They vary based on the environment in which individuals are responding to a conflict.

Much of the psychological research on responses to conflict focuses not on this individual predisposition, but on conflict-resolution strategies and outcomes in specific interpersonal settings—dating, marital conflict, and organizational or managerial situations. The majority of research in this discipline builds on Blake and Mouton's managerial grid theory, which argues that differences in conflict-handling approaches stem from relative concerns for production and for people. These relative concerns produce five types or styles of handling office conflict: impoverished, country club, dictatorial or "produce or perish," middle-of-the-road, and the team (Blake and Mouton 1964). For example, an employer who is more concerned about ensuring high production than about the well-being of his employees will handle conflict in a dictatorial style. He will force the resolution of any disagreements and do so in a way that does not damage his firm's output but likely leaves his employees unhappy and unsatisfied. Alternatively, a manager who cares about both production and people will take a team-building approach to conflict resolution, encouraging his team to air disagreements in a way that does not sacrifice either their happiness or the success of the organization.

In this and similar types of conflict-resolution instruments, participants are asked to choose between two statements that describe behavior—for example, "I try to find a compromise solution" and "I sometimes sacrifice my own wishes for the wishes of the other person" (Kilmann and Thomas 1977). These solution-oriented measures are effective in determining how people attempt to problem-solve in the face of conflict, but choosing one statement over the other does not clearly represent that person's conflict orientation. For example, an individual who does not enjoy conflict might immediately try to find a compromise solution in order to stop an argument, but someone who is conflict-approaching could also report that they try to find a compromise solution because they enjoy working through all of the differences between their opinion and that of others. Similarly, concerns for people and production explain why one might choose a particular conflict-resolution strategy in a "country club" environment and behave differently in a team-based situation, but these motivations are orthogonal to one's disposition toward conflict itself. Conflict orientation and conflict resolution are distinct concepts; focusing on the strategies for resolving conflict does not adequately capture the stable personality trait that guides individuals to those strategies.

This distinction between conflict orientation and conflict-resolution strategies is captured in the second wave of the Qualtrics Panel survey. Participants completed both the CCS and Blake and Mouton's Leadership Questionnaire. Whereas the two components of the managerial grid—concern for people and concern for production—were highly correlated ($r = 0.87$), each individual component was only slightly correlated with participants' conflict orientations ($r_{task} = 0.13$ and $r_{people} = 0.15$). While both correlations are statistically significant at $p = 0.05$, they are loose enough to leave us feeling confident that conflict avoidance is not the same as low concern for people or production, nor is conflict-approaching motivation equivalent to high concern for people or production. Conflict orientation and conflict-resolution strategies are related, but they are not different ways of assessing the same underlying concept. Instead, one's conflict orientation may make one more or less likely to turn to specific strategies for resolving conflict.

Conflict orientation is a psychological trait that is pre-political—developed and engrained in our personalities throughout childhood and relatively firmly entrenched by the time we enter adulthood. As such, it is expected to be closely related to other personality measures—specifically, the Big Five traits that are thought to present a holistic assessment of an individual's personality (McCrae and Costa 2008). These five traits—extraversion, openness to new experience, emotional stability, conscientiousness, and agreeableness—are heritable and stable over time. Because they are determined by biological differences, whereas conflict orientation has been shown to vary with cultural and other demographic characteristics, the Big Five can be thought of as causally prior to both our conflict orientation and our political behaviors (Mondak 2010).

Research into the influence of Big Five traits on disagreement in political discussion reinforces this expectation of a connection. Looking at interpersonal relationships, Graziano, Jensen-Campbell, and Hair (1996) found that individual differences in agreeableness are systematically related to patterns of conflict and conflict resolution. Specifically, individuals who received a low score on a scale of agreeable tendencies were more likely than highly agreeable individuals to see "power-assertion" tactics as solutions to conflict. While this finding highlights the connection between agreeableness and a behavioral strategy for resolving conflict, it also suggests that an individual high in agreeableness should have a negative reaction to conflict situations. Findings in political science reinforce this hypothesized relationship. In a study of personality's impact on an individual's exposure to disagreement on topics ranging from politics to sports, researchers have found that higher levels of agreeableness are weakly associated with increased willingness to engage in discussion (Gerber et al. 2012).

Beyond agreeableness, political scientists also find that openness to new experiences, extraversion, and emotional stability are also related to the willingness to engage in political discussion where there may be disagreement (Gerber et al. 2010, 2012; Testa et al. 2014). A highly open person should find conflict stimulating and exciting, while an extrovert's tendency to be more assertive and outgoing should also lead toward more comfort in experiencing conflict. Those high in emotional stability are also more likely to have high self-confidence, ultimately making them feel less threatened by conflict. Finally, while there is less conclusive evidence about the relationship between conscientiousness and political disagreement, highly conscientious people are likely to be highly aware of violations of social norms (Mondak 2010). Therefore, they should be particularly attuned to the use of conflict communication like incivility that infringes on conversational norms of politeness.

Ultimately, previous research suggests that a conflict-approaching orientation, measured as positive values on the adapted CCS, should be positively associated with extraversion, emotional stability, and openness but negatively associated with agreeableness and conscientiousness. In the Project Implicit and Qualtrics Panels studies, participants were asked to complete the Ten-Item Personality Inventory (TIPI), which gives them scores from –6 to 6 on each of the five personality factors, with –6 indicating low levels of that trait and 6 indicating high values (Gosling, Rentfrow, and Swann 2003). The results for Project Implicit are presented here; the Qualtrics Panels results are available in appendix B. I test the relationship between these characteristics and conflict orientation by examining the correlations between each of the five factors and the full CCS and the results of ordinary least squares (OLS) regressions of conflict orientation on each characteristic, holding the other four constant. As table 2.1 shows, the Pearson's correlations between each personality trait and the scale are in the expected direction, and all are significant. Extraversion and agreeableness are correlated more strongly than the other three traits. These relationships hold in the regression results, as seen in figure 2.2.

TABLE 2.1 PEARSON'S CORRELATIONS BETWEEN BIG FIVE
PERSONALITY TRAITS AND THE ADAPTED CCS

	CORRELATION: FULL CCS
Extroversion	0.22[*]
Agreeableness	−0.37[*]
Conscientiousness	−0.11[*]
Emotional stability	0.11[*]
Openness	0.12[*]

Source: Project Implicit.

[*]$p < 0.01$

The higher an individual's score on emotional stability, extraversion, or openness, the higher that individual's predicted conflict orientation. In other words, an individual who is extraverted, open, or emotionally stable is more likely to be conflict-approaching, holding the other factors constant. The greater one's score on agreeableness or conscientiousness, however, the lower the predicted CCS score, or the more likely one is to be conflict-avoidant. This effect is particularly strong for agreeableness, where there is a 15-point difference in the likely CCS score of individuals on the two extremes of the personality factor. These results are consistent with previous findings by psychologists and political scientists, suggesting that conflict orientation may mediate the relationship between these standard measures of personality, political communication, and political behavior.

In chapter 1, I suggested that conflict orientation has the potential to exacerbate existing inequalities in political participation. This argument rests on the assumption that conflict orientation is connected to political and demographic characteristics that shape political behavior. Specifically, I am concerned with the relationship between conflict orientation and age, gender, race, education, and income.

Years of political science research has found that these demographic characteristics are correlated with an individual's likelihood of participating in politics, both by voting and by engaging in more effortful political

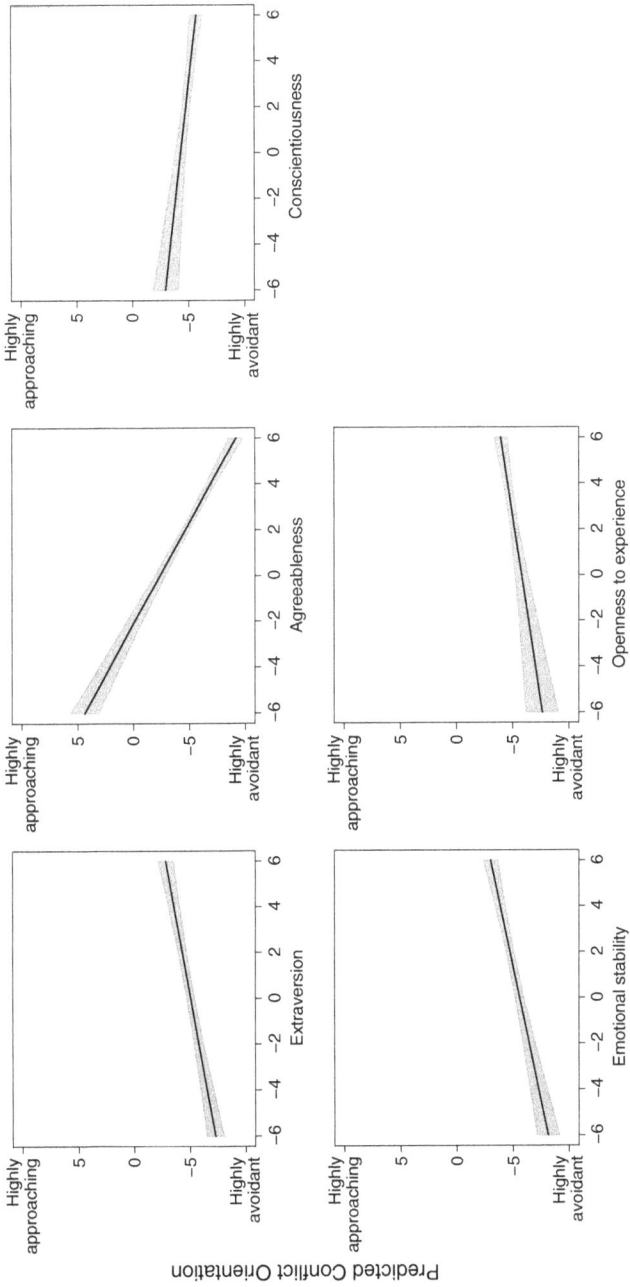

FIGURE 2.2 Relationship between conflict orientation and the five personality factors.

Note: Linear predictions derived from bivariate regressions of personality dimensions on conflict orientation. Shaded areas represent 95% confidence intervals.

Source: Project Implicit.

acts such as donating money, working for a campaign, or protesting. Those in the highest income quintile are more likely to vote, more likely to donate their time, and substantially more likely to contribute financially to a political candidate than those in the lowest quintile (Brady, Verba, and Schlozman 1995; Schlozman, Verba, and Brady 2012; Verba, Schlozman, and Brady 1995). Citizens are more likely to participate as they get older (with a drop-off as they approach the oldest 10 percent) and as they gain more education (Rosenstone and Hansen 2002; Verba et al. 1995). Finally, men are more likely to participate than women, and white citizens are more likely to participate than minorities (Schlozman, Burns, and Verba 1999; Verba, Burns, and Schlozman 1997; Verba et al. 1995).

According to psychological research, these demographic characteristics are also related to conflict orientation. Literature on aging and developmental psychology suggests that as people age, they experience fewer problems and tensions in their interpersonal relationships. They become less aggressive, more conciliatory, and are more capable of regulating their reactions to problems (Birditt et al. 2005; Blanchard-Fields and Cooper 2004; Carstensen, Isaacowitz, and Charles 1999). In other words, citizens should become more conflict-avoidant as they age.

Women are generally more conflict-avoidant than their male counterparts. Tannen suggests that the U.S. education system trains students to stake out one position in opposition to another, but also notes that this particular form of learning—directly criticizing or contradicting colleagues' or authors' perspectives—is not always as effective in teaching women as men. She concludes, "Clearly, women can learn to perform in adversarial ways. . . . [It is not written in stone that] individual women may not learn to practice and enjoy agonistic debate or that individual men may not recoil from it" (Tannen 1998). If conflict avoidance deters political participation, and women are also more likely to be conflict-avoidant, as Tannen suggests, then gender is one area in which we would expect conflict orientation to exacerbate existing political divides.

Tannen's argument also suggests that education should be positively associated with conflict-approaching behavior. As people spend more time in an adversarial education system, they should become more comfortable with conflict, particularly conflict as expressed through academic practices like debate. However, increased education also serves to delineate social expectations for speech and tone, so that those with greater education may be less tolerant of incivility. A similarly ambivalent expectation holds for the relationship between conflict orientation and income. On one hand, income is something one acquires in adulthood, at which point one's conflict orientation is relatively established. However, income is also closely related to education, so that if education influences conflict orientation in predictable ways, it is possible that income follows the same pattern.

Finally, research on the cultural differences in conflict orientation suggests that racial minorities in the United States may react differently to conflict than whites (Gudykunst and Ting-Toomey 1988; Leong, Wagner, and Tata 1995; Trimble et al. 1996). From this research, we would expect African American and Hispanic participants to be more conflict-avoidant than their white counterparts. This relationship, like that for gender, has the potential to exacerbate existing political inequalities.

Pearson's correlations from five of the six studies buttress these findings (see table 2.2). Linear predictions of the relationship between age and conflict orientation suggest that conflict orientation moves from an average score of -4 (slightly conflict-avoidant) for an 18-year-old to -6

TABLE 2.2 PEARSON'S CORRELATIONS: CONFLICT ORIENTATION AND DEMOGRAPHIC CHARACTERISTICS

	QUALTRICS PANELS (T1)	MTURK STUDY 1	SSI	PROJECT IMPLICIT	MTURK STUDY 2	GFK
Age	−.05	−0.11*	−0.11*	−0.08*	−0.09*	−0.11*
Female	−0.06	−0.25*	−0.24*	−0.30*	−0.28*	−0.25*
White	−0.08	−0.01	0.11*	−0.02	−0.01	−0.08
Education	−0.02	0.08*	0.15*	0.01	0.02	0.11
Income	0.05	0.07*	0.04	—	0.03	0.08

$^*p < 0.05$

(more conflict-avoidant) for a 65-year-old in the Project Implicit study. An examination of 18-year-old and 65-year-old Mechanical Turk Study 1 participants yields a similar difference in conflict orientation, with scores of -3.5 and -6.5, respectively. This change occurs for both men and women.

The correlations in these studies provide further evidence of the claim of gender differences, with the gender-CCS relationship matching only the strength of political interest and the personality trait agreeableness. A female Mechanical Turk Study 1 participant scores, on average, around a -7.2 on the full CCS, while her male counterpart scores -2.4. Similarly, male and female Project Implicit participants score -2.3 and -6.3, respectively, demonstrating that women in these studies are substantially more conflict-avoidant than men. For the most part, the adapted CCS used throughout this book mirrors the relationships with key demographic variables that have been found in other research.

CONFLICT ORIENTATION AND POLITICS

I am arguing that conflict orientation shapes individuals' political behavior and patterns of media consumption in part by affecting individuals' emotional responses to mediated incivility. However, one's response to political incivility may depend on whom the rude language is directed toward. For example, Republican citizens may respond negatively to incivility when it is directed toward Republican politicians but find it entertaining when like-minded political commentators are uncivil toward their political opponents (Gervais 2015). Furthermore, this reaction could be stronger for those who strongly identify with a particular party than for weak identifiers. Given these possibilities, it is important to demonstrate that conflict orientation is distinct from certain political variables—specifically, partisan identification, the strength of that identification, and political interest.

Recent research into a trait-based understanding of ideology suggests that conservatism is strongly connected to an individual's risk aversion or threat sensitivity (Jost et al. 2003). Although I do not simultaneously

measure conflict orientation and risk aversion in any of the studies presented here, one could imagine that there is a relationship between the
two, such that those who are conflict-avoidant are also more likely to be
risk-averse or sensitive to threat. These hypothesized relationships, in turn,
suggest that conflict avoidance could be correlated with conservatism and
Republican partisan identification.

There is an additional argument to be made for the connection between
conflict orientation and partisan strength. Those who are stronger partisans
could be more likely to embrace conflict because they are more invested in a
particular party or set of policy preferences. Incivility also appears to be more
prevalent among media outlets that present strong partisan perspectives,
suggesting that individuals who tune in to Hannity or Rush Limbaugh are
accepting not only of their political perspective but also of the tone in which
they deliver that perspective (Jamieson and Cappella 2008; Sunstein 2011).

However, there is little evidence of a relationship between ideology,
partisan identification, or partisan strength and conflict orientation in any
of my studies. Across all six samples, the full Conflict Communication
Scale and the three political characteristics have essentially no correlation,
as measured by the Pearson's correlation coefficients displayed in table 2.3.
This provides strong evidence that conflict orientation is not tied to these
specific political characteristics.

TABLE 2.3 PEARSON'S CORRELATIONS BETWEEN CONFLICT
ORIENTATION AND POLITICAL CHARACTERISTICS

	QUALTRICS PANELS (T1)	MTURK STUDY 1	SSI	PROJECT IMPLICIT	MTURK STUDY 2	GFK
Republican	0.06	−0.03	−0.01	0.01	−0.01	−0.04
PID Strength	−0.01	0.06	−0.01	−0.03	−0.03	−0.05
Pol. Interest	−0.08	0.23*	n/a	0.23*	0.17*	n/a
Conservative	0.02	0.03	−0.03	−0.04	−0.01	−0.02

Note: The SSI and GfK studies did not ask participants to report their interest in politics.

$^{*}p < 0.05$

This argument is more compelling if conflict orientation does not strongly correlate with other political characteristics that might also shape these emotions, and ultimately individuals' engagement—specifically, party identification (and the strength of that identification) and political interest. We know that partisan identification, and the strength of that identification, can determine to which media citizens turn for their political news, for which candidates citizens vote, and many other political attitudes (Arceneaux, Johnson, and Murphy 2012; Iyengar and Hahn 2009; Rosenstone and Hansen 2002; Stroud 2011). Furthermore, we know that political interest drives the decision to vote (Brady et al., 1995). Given these almost overpowering relationships between partisanship, political interest, and political behavior, it is important to distinguish conflict orientation as a psychological trait that is independent of an individual's decision to affiliate with a party or the person's interest in politics generally.

Political interest is the only political variable that approaches a midrange correlation with conflict orientation. It is significant across almost every CCS subscale in both studies in which participants were asked about their level of political interest. Across all three subscales and the full scale, there is a significant positive correlation between the two variables, so that as individuals report greater interest in politics, they are also more likely to be conflict-approaching: more tolerant of conflict, more willing to air disputes publicly, and more willing to confront their opponent head-on. This relationship could raise concerns about the theoretical relationships I outline in the book. If the conflict-approaching individuals are also the most politically interested, then it is possible that any relationship between conflict orientation and political behavior is confounded by their high political interest, which we know leads to greater political engagement and media consumption (Verba et al. 1995).

In the analyses in the following chapters, I examine the relationship between conflict orientation and political engagement across different levels of political interest—particularly among the most politically interested. While political interest does play a major role in shaping political participation, conflict orientation continues to have an independent effect, a phenomenon I will discuss more in chapters 4 and 5.

CONFLICT ORIENTATION, UNCIVIL MEDIA, AND POLITICAL BEHAVIOR

So far, this chapter has characterized conflict orientation as a specific type of approach/avoidance motivation, stable within an individual but with variation across different people. Variation in conflict orientation is tied to psychological and demographic characteristics such as gender, extraversion, and agreeableness, but is distinct from the strategies an individual uses to resolve conflict, as well as political ideology and partisanship. However, if it is so distinct from political characteristics, how does it end up playing a role in political behavior? In order for conflict orientation to influence an individual's political choices, it first has to be made salient by the presence of conflict in political communication. Incivility is just one way in which this conflict can be manifest. In order to ensure that it is incivility and not other forms of communication conflict, such as disagreement, that is driving individual behavior, each of the experiments described in this book attempts to hold disagreement and other elements of the political exchange constant.

Much research has already been done on the impact of incivility on political behavior. In line with theoretical work that argues incivility reduces the deliberative capacity of the American public, scholars have shown that exposure to incivility leads Americans to be more closed-minded, more polarized in their opinions, and less trusting of government and politicians (Brooks and Geer 2007; Geer and Lau 2006; Mutz 2007; Mutz and Reeves 2005). At the same time, incivility can be seen as a boon for participatory democracy, as it energizes citizens and encourages them to fight for their opinions and preferences (Ferree et al. 2002). Empirical findings also support this claim. People are more likely to participate in political activities and discussion across a range of media platforms when exposed to incivility (Borah 2014; Kahn and Kenney 1999; Papacharissi 2004).

These findings demonstrate that, from a macro perspective, it is difficult to determine whether incivility is normatively good or bad; its value depends on what your end goal is within democracy. But if incivility cues an individual's conflict orientation, incivility's effects depend not only on your perspective on democracy, but also on characteristics of the environment and the individual being exposed to that incivility. Political-communication scholars have already begun to investigate the ways in which context changes the effects of uncivil communication. For example, news stories embedded in uncivil blog posts are seen as more credible, because the news article appears to be relatively objective in contrast to the blogger's opinions (Thorson, Vraga, and Ekdale 2010). Incivility is more easily perceived in visual media than on auditory or textual platforms, and the anonymity and lack of moderation in some online comments sections make them more likely to contain uncivil discourse (Stroud et al. 2015; Sydnor 2018). In other words, we know that the media context in which political incivility is presented can play a role in how it affects those who are exposed to it.

Incivility's effects are also dependent on characteristics of individuals. Mutz (2015; Mutz and Reeves 2005) has already demonstrated a link between conflict orientation and incivility, while Gervais (2015) argues that uncivil attacks on one's partisan in-group produce different affective responses than attacks on a partisan out-group. The basic expectation for behavioral effects of incivility—an increase in engagement and a decrease in deliberative discussion, perceptions of trust, and legitimacy—is no longer adequate. Instead, the effects of incivility are context- and individual-specific.

These increasingly nuanced explanations for the impact of incivility on behavior lead to a series of hypotheses about the heterogeneous, interactive effects of conflict orientation and incivility on emotion, information processing and media search, and political discussion and engagement. I will describe the three overarching hypotheses here, then elaborate on the specifics of each in the following chapters, which offer empirical evidence for the interaction between conflict orientation and incivility.

Each set of hypotheses begins with the same assumption, developed in this chapter, that conflict orientation is an approach/avoidance motivation, such that the conflict-avoidant experience incivility as a negative stimulus to shy away from while conflict-approaching individuals experience incivility as a positive stimulus to approach and with which they should continue to engage. Psychologists have demonstrated that emotions result in part from motives; the realization that a stimulus or an event will have implications for the attainment of a particular motive produces an emotional response (Roseman 2008). In this case, incivility is the stimulus, and its presence has different implications for the conflict-avoidant and the conflict-approaching. The conflict-avoidant should experience a negative affective response to arguments or incivility because they are looking to avoid what they see as a negative incident, while the conflict-approaching will report more positive emotional experiences when exposed to incivility.

> *Emotion hypothesis:* The more conflict-avoidant an individual is, the more he or she will report experiencing negative emotions when exposed to incivility. The more conflict-approaching an individual is, the more he or she will report experiencing positive emotions in the face of incivility.

Given what we know about both approach/avoidance motivations and the behavioral implications of affective reactions to stimuli, I also expect incivility and conflict orientation to interact to produce divergent approaches to the search for and processing of political information, as well as engagement in political activities and discussion. Media consumption is the result of a range of choices: an individual must first choose to engage with news at all, and then choose the outlet through which to learn about politics. A range of psychological theories suggest that the conflict-avoidant would look to minimize their exposure to incivility in selecting sources of political news while the conflict-approaching would seek out incivility repeatedly. This is a basic assumption of approach/avoidance motivations—that individuals who have an approach motivation will continue to seek out the stimuli with which they have positive associations, and those with an avoidance motivation will try to remove themselves from the presence of negative stimuli (Elliot 2006). Similarly, psychologists have found that people want congruence between their personal predispositions and their environment and will take action to increase that congruence (Deutsch 1985). Therefore, while individuals who enjoy conflict will be content in a highly uncivil or argumentative environment, their conflict-avoidant counterparts will adapt their behavior and environment to minimize incivility. People also try to minimize their experience of negative emotions and repeat events that produce positive emotions. Each of these psychological tendencies suggests that conflict-avoidant individuals will avoid political news generally and, more specifically, avoid media outlets that would expose them to incivility. Conflict-approaching people, on the other hand, would be more likely to engage with political news, regardless of whether the source was likely to expose them to incivility.

That being said, we all know that it is impossible to avoid political incivility once we have turned on the news. Therefore, I also examine what happens once someone has been exposed to incivility. How does exposure to political incivility shape our strategy for seeking out additional media content? The intuitive response might be that the same patterns play out: the conflict-avoidant immediately look for alternatives, while the conflict-approaching dive in and look for more. But research into the effects of anxiety and the way we manage our mood more generally suggests that this may not be the case. Anxious individuals engage in biased information-processing. They spend more time looking for information about threatening stimuli and recall more details about that information (Albertson and Gadarian 2015). Once the conflict-avoidant are exposed to political incivility, they are unable to look away. The conflict-approaching, in contrast, are quick to move on. Because their good moods are not diminished by exposure to uncivil politics, they actually expand the types of content they are looking for. As mood-management theory suggests, overall positive affect can lead us to widen our media exposure and look beyond those things that entertain us.

Information-seeking hypothesis: Conflict-avoidant individuals will avoid political news, but when exposed to incivility, will be more likely to seek out additional uncivil content. By contrast, the conflict-approaching will spend more time with political programming, but will be less motivated to seek out incivility after seeing it once.

Lastly, I expect the interaction between incivility and conflict orientation to influence the quality and quantity of political engagement. Political scientists have already established that both incivility and conflict orientation have direct effects on participation in certain political activities (e.g., Brooks and Geer 2007; Kahn and Kenney 1999; Testa et al. 2014; Ulbig and Funk 1999) and interactive effects on political attitudes (Mutz 2015; Mutz and Reeves 2005). However, I argue that incivility and conflict orientation interact to produce variation not only in the amount of political engagement, but also in the quality of participation. In other words, incivility leads certain types of people to participate in certain types of political activities—protest, persuasion, or blog commentary. It also shapes the language they use in those activities. I hypothesize that the conflict-approaching are more likely to use incivility in political discussions, at least in part because they are comfortable with uncivil expression to begin with. Therefore, the conflict-approaching are not only more engaged in the kinds of political activities where people are likely to be most vocal about their opinions, but also less civil in expressing their opinions.

Engagement quantity hypothesis: The more conflict-approaching an individual is, the more he or she will report participating in political activities in which exposure to incivility is high.

Engagement quality hypothesis: The more conflict-approaching an individual is, the more likely he or she will be to use uncivil language in political discussion.

* * *

Individuals' predispositions toward conflict—their reactions to and experience of disagreement and argument—are stable, trait-based characteristics that are tied to several key demographic characteristics, including gender, age, personality, and political interest. Because we know that the *Humans of New York* interviewee to whom we were introduced at the beginning of the chapter is conflict-avoidant, we might expect him to be more agreeable and conscientious, but less extraverted and less interested in politics. Because his conflict orientation was established in child- and early adulthood, it is a pre-political trait that likely has little influence on his partisan identification or the strength of that identification. Furthermore, conflict orientation is distinct from decisions about how to resolve conflict. While he notes that his solution is to agree "with pretty much everything anybody says," that tendency is distinct from his experience and reaction to conflict situations, particularly conflict communication. As I will demonstrate in the coming chapters, conflict orientation influences the affective response individuals have to political incivility and ultimately the ways in which citizens like our interviewee engage with the media and in political activities. Per the hypotheses outlined here, our conflict-avoidant interviewee is far less capable of effective engagement in the political world than his conflict-approaching counterparts: he is more likely to experience negative emotional reactions to politics, to consume less political news, to engage in biased information search, and to participate in fewer political activities.

3

TO LAUGH OR CRY?

Emotional Responses to Incivility

Incivility at times provides wonderful entertainment,
but it creates anxiety.

—SUSAN HERBST (2010, 130)

I HAVE A short clip from a 2013 episode of Fox's *Hannity* that I like to use to start classroom discussions of incivility. In it, Tamara Holder, a Democrat and *Fox News* contributor, and conservative radio host Billy Cunningham are having a conversation about raising the debt ceiling. Their disagreement escalates as Cunningham praises Rand Paul's balanced budget and jabs his finger toward Holder, saying "Your ilk, people of your ilk. . . ." Holder cuts him off, shouting, "Get your finger out of my face!" ("Holder and Cunningham Blow Up" 2013). As they watch, students tend to have one of two reactions. Some stare at me in shock, clearly uncomfortable with the behavior of the two television commentators. Others start chuckling at the politicos' behavior, finding the exchange to be just another example of the ways in which politics becomes theater. Either way, the segment elicits a series of emotions in the students that shape their comments in class and their attitude toward the show and the argument being made about Obama's economic policy.

In a move away from an emphasis on the "rational voter" (e.g., Downs 1957; Enelow and Hinich 1984; Page and Shapiro 1992), contemporary scholars of political behavior have welcomed affect into their theories. Emotions have been found to increase persuasion, shape candidate evaluations, and inspire engagement in "effortful" political activities like protest and letter-writing (Brader 2005; Cassino and Lodge 2007). Generally, different emotions are associated with approach and avoidance tendencies: an approach motivation is linked to positive feelings, and negative feelings are associated with avoidance (Cacioppo, Priester, and Berntson 1993; Elliot, Eder, and Harmon-Jones 2013). However, anger stands out as a negative emotion that is tied to an approach motivation. In politics, anger encourages citizens to get involved—to protest, write letters, or express their opinions—while disgust and anxiety turn citizens away from political engagement (Brader 2006).

The general assumption behind much of this research is that most people have similar emotional responses to political stimuli: negative advertisements produce negative emotional responses across all study participants, and positive advertisements produce positive emotional responses. When individual differences have been incorporated, the most common focus is on the effects of partisanship. However, in the previous chapter, I hypothesized that conflict orientation influences affective and behavioral responses to political incivility, producing heterogeneous effects on individuals' emotional responses, information-seeking patterns, and political engagement. The first of these hypotheses, the *emotion hypothesis*, suggests that in the face of incivility, individual citizens will have different responses, and these different responses will be conditional on the person's conflict orientation. Conflict-avoidant citizens will have stronger negative emotional responses to incivility than their conflict-approaching counterparts. Conflict-approaching individuals will have more positive emotional responses to the same information and tone. Returning to the earlier example, my theory suggests that the conflict-approaching students were the ones who laughed at the Holder-Cunningham exchange, while my conflict-avoidant students cringed or looked uncomfortable.

These expectations are borne out in the data. This chapter reports the results from two survey experiments in which participants were shown either a civil or an uncivil video clip and then asked about their emotional response to that clip. I found, as expected, that conflict-avoidant individuals recoil from expressions of incivility in the media, while conflict-approaching individuals relish it. Conflict-avoidant participants reported greater feelings of disgust, anxiety, and anger after watching uncivil media, whereas conflict-approaching participants overall reported less of these emotions at roughly equivalent levels for both civil and uncivil video clips. Conversely, the most conflict-approaching participants reported significantly higher feelings of amusement and entertainment when assigned to watch the uncivil treatment. The conflict-avoidant, however, were no more entertained by incivility than by civil presentations of information. These results demonstrate that the interaction of incivility and conflict orientation leads to very different emotional responses across individuals.

These divergent outcomes complicate our understanding of the role of incivility in politics. On the one hand, incivility elicits emotions that draw people into the political arena, potentially increasing participation and citizen engagement. On the other hand, it systematically discourages involvement by the conflict-avoidant—people who are more likely to articulate positions in nonconfrontational ways. Furthermore, these findings suggest that incivility breeds incivility: nasty online comments and hateful outbursts at political rallies may be the result of the conflict-approaching individual's enthusiasm for argument and confrontation.

EMOTIONAL POLITICS

Research on emotion and affect spans psychological subfields as cognitive, social, and neuro-psychologists attempt to determine the extent to which emotions are conscious or unconscious, a result of cognitive processes or the inspiration for cognitive action (Frijda 1986; James 1884; Lazarus 1994). Multiple theories seek to explain the nature of emotion and connect it to behavior and decision-making, and many of them have been applied to politics.[1] One such theory suggests that emotion sparks different motivations that ultimately shape citizen behavior. Generally, this line of research suggests that positive emotions are associated with an approach motivation and negative emotions encourage avoidance (Cacioppo et al. 1993; Carver and Scheier 1990; Elliot et al. 2013). However, anger is often associated with both an approach motivation and negative feelings (Carver 2004; Harmon-Jones 2003; Harmon-Jones, Harmon-Jones, and Price 2013). These general emotion-motivation-behavior patterns play out in a range of social and political scenarios, with emotions shaping candidate preferences, persuasion, reliance on prior beliefs, and political interest (Brader 2006; Cassino and Lodge 2007; Huddy, Feldman, and Cassese 2007; MacKuen et al. 2007; Parsons 2010).

Political communication, and incivility in particular, can produce different emotional responses in citizens. For example, Brader (2006) shows that positive music in campaign ads cues enthusiasm while negative music and images evoke fear. While Brader focuses on nonverbal communication in order to ensure his effects are in response to the processing of emotions rather than a cognitive response to the substance of the message, others have focused on emotional responses to language (e.g., Gross 2008; Druckman and McDermott 2008), and particularly the language used in uncivil communication (Mutz 2015; Gervais 2014, 2015). Sociologists interested in Australians' responses to situations of "everyday incivility" found that individuals' emotional responses to uncivil experiences depend on whether the person is a witness or participant in the event. In focus-group recollections of these experiences, individuals who had participated were more likely to report feelings of anger, while observers reported more feelings of fear, unease, and disgust (Phillips and Smith 2004). Similarly, Gervais (2015) found that exposure to like-minded incivility provoked less of an emotional response in participants in an online discussion forum than did exposure to disagreeable incivility. Characteristics of the individuals receiving the message—their position vis-à-vis the person communicating through incivility—shaped their emotional and behavioral responses to the communication.

Like Phillips and Smith and Gervais, I argue that our responses to political incivility are more nuanced. Incivility does not elicit the same emotions across all individuals. Appraisal theory suggests that emotions are elicited based on an individual's assessment of the personal significance of a situation, object, or stimulus (Lazarus 1994; Roseman 2008; Scherer 1999). From this perspective, we are constantly assessing the congruence between situations and our own motivations. If individuals are motivated to approach conflict situations, then they will have a different emotional response than if they are motivated to avoid conflict. In the case of political incivility, individuals' motivations are tied not only to partisan identity but also to their conflict orientation: their desire to approach or avoid argumentative or confrontational situations.

EXPECTATIONS

Previous research has demonstrated that incivility can produce a range of emotional responses, from disgust, fear, and frustration to anger to excitement (Gervais 2015; Mutz and Reeves 2005; Phillips and Smith 2004). Certain individuals are more likely to experience these emotional reactions than others because of the interaction between conflict orientation and incivility. More conflict-avoidant individuals will be more likely to react negatively to incivility while conflict-approaching individuals will have positive responses to the same tone. I focus on three negative emotions—anxiety, disgust, and anger—and three positive emotions—amusement, entertainment, and enthusiasm.

I expect that when conflict-avoidant individuals are faced with political information that is expressed in a highly argumentative or uncivil manner, they will have a negative reaction, regardless of whether they agree with the information being conveyed or the people presenting that information. The conflict-approaching, on the other hand, will more likely react with enthusiasm or amusement to the expression of incivility in political media.

Looking first at negative emotions, the literature suggests that incivility could easily tap into the distinct appraisal themes and action tendencies of each. Perceptions of threat and uncertainty produce anxiety (Albertson and Gadarian 2015; MacKuen et al. 2007). If individuals prefer a world in which conflict is minimized, it seems obvious that they will perceive incivility as threating to the stability and habitual nature of their world. If an individual enjoys conflict, incivility is far less likely to produce the same feelings of threat or uncertainty.

Anxiety hypothesis: The more conflict-avoidant the individual, the more anxiety he or she will report feeling when exposed to incivility.

Whereas anxiety stems from feelings of uncertainty, disgust arises when a situation or stimulus violates expectations of moral purity (Horberg et al. 2009; Pizarro, Inbar, and Helion 2011; Rozin, Haidt, and McCauley 2008). The use of obscenity or other uncivil language has been tied to morality throughout American culture (Carter 1998; Feinberg 1988; Horberg et al. 2009), making it plausible that uncivil language would elicit feelings of moral disgust toward politics or the political discussion.

Disgust hypothesis: More conflict-avoidant individuals than conflict-approaching individuals will report feeling disgusted by incivility.

Appraisal theory suggests that individuals are more likely to experience anger when they assess a situation as wrong or unjust in some way (Lerner and Tiedens 2006; Russell and Giner-Sorolla 2011). Incivility's ability to provoke anger, therefore, would depend not only on how an individual feels about conflict, but the person's assessment of the situation in which incivility is used. In a political situation, this could be tied to partisanship; as Gervais (2015) has shown, partisans are more likely to experience anger when incivility is directed toward their own party than when it is directed at the opposing party. We can imagine that exposure to incivility might prompt greater anger among the conflict-avoidant—toward the media for sanctioning this type of language, toward political elites for using it, or toward politics generally. Furthermore, conflict-avoidant individuals who share the partisan perspective being attacked might be more likely to report anger than those who share the perspective of the attacker.

Anger hypothesis: Conflict-avoidant individuals will be more likely to report feelings of anger after exposure to incivility.

Partisan-anger hypothesis: Conflict-avoidant individuals who are exposed to disagreeable incivility will report greater anger than those who see the exchange as like-minded incivility.

While the conflict-avoidant are more likely to experience negative emotions, I expect those who are more conflict-approaching to have more positive reactions to incivility. Experiences generated by others that are also consistent with an individual's personal motives evoke "liking" (Arnold 1960; Roseman 1984). Translated directly into my framework, mediated incivility is consistent with the conflict-approaching individual's motivation to experience conflict and therefore will be liked. Similarly, affective-intelligence theory suggests that enthusiasm and satisfaction stem from the successful repetition of behavioral outcomes (Marcus, Neuman, and MacKuen 2000). From both perspectives, an individual who enjoys conflict situations will report experiencing incivility positively. Indeed, this is what Mutz and Reeves (2005) found: individuals who are excited by conflict also report that incivility has greater entertainment value. I assess individuals' reporting of three positive affective states in the face of incivility: entertainment, amusement, and enthusiasm. I expect the patterns here to be the opposite of those found in the investigation of negative emotions. Whereas the conflict-avoidant will report no difference in their positive experience of the civil or uncivil video clips, the conflict-approaching will have a stronger positive reaction to incivility.

Entertainment hypothesis: The more conflict-approaching the individual, the more he or she will report being entertained by incivility.

Amusement hypothesis: The more conflict-approaching the individual, the more he or she will report being amused by incivility.

Enthusiasm hypothesis: The more conflict-approaching the individual, the more he or she will report enthusiasm about incivility.

EXPERIMENTAL MANIPULATION OF INCIVILITY

My first test of these hypotheses uses data from the six hundred participants in the Survey Sampling International (SSI) study. In the SSI study, after participants responded to the Conflict Communication Scale, they were told that they would watch a short clip from a recent political newscast and then be asked a series of questions based on the video. Participants were assigned to one of four treatments that varied in their level of civility. The clips were either civil or uncivil[2] and came from either MSNBC's *Morning Joe* or *The Dylan Ratigan Show*.[3] Because a pilot test of the treatments suggested that the clips from the two shows were viewed similarly across key measures, the analyses in this chapter focus only on the difference between the civil and uncivil treatments and not on distinctions between those participants who saw *Morning Joe* and those who saw *Dylan Ratigan*. The use of both civil and uncivil treatments allows me to compare reactions to the two treatments at the same value of conflict orientation, as well as responses to the same treatment across different levels of conflict orientation. To encourage realism, the clips were excerpts from live cable news broadcasts, with the same two- to three-minute segment shortened to highlight either the civil or uncivil components of one conversation among the same set of commentators. The segments from both *Dylan Ratigan* and *Morning Joe* dealt with major economic debates from 2009 and 2011: the AIG bonus scandal and the budget deficit. As with any experimental treatment, the videos represent a balance between the desire for ecological validity and a realistic experience on the part of participants versus the need to control as much of the content as possible to ensure that the treatments differ only on the construct of interest (Druckman et al. 2011).

To ensure that the civil and uncivil treatments differed in incivility rather than simply the level of disagreement, I chose videos in which political elites—journalists and elected officials—disagreed about a political outcome. Substantively, the clips focus on policy and do not contain the sort of antidemocratic content that Papacharissi (2004) identifies as uncivil. Therefore, the findings reported here only compare emotional responses to incivility as captured by the tone of communication rather than the substance. Both uncivil clips contain indicators of incivility similar to those used in other experimental research (e.g., Berry and Sobeiraj 2014; Brooks and Geer 2007; Gervais 2015; Mutz 2015), including interruption, shouting, and verbal sparring (phrases like "wait a second" or "well, listen"). The uncivil clips also contain visual cues that could signal incivility. In *Morning Joe*, cohost Mika Brzezinski touches Joe Scarborough's forearm as he emphatically interrupts Representative Cantor, as if to encourage him to tone down his response. In the *Dylan Ratigan* clip, one of the female speakers holds her hands up while fighting against an interruption, reinforcing her words, "wait a minute," with a hand gesture that indicates the same thing. While neither gesture is uncivil in itself, both could be incorporated into an individual's mental picture of the scene as evidence that incivility is occurring. Finally, the civil clips contain an exchange between the same journalists and political elites in which they had some disagreement but without the indicators of incivility such as name-calling or shouting.

As figure 3.1 shows, participants in the survey interpreted the uncivil treatment as approximately one-half point less civil than the civil treatment, a statistically significant but perhaps not substantively significant difference $(\overline{x}_{uncivil} = 3.1, sd = 1.0; \overline{x}_{civil} = 2.5, sd = 1.1, t = 6.6)$. The most conflict-avoidant and the most conflict-approaching participants perceived the civil treatment as similarly civil and the uncivil treatment as similarly uncivil. These treatments present a hard test of my theory: if only a slight difference in incivility can produce different emotional effects, it is likely that a more extreme case would produce larger variation. Furthermore, because perceptions of incivility do not vary with conflict orientation, we can be more confident that conflict orientation is directly shaping emotional reactions, rather than orientation affecting perceptions of incivility, which then influence one's affective response.

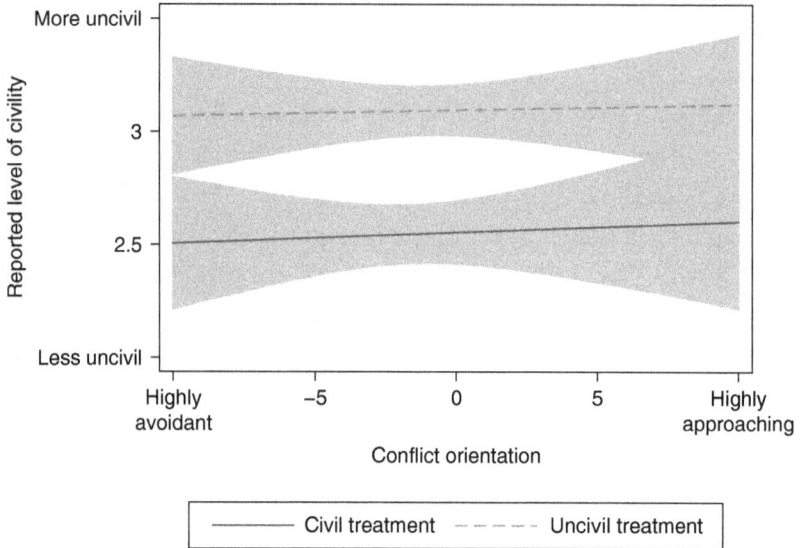

FIGURE 3.1 Perceived civility of the MSNBC clips.

Note: Linear predictions derived from bivariate regressions of perceived civility on conflict orientation and experimental treatment. Shaded areas represent 95% confidence intervals.

Source: SSI.

INCIVILITY SPARKS EMOTIONAL RESPONSES

Before getting into the differences across conflict orientations, I looked for a general relationship between exposure to incivility and reported emotional responses. Drawing on Mutz and Reeves (2005) and Brader (2006), I expected the uncivil treatment to increase individuals' reported experience of all emotions, positive or negative.

These relationships are borne out in the data, although the results are more pronounced for negative emotions than for positive ones. The graph on the left side of figure 3.2 shows that incivility only weakly increases individuals' positive feelings. Participants in the incivility treatment only report a significant increase in their feelings of amusement when compared

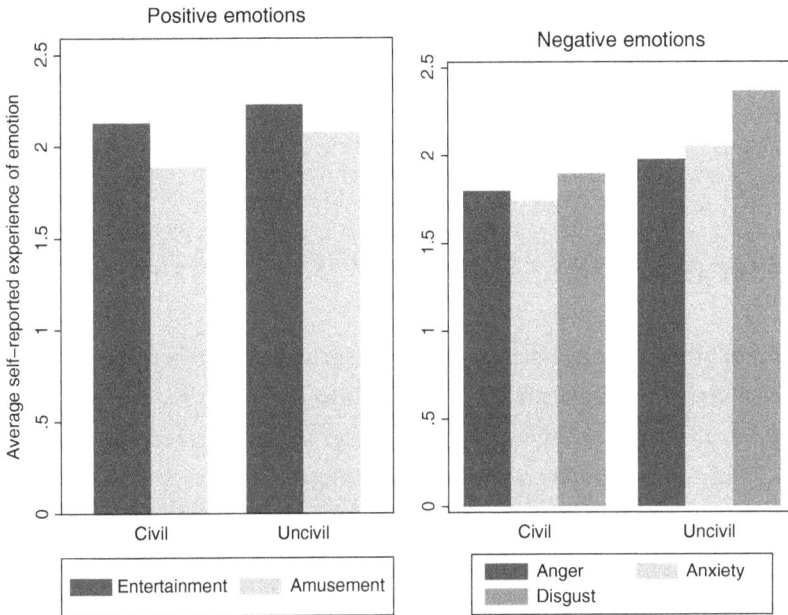

FIGURE 3.2 Average emotional responses to treatments.
Source: SSI.

to those who watched the civil clip ($\bar{x}_{\text{civil}} = 1.89$, $\bar{x}_{\text{uncivil}} = 2.08$, $p < 0.041$).[4] This difference is relatively small: the participants in the uncivil condition reported their amusement as, on average, two-tenths of a point higher on a five-point scale than did those participants in the civil condition. A two-sample, two-tailed t-test indicates there was no significant difference in their reported entertainment ($\overline{x_{\text{uncivil}}} = 2.2$, $\overline{x_{\text{civil}}} = 2.1$, $p = 0.30$).

The treatment has a greater effect on participants' reported experience of negative emotions—anger, disgust, and anxiety. Participants reported statistically significantly greater feelings of each negative emotion in the uncivil condition than in the civil condition. The effects are still relatively small for anger and anxiety, an increase of between two- and three-tenths of a point (*Anger : $\overline{x_{\text{uncivil}}} = 2.0$, $\overline{x_{\text{civil}}} = 1.8$, $p < 0.02$; Anxiety : $\overline{x_{\text{uncivil}}} = 2.1$, $\overline{x_{\text{civil}}} = 1.7$, $p < 0.041$*), but they are much greater for feelings of disgust. On average, participants report feeling a little disgusted after watching the civil treatment ($\bar{x} = 1.90$), but this average jumps half a point on the scale to 2.37, or somewhere between "a little" and "somewhat" disgusted for participants in the uncivil condition ($p < 0.01$).

EFFECTS AS MODERATED BY CONFLICT ORIENTATION

Overall, these findings demonstrate that incivility elicits a range of emotional responses from citizens, both positive and negative. But the main effects of incivility on emotional response also suggest an interesting tension: incivility increases reported negative feelings like anger, disgust, and anxiety, but it also increases positive feelings of amusement. Breaking the results down across the range of conflict orientations reveals why incivility seems to produce both positive and negative emotional reactions in individuals. In comparison to civil coverage of the same issue, incivility is more likely to elicit positive emotions in more conflict-approaching individuals, but more likely to induce negative emotions in the conflict-avoidant.

Table 3.1 displays the results of five OLS regression models that investigated the relationship between each emotional response, conflict orientation, the treatment condition, and a variety of demographic and political characteristics. Looking first at the negative emotions—anxiety, anger, and disgust—I expected that exposure to incivility would increase feelings of all three among the conflict-avoidant and that partisanship would also play a role in evoking anger. When I compare the findings from the civil and uncivil treatments across the range of conflict orientations, it is clear that individuals who are more conflict-avoidant experience greater negative emotional reactions to incivility than they do to a civil discussion of the same issue. As table 3.1 shows, a similar pattern emerges in individuals' self-reported feelings of anxiety, disgust, and anger in response to civility and incivility. Individuals who are more conflict-avoidant report greater negative emotional reactions to the uncivil clip than they do to the civil clip. However, this difference disappears when we look at individuals who are more conflict-approaching.

TABLE 3.1 THE INTERACTION BETWEEN CONFLICT ORIENTATION AND INCIVILITY INFLUENCES EMOTIONAL RESPONSES

	ANXIOUS	DISGUSTED	ANGRY	AMUSED	ENTERTAINED
Conflict orientation	−0.0080	0.022	0.0087	0.037*	0.014
	(0.0144)	(0.016)	(0.015)	(0.015)	(0.015)
Uncivil treatment	0.26**	0.41**	0.15	0.28**	0.21*
	(0.094)	(0.107)	(0.097)	(0.098)	(0.099)
C.O. x Treatment	−0.031	−0.059*	−0.030	0.031	0.050*
	(0.021)	(0.024)	(0.022)	(0.022)	(0.022)
Political knowledge	−0.099**	−0.041	−0.074*	−0.16**	−0.17**
	(0.036)	(0.041)	(0.037)	(0.373)	(0.038)
Democrat	−0.14	−0.26	−0.17	0.039	0.029
	(0.122)	(0.136)	(0.124)	(0.125)	(0.126)
Independent	−0.19	−0.099	−0.21	0.049	−0.072
	(0.141)	(0.159)	(0.144)	(0.145)	(0.147)
Strong partisan	0.12	0.12	−0.011	0.26*	0.27*
	(0.111)	(0.125)	(0.113)	(0.114)	(0.115)
Female	−0.22*	−0.15	−0.24*	−0.20*	−0.14
	(0.092)	(0.104)	(0.094)	(0.095)	(0.097)
Constant	−0.22**	2.21**	2.28**	2.35**	2.60**
	(0.092)	(0.187)	(0.170)	(0.17)	(0.174)

Source: SSI.

Note: Cell entries are regression coefficients with standard errors in parentheses.

*$p < 0.05$, **$p < 0.01$

Figure 3.3 displays these regression results graphically. Feelings of disgust among the conflict-avoidant are most influenced by the presence of incivility, with the highly conflict-avoidant (those who score a −10 on the Conflict Communication Scale) reporting average feelings of disgust at around 2.6 on the 5-point scale when shown the uncivil video clip. This translates to feeling somewhere between "slightly" and "moderately" disgusted. Those conflict-avoidant individuals who viewed the civil clip

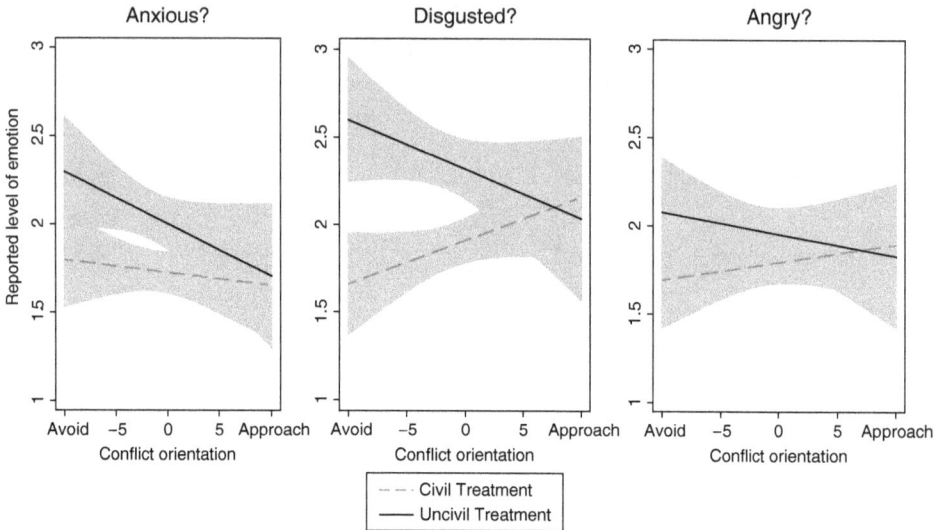

FIGURE 3.3 Conflict-avoidant individuals experience more negative emotions in response to incivility.

Note: Linear predictions are from an OLS regression of emotion and the interaction between conflict orientation and experimental treatment, controlling for demographic and political variables. Each emotion was measured on a 1 to 5 scale, with 1 indicating a respondent experienced a given emotion "not at all" and 5 indicating "extremely." *Source*: SSI.

reported feelings of disgust that averaged around 1.6, a full point lower than those who viewed incivility, somewhere between "not at all" and "slightly" disgusted. The gap between those who viewed the uncivil clip and those in the civil condition declines as conflict orientation moves toward greater conflict-approaching tendencies, becoming statistically indistinguishable around the conflict-ambivalent zero point.

Incivility also has a greater effect on individuals' reported feelings of anxiety if they are highly conflict-avoidant. The gap between average reported anxiety for the highly conflict-avoidant in civil and uncivil treatments is about half a point on the five-point scale, with those who watched the uncivil video clip reporting more anxiety than those in the civil treatment. The difference between the treatments at the highest levels of conflict avoidance is not statistically significant, but this is likely due to the relatively small set of participants who score the highest and lowest values of the CCS. The difference is clear for those participants who are slightly conflict-avoidant (those who scored between -7 and zero), and the gap between reported feelings of anxiety for these individuals is between a quarter and a third of a point. As with reported feelings of disgust, the difference between the civil and uncivil treatments disappears for those participants who are conflict-approaching. The responses for reported feelings of anger also follow this pattern, although these differences are not statistically significant. The conflict-approaching do not experience any greater feelings of anger, anxiety, or disgust when viewing an uncivil video clip than when viewing a civil clip. However, the conflict-avoidant report feeling more anxious and disgusted when they watch uncivil coverage of politics than when they watch a civil discussion of the same issue, thereby offering support for the *anxiety*, *disgust*, and *anger hypotheses*. There was no support for the *partisan-anger hypothesis*. Neither partisanship nor the strength of party identity had a statistically significant effect on participants' report of negative emotional reactions.

The pattern for the experience of positive emotions mirrors that for negative emotions. Looking at figure 3.4, we see that the conflict-approaching are more likely to report feeling amused or entertained when watching an uncivil clip than when exposed to the civil treatment. However, more conflict-avoidant individuals report feeling no more positive when watching the uncivil video than when watching the civil one. The effects for both amusement and entertainment are relatively similar, with highly conflict-approaching participants in the uncivil condition reporting levels of both reactions that are about three-quarters of a point higher than those in the civil condition. In other words, the most conflict-approaching people found the uncivil clip to be moderately amusing or entertaining, while they found the civil clip to be only slightly amusing or entertaining. Those who identified as more conflict-avoidant reported no difference in their feelings of amusement and entertainment when watching the uncivil or civil video clips.

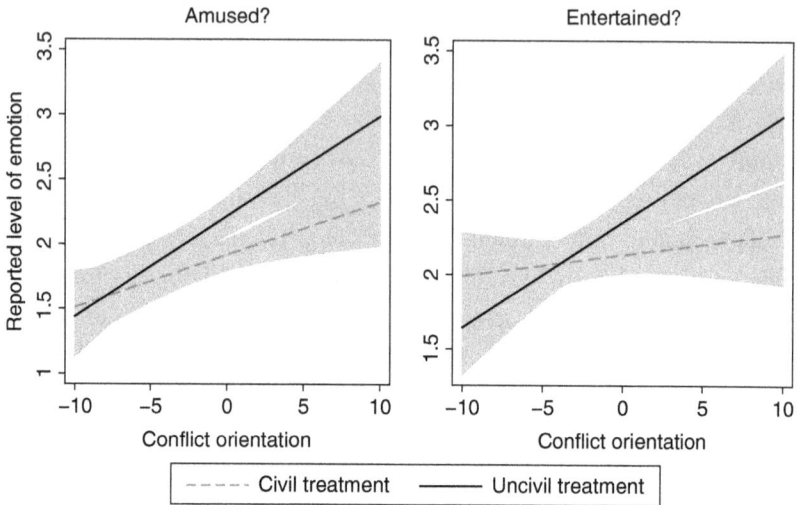

FIGURE 3.4 Conflict-approaching individuals experience positive emotional reactions to incivility.

Note: Linear predictions are from an OLS regression of emotion and the interaction between conflict orientation and experimental treatment, controlling for demographic and political variables. Each emotion was measured on a 1 to 5 scale, with 1 indicating a respondent experienced a given emotion "not at all" and 5 indicating "extremely."
Source: SSI.

To summarize, the SSI study results suggest that conflict orientation and incivility interact to produce different emotional responses in the conflict-avoidant and conflict-approaching. Participants who are more conflict-avoidant are more likely to report negative emotions such as disgust and anxiety when shown an uncivil news clip than when shown a civil portrayal of the same information. Conversely, more conflict-approaching people report greater amusement and entertainment when watching an uncivil clip than a civil one. These findings hold even when controlling for other facets of individuals' political lives, including their partisanship, political interest and knowledge, and demographic characteristics such as gender. While these demographic and social characteristics do have an impact on individuals' emotional responses above and beyond the treatments, incivility and conflict orientation continue to play a significant role in emotional response, particularly in evoking disgust and entertainment.

BEYOND POLITICAL INCIVILITY

The SSI study demonstrates that political incivility elicits different emotional reactions based on our conflict orientations. But these results raise a second question: Can we be conflict-avoidant when it comes to politics, but conflict-approaching in our professional lives? If our conflict orientation is specific to politics, then we would not have the same reactions to political incivility as we would to other types of incivility.

The GfK study was designed in part to test the extent to which conflict orientation shapes our responses to incivility in the mediated world more generally The 3,101 participants recruited for this study completed a four-question version of the Conflict Communication Scale[5] and were randomly assigned to one of four 45-second clips that varied in the presence of civility or incivility and their substantive content. One set was political in nature, featuring CSPAN coverage of congressional hearings on Planned Parenthood. The second set of clips was entertainment-based and centered on two judges' evaluations of food prepared by a contestant on the reality cooking show *Master Chef*. Each of the clips was pretested by a different online convenience sample and selected to maximize differences in perceived civility between the civil and uncivil clips while minimizing differences across the substantive topics.

The Planned Parenthood clips showed an exchange between members of the Congressional Oversight and Government Reform committee and Planned Parenthood president Cecile Richards. In the civil condition, Representative Elijah Cummings (D-Md.) argues in a reasoned, calm tone that the rule of law must be followed even if he or others wish that it said something else. The uncivil clip depicts an exchange between Richards and Representative Jim Jordan (R-Ohio). Jordan frequently interrupts Richards, raises his voice, holds his finger up as if he's point-ing or telling her to wait a minute, and ultimately accuses her of avoiding his questions. Using a 5-point scale on which 1 signified the clip was not at all civil and 5 indicated extreme civility, participants saw a statistically significant difference in the civility of the two clips ($\overline{x_{\text{civil}}}$ = 3.2, sd = 1.3; $\overline{x_{\text{uncivil}}}$ = 1.7, sd = 0.90, $p(two - tailed) < 0.01$).

In the *Master Chef* clips, a male contestant's pasta dish is being judged. In the civil condition, a female judge is critical of the food but keeps an even tone and does not malign or otherwise insult the contestant. The uncivil condition presents an assessment of the same meal by a second, male judge. This judge is also critical, but he criticizes in a way that belittles the contestant, pointing to his "cavalier" and "oh poor me again, I screwed up" attitude. He continues: "You want to show us how cutesy and intelligent and crafty you are. Well that's going to get you a one-way ticket back to where you came from. And then you can show your friends and the six people who told you you were good how cutesy and smart you are while you're at home cooking at dinner parties" ("Joe vs Howard Pasta Challenge" 2013). As with the Planned Parenthood clips, the *Master Chef* clips were perceived as significantly different from one another ($\overline{x_{\text{civil}}}$ = 2.5, sd = 1.20; $\overline{x_{\text{uncivil}}}$ = 1.6, sd = 0.89, $p(two - tailed) < 0.01$).

Before moving into the relationships between conflict orientation, incivility, and emotional responses to these new clips, I offer a brief char-acterization of the participants and treatments. The average participant was slightly conflict-avoidant ($\overline{x}$ = −2.4, sd = 2.95). There was a statisti-cally significant difference between the perceived civility of the civil and uncivil clips, as well as between the coverage of the two topics. Specifically, the civil Planned Parenthood clip was found to be almost half a point more civil than that from *Master Chef* ($\overline{x}$ = 3.2, sd = 1.31; $\overline{x}$ = 2.6, sd = 1.20, respectively) on a 5-point scale where 5 signified extreme civility. The dif-ference between the two uncivil clips was smaller and statistically insignifi-cant ($\overline{x_{PP}}$ = 1.7, sd = 0.90; $\overline{x_{MC}}$ = 1.6, sd = 0.89).

As in the previous experiment, participants' experience of discrete emo-tions was self-reported on a 5-point scale where 1 demonstrated that a participant did not feel a particular emotion at all and 5 indicated extreme emotion. For the most part, the uncivil treatments produced more emotional responses, particularly negative ones, than the civil treatments.

An OLS regression of each emotion on the interaction between conflict orientation and incivility, holding constant partisanship, ideology, gender, education, and race, displays patterns similar to those seen in the SSI study. Figure 3.5 graphically depicts these results.[6] For the *Master Chef* clip, there is no significant difference in the reported anger, disgust, or anxiety of the highly conflict-approaching. However, the most conflict-avoidant individuals were likely to report substantially more anger, disgust, and anxiety after watching the uncivil clip than the civil one. The uncivil Planned Parenthood clip produced a strong direct effect but weaker interactive effects on anger and disgust. Regardless of conflict orientation, the uncivil clip elicited greater disgust and anger on the part of participants. However, the interactive pattern for anxiety matches that found in the SSI study and with the *Master Chef* clips. The conflict-avoidant reported greater feelings of anxiety—almost a point higher on the scale—when shown the uncivil clip, whereas there is no difference in the emotion evoked by the two clips in the conflict-approaching. Once again, there is support for the *anxiety, disgust*, and *anger hypotheses*. Party identification fails to obtain statistical significance, so once again there is no support for the *partisan-anger hypothesis*.

As in the SSI study, incivility and conflict orientation produce weaker effects on positive emotional responses (see figure 3.6). Both conflict orientation and incivility produce statistically significant direct effects for the Planned Parenthood and *Master Chef* videos; however, the interaction between the two is only statistically significant for amusement in the Planned Parenthood condition. While the remaining interactions fail to achieve statistical significance, they do follow a similar pattern to that found in the SSI sample. Therefore, there is at least some support for the *amusement* and *entertainment hypotheses*, as well as an indication that conflict orientation and the presence of incivility can evoke enthusiasm in participants, thereby substantiating the *enthusiasm hypothesis*.

* * *

To what extent did the clip make you feel...

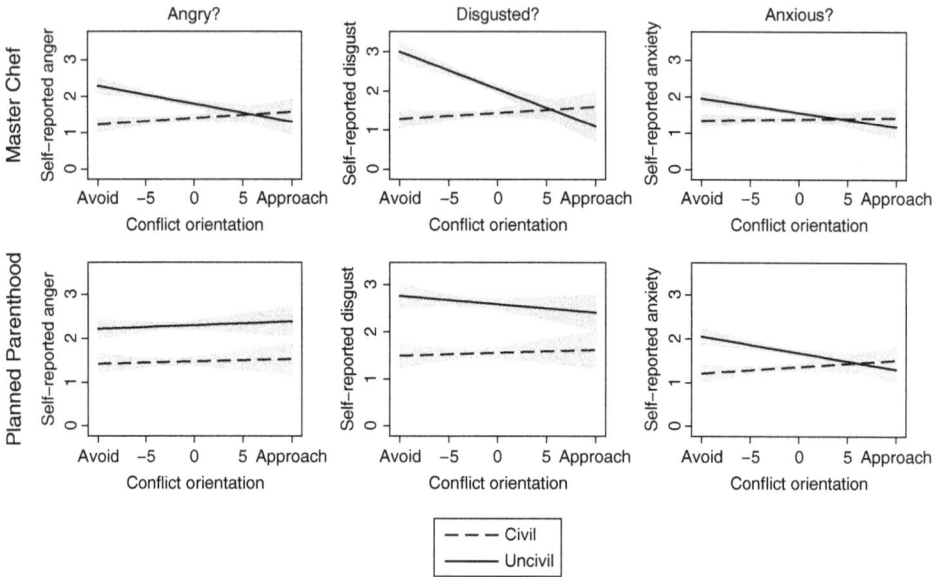

FIGURE 3.5 GfK study also demonstrates conflict-avoidant have negative reactions to incivility.

Note: Linear predictions are from an OLS regression of emotion and the interaction between conflict orientation and experimental treatment, controlling for demographic and political variables. Each emotion was measured on a 0 to 4 scale, with 0 indicating a respondent experienced a given emotion "not at all" and 4 indicating "extremely."

Source: GfK.

Current research on incivility emphasizes its dual nature: on one hand, it decreases trust in government and perceptions of legitimacy; on the other, it increases participation. This book offers one reason for these contrasting outcomes: incivility affects people differently because people respond to conflict in different ways.

Specifically, the studies described in this chapter demonstrate that people who do not enjoy conflict—the conflict-avoidant—will experience greater negative emotions when exposed to incivility than when asked to watch a civil video clip. Alternatively, the conflict-approaching will report

To what extent did the clip make you feel...

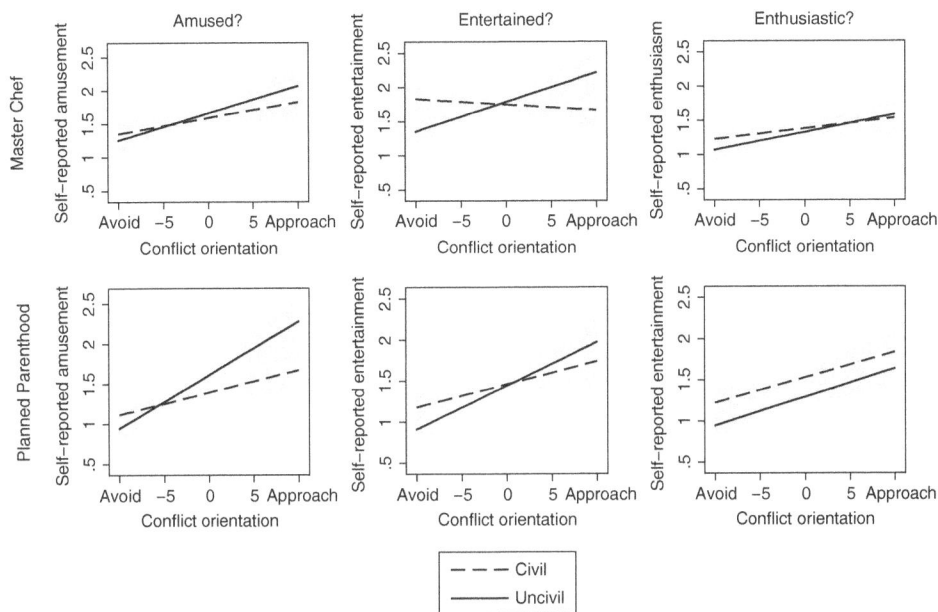

FIGURE 3.6 Incivility evokes positive emotions among GfK participants.

Note: Linear predictions are from an OLS regression of emotion and the interaction between conflict orientation and experimental treatment, controlling for demographic and political variables. Each emotion was measured on a 0 to 4 scale, with 0 indicating a respondent experienced a given emotion "not at all" and 4 indicating "extremely."

Source: GfK.

stronger positive emotions in the face of incivility. These patterns hold up across different samples and using different video clips on both political and entertainment topics.

The fact that conflict orientation and incivility interact to provoke different emotional responses has implications for a range of political behaviors and decisions. Much of the evidence suggests that emotion has a positive effect on political participation (Marcus et al. 2000). Research by Brader (2006) suggests that anxiety propels people to seek more information, while enthusiasm stimulates the desire to vote. This increased engagement in the political sphere is typically seen as normatively positive, but it raises concerns about the quality of citizens' engagement. Conflict-approaching individuals are being drawn into politics, but not in a way that facilitates reasoned, respectful conversations about the issues. Previous research (Anderson et al. 2013; Stroud et al. 2015) demonstrates that preventing anonymous postings and moderating comment forums can reduce uncivil comments, but this does not explain why individuals are driven to make uncivil comments in the first place, nor does it explain why they are willing to use their Facebook accounts to do so. My research suggests that the presence of incivility in the media, coupled with greater engagement by people who are comfortable with conflict, could increase the likelihood that discourse will become uncivil.

While there is a clear relationship between conflict orientation, exposure to incivility, and affective responses, the impact of that relationship on behavioral outcomes is less clear. If incivility makes the conflict-avoidant anxious, are they looking for more information about politics, and if so, how and where are they doing so? The greatest effects were in eliciting disgust reactions, which have been shown to lead to avoidance behaviors (Neuberg, Kenrick, and Schaller 2011; Rozin et al. 2008). Are most of the conflict-avoidant deciding to simply avoid politics instead? Or, because anger motivates political action, could we see the conflict-avoidant become more engaged in political activity? Positive emotions like enthusiasm also encourage engagement, so it is possible that the conflict-approaching are also more likely to participate in certain types of political activity. In the next two chapters, I investigate how conflict orientation and political incivility interact to influence political engagement.

4

CHOOSING OUTRAGE

Selective Exposure and Information Search

The day after the election, the hate and darkness got to be too much. I unfriended nearly everyone. Now I have three friends: my husband and children. . . . I do hold (Facebook) responsible for helping to spread disinformation that contributed to both the election results and the level of vitriol and hate in this country. I am building my own wall now.

—SUSAN BRUBAKER KNAPP, QUOTED IN SELYUKH (2016)

IN NOVEMBER 2016, National Public Radio asked listeners how their attitudes toward social media were changing in the wake of the presidential election. As the epigraph for this chapter suggests, a majority of the responses described difficulty focusing, questioning of friendships, and overall feelings of frustration and exhaustion. Some individuals explicitly noted that they were turned off by the incivility and vitriol expressed by friends and family on Facebook. As reporter Alina Selyukh (2016) wrote, "People are turning off TVs (one even canceled her cable—mass media are not off the hook, either), deleting social apps from their phones, rationing time spent on Facebook and Twitter, and shrinking their digital friend lists." However, Selyukh also noted that another set of respondents expressed regret at not being more outspoken on social media and vowing to speak their minds more during Trump's presidency. What led to these two opposing outcomes? Why did some people stop looking for information on Facebook while others turned to it even more frequently to air their views and learn about politics?

These divergent paths are the result of the different experiences the conflict-avoidant and conflict-approaching have in the face of incivility. Conflict orientation shapes media choice; we consciously and unconsciously associate certain types of media or specific media outlets with varying levels of conflict and incivility. Because politics is an inherently conflictual domain, conflict orientation affects the frequency with which people choose political news over entertainment. Once Americans decide to tune in, they are constantly faced with the decision of which outlet or which program to choose. Based on headlines, Twitter comments, or blog posts, do they click the link to a news story or keep scrolling? Do they watch *The Bachelorette* or the national news? Once they decide to watch a news program, what do they do when exposed to political incivility? In this chapter, I evaluate evidence for the *information-search hypothesis* that these choices are in part a function of the interaction between conflict orientation and the incivility we are exposed to in political programming.

WHAT TO WATCH?

In her NPR story, Selyukh noted that many people were canceling cable, turning off their televisions, and deactivating Facebook—they were exiting the political media environment entirely. With so many channels, websites, streaming services, and other media available, an increasing proportion of Americans choose not to engage with political media at all (Arceneaux and Johnson 2013; Arceneaux, Johnson, and Cryderman 2013; Prior 2007). Recent changes in the media environment suggest that viewers engage in a two-step process when making consumption decisions. First, they decide whether to tune in to political news. Then, if they choose news over entertainment, they select a program or channel on the basis of a variety of characteristics, including partisanship and the amount of conflict they will likely be exposed to once they tune in.

The decision to select political news over entertainment is in part a function of individual characteristics, especially political interest (Prior 2007).

Looking at data from a 2010 Pew survey about media habits, Arceneaux and Johnson (2013) found substantial information differences among four types of audiences: the inattentive, broadcast-news viewers, Fox viewers, and MSNBC viewers. Those who choose to watch political news enjoy it more than their inattentive counterparts; they are more likely to report following major political issues, are more likely to vote, and answer more political knowledge questions (e.g., identifying the majority political party in the U.S. House of Representatives) correctly. Cable-news viewers are even more engaged with politics and political information. About 80 percent of talk-show viewers reported that they enjoy keeping up with the news "a lot," while only 62 percent of broadcast-news watchers said the same (Arceneaux and Johnson 2013). In other words, people who tune in to political news enjoy and are more interested in politics than their inattentive peers. In chapter 2, I offered evidence that conflict orientation is correlated with political interest, such that people who are conflict-approaching are also more likely to be interested in politics. Given this relationship, we might also expect that the conflict-approaching are more likely to pay attention to political news across all formats and platforms. Indeed, Arceneaux and Johnson (2007) found that, when given a choice, the conflict-approaching will spend more time watching the uncivil punditry of Fox's *Hannity & Colmes* than their conflict-avoidant peers. Based on this research, the *tune-in hypothesis* proposes that the conflict-approaching will be more likely to watch, listen to, or read political news than their conflict-avoidant friends.

> *Tune-in hypothesis:* Conflict-approaching individuals will report consuming political media generally at a greater frequency than their conflict-avoidant counterparts.

Once an individual decides to tune in to political news, she is immediately faced with a new conundrum: where does she want to turn for that news? The increasingly diverse media environment spurred by the growth of cable and Internet sources only increases the likelihood that individuals will be aware of, and use, information about the tone of a show or format to make decisions about their media consumption. Communication scholars have long investigated the "gratifications" that attracted audiences to certain media and the ways in which individuals use media to fulfill social and psychological needs (Cantril 1942; Katz, Gurevitch, and Haas 1973; Papacharissi 2007; Ruggiero 2000). Rubin (1994) differentiates between ritualized, habitual use of media and instrumental use, in which people watch a show because it offers useful information or allows them to engage in social discussion of that show with their friends or peers. Those who have greater exposure to or affinity for media are more likely to engage in habitual media use, while more specific motives drive instrumental use of media. Applying uses-and-gratifications theory to the dynamic between conflict orientation and mediated incivility suggests that the conflict-avoidant and the conflict-approaching use media differently and receive differential benefits from that use. At minimum, given the emotional responses seen in chapter 3, the conflict-avoidant are less likely to feel psychologically fulfilled after being exposed to incivility than the conflict-approaching. Therefore, when choosing media to consume, they will actively avoid outlets or platforms that they know might increase their likelihood of exposure.

Building on uses-and-gratifications theory (or at least similar foundational assumptions), political scientists have also started to theorize about how and why individuals make their political news choices. Prior notes that "more choice leads to better sorting of the television by taste" (2007, 95). As a result, Americans are able to choose whose opinions they want to hear, exacerbating knowledge gaps and echo chambers. In an increasingly choice-driven media environment, academics and public figures have become concerned about partisan selective exposure—the individual's decision to watch, read, or listen to like-minded media outlets. While evidence suggests that media are the venue most likely to expose citizens to diverse viewpoints, other research has shown that Americans select news reports based on the perceived affinity between their political preferences and those of the particular media outlet (Iyengar and Hahn 2009; Mutz and Martin 2001; Stroud 2011).

Partisan selective exposure is a concern because of its potential to increase polarization among the electorate (Stroud 2011; Sunstein 2009) and reduce cross-cutting exposure, or opportunities to "hear the other side"

(Jamieson and Cappella 2008; Mutz 2006). However, others have argued that these findings are in part an artifact of experimental design: randomized exposure to ideologically biased programming leads to further entrenchment of attitudes in situations where individuals are forced to watch counter-attitudinal programming. When participants are given the ability to choose, they are found to be more open to arguments from across the political spectrum (Arceneaux, Johnson, and Cryderman 2013).

Arceneaux and Johnson's (2013) active-audience theory specifically incorporates choice in the media environment into models of the relationship between media coverage and individual attitudes. Their theory rests on two propositions. First, an active audience is scrutinizing and evaluating the messages it receives, engaging in motivated reasoning to accept viewpoints that fit in their worldview and to dismiss those that challenge their beliefs. Second, their active audience makes "purposive viewing decisions" (10). Entertainment seekers select out of the news environment, diluting the effects of highly partisan cable talk shows by removing the "inadvertent audience." The effects of partisan news coverage on those who remain— those who chose to watch broadcast or cable news—will be different from the effects on the inadvertent audience. Many of the same concerns can be raised about exposure to incivility and conflict in political media. If you never watch talking heads shout at one another on cable television, being exposed to that sort of exchange in an experimental context could be more startling or remarkable than if you regularly watch cable shows. Incivility's effects on willingness to hear the other side, consumption of political information, and beliefs about government legitimacy could be exacerbated by an individual's ability to *choose* to be exposed to it, or that ability to choose might actually mitigate incivility's problematic impact on political behavior. Arceneaux and Johnson's (2007) findings provide some support for both sides of the question. On one hand, the negative effects of televised incivility on trust go away once people can avoid being exposed to it. On the other, even those who chose to watch incivility felt as though they had less say in government functions—less internal efficacy—than those who were not exposed.

Citizens select the media they use to gather political information on the basis of an outlet's partisan congruence, but also on a particular format's likelihood of introducing information in an uncivil, confrontational manner. For some citizens—the conflict-avoidant—the fact that a media personality is known for her vitriolic approach to the news will dissuade them from seeking her perspective. Recall my students watching the *Hannity* clip. Some remarked in class discussion that they never watched cable news because they knew that it would lead to the kind of finger-pointing and name-calling they had just witnessed. For others, this knowledge was enough to draw them in and make them regular viewers. While some of us are capable of making this distinction on a show-by-show basis, others form more general, format-based assessments of the likelihood of exposure to incivility. In other words, Americans' preferences for newspapers or cable television are shaped by their perceptions that these types of media are more or less uncivil.

In order to assess the extent to which individuals choose particular media environments on the basis of their likelihood of being exposed to incivility, we must first categorize different types of media outlets as either high- or low-conflict. Because the swath of possible media outlets is so vast, I limit my categorizations to the platform level, seeking to distinguish cable television from network television, and Internet sources like blogs from social media like Twitter, but without delving into the differences between, say, *Hannity* and the *Nightly News with Lester Holt*. By virtue of their breadth, these categories are naturally a bit unwieldy, but they are grounded in research into the presence and perception of conflict and incivility on each platform.

Just as citizens intuitively (albeit at times incorrectly) sort media outlets into liberal or conservative camps, they also believe that certain types of media are more likely to use uncivil tone and language than others. These perceptions are partially a function of the attributes of each platform; individuals perceive visual and audio media as more uncivil than textual media even when the message is the same (Sydnor 2018). The sources used, topic of an article, and outlet—blog or news site—can influence perceptions of incivility in the same message (Anderson et al. 2014; Coe, Kenski, and Rains 2014; Thorson, Vraga, and Ekdale 2010). However, some media are also more likely to present uncivil messages than others. Sobeiraj and Berry

(2011; Berry and Sobeiraj 2014) developed thirteen categories of language and expressions that comprise outrageous behavior to reach their conclusion that cable news and talk radio are much more likely to introduce uncivil discourse than blogs (Berry and Sobeiraj 2014, 45). Papacharissi (2004) also investigates incivility in online forums and, even when separating uncivil and impolite talk into two categories, finds that around 50 percent of messages contain either impolite or uncivil commentary. Looking at comments posted in response to newspapers' online articles, Coe et al. (2014) found that more than one in five comments on online articles (22 percent) written for the *Arizona Daily Star* were uncivil. Research suggests that cable television, talk radio, and Internet sources are the most likely venues for uncivil political communication.

The Internet has been identified as particularly hospitable to incivility. As Chen (2017) writes, "the de-individuation of online discourse along with the lack of conversational cues plus the speed with which a comment can go public and viral online foments a perfect storm of sorts for incivility to flourish and cause harm" (64). Deindividuation, or the subsuming of one's individual identity to a group identity, makes people feel more connected to their weaker social ties than they really are, leading them to share personal information that they might not typically share face to face. However, this same tendency can make individuals online feel freer to act in socially undesirable ways. Just like Eagles fans who smashed windows and overturned a car after their team's 2018 Super Bowl win, commenters online feel more uninhibited because there is a perception that their words are more difficult to trace back to them. Many comment streams or Internet forums allow participants to post anonymously, which has been found to increase the amount of incivility in the comments section (Santana 2014), but even when people have to sign their own name or link to their Facebook account, they feel hidden in the vast expanse of the web (Chen 2017).

This sense of deindividuation is more complicated on social media. Some 67 percent of American adults report getting at least some of their news from social-media sites (Shearer and Gottfried 2017). Although these sites primarily link to other outlets such as blogs and traditional news organizations' websites, networked individuals frequently share these links while adding their own opinions, commentary, or reactions. Incivility is alive and well on platforms like Twitter and Facebook, where journalists, politicians, and thousands of other people regularly experience gendered harassment, flaming, and trolling (Chen 2017; Oz, Zheng, and Chen 2017). However, affordances of different social media lead to variation in the presence of incivility. For example, Oz, Zheng, and Chen (2017) found that posts responding to White House tweets were more likely to be uncivil than posts responding to the White House on Facebook. In part, this is because users control who they are "friends with" on Facebook or "following" on Twitter, and these connections are frequently driven by real-life acquaintance or shared interests. While these sites might slightly increase the diversity of one's social network (Kim, Hsu, and de Zúñiga 2013), other research suggests that Twitter users, in particular, tend to seek out clusters of other users who are politically homogeneous (Himelboim, McCreery, and Smith 2013). Though homogeneity does not preclude the use of uncivil language, in many cases it reduces the presence of incivility. This tendency toward like-minded networks allows me to categorize social media as a low-conflict source of political information, even while the Internet more generally is labeled high-conflict.

While "new" media like cable, talk radio, and blogs are frequently uncivil, traditional forms of political media do not demonstrate the same level of rude and impolite language. Berry and Sobeiraj (2014) use newspapers as a control in their evaluation of outrage on blogs and cable television, finding that newspaper columnists are likely to have about six instances of outrage in a column (in comparison, cable television and radio segments contain, on average, twenty-three to twenty-four incidents). Cable programming is frequently tied to political incivility (York 2013; Gervais 2014), whereas network news has been found to minimize individuals' assessments of politics as uncivil (Forgette and Morris 2006).

To find further evidence that cable and network news differed in their level of incivility, I conducted content analysis of 666 television news segments from MSNBC, Fox, CNN, NBC, and ABC.[1] I assessed the presence of civility and incivility by looking for language similar to that coded by Sobieraj and Berry and recorded whether each source, throughout the course of the segment, used any of three civil and four uncivil communication strategies. Specifically, I measured the presence or absence of the following civil approaches: indication that an opponent's policies would positively change American values or institutions, acknowledgment of common ground, and use of complementary language or praise of an opponent. Incivility was coded as present if a source placed blame on his or her opponents, used hyperbolic language to characterize his or her opponent ("outrageous"), used pejorative language ("racist," "liar"), and/or described the opposition with derogatory adjective ("reckless," "weird"). From these seven items, I created additive measures of incivility and civility for each segment, counting the total number of uncivil and civil incidents present, regardless of type.

In this analysis, certain types of uncivil language are used more frequently across all television news outlets, while other types are much more prevalent on cable news. Table 4.1 shows the percentage of segments that contain at least one use of each type of language. While not approaching Sobeiraj and

TABLE 4.1 PERCENTAGE OF SEGMENTS WITH CIVIL OR UNCIVIL LANGUAGE, BY MEDIA OUTLET

	FOX	MSNBC	CNN	ABC	NBC	TOTAL
Any Uncivil Language	78	80	68	55	50	70
Blame	63	54	48	31	39	51
Hyperbole	37	54	30	24	24	34
Accusations of lying	17	24	9	6	2	12
Name-calling	39	47	21	22	19	28
Threatens American values	26	35	20	14	11	22
Any Civil Language	17	23	20	20	7	18
Praise	7	5	7	2	4	6
Common ground	11	18	14	12	4	13
Bolsters American values	4	4	4	6	2	4

Berry's finding of outrage incidents in 100 percent of the cable-television news sample, I did find that 70 percent of my sample contained at least one of the five measures of uncivil language. Sources were most likely to use blame in dealing with their opponents, and least likely to accuse others of lying. There was substantially less evidence of civil language, with only 18 percent of the total sample demonstrating any of the three types of civility coded: praise for the other side, acknowledgment of common ground, or support for American values. Of those three, sources were most likely to acknowledge common ground with their detractors.

Table 4.1 records what percentage of segments contained particular types of civility and incivility. It does not capture how frequently multiple forms of incivility were present within the same segment. It is one thing to blame one's opponents for political problems, but another to do so while also calling them lying idiots who are destroying America. Segments were not likely to contain multiple identifiers of civil language. On average, across all five news outlets, a segment contained less than one incident of civil language ($\overline{x_{civil}} = 0.25$). However, when incivility was used, it was frequently used multiple times. Cable and network news averaged two types of uncivil language per segment ($\overline{x_{uncivil}} = 2.0$). However, the distribution of uncivil incidents per segment is strongly right-skewed; while the averages for both types are relatively low, 25 percent of segments contain more than three uncivil incidents.

There is also variation in the prevalence of highly uncivil segments across media outlets, with Fox and MSNBC containing averages of 3.2 and 2.5 incidents per segment, respectively. CNN, NBC, and ABC contained, on average, 1.7 or fewer incidents of uncivil language.[2] Cable networks had 10 percent more overall uncivil language than network television. These results suggest that network news programming is more civil than the shows on cable news. This distinction reinforces previous findings that television news is highly uncivil and provides clear evidence that it is cable, not network television, that drives this association.

To summarize, the research outlined here establishes that political media can be divided into high- and low-conflict sources. Specifically, cable television, Internet news and blogs, and talk radio are classified as high-conflict, while newspapers, network television, and social media are low-conflict. These categorizations can be summarized as follows:

CATEGORIZATION OF MEDIA BY LEVEL OF CONFLICT

High-Conflict Media	Low-Conflict Media
Cable television	Newspapers (including their online versions)
Internet news/blogs	Network television
Talk radio	Social media (Twitter, Facebook)

Survey data suggest that citizens perceive these differences in incivility across media platforms and blame cable, Internet, and talk radio for the increase in political incivility (Weber Shandwick, KRC Research, and Powell Tate 2013).

Individuals will seek to match their attitudes toward conflict to media that fit their predispositions. Those who are entertained by incivility and argumentation can select the high-conflict media programming found on cable television, online blogs, and talk radio, while their conflict-avoidant counterparts can seek information from low-conflict environments such as newspapers, network television, and social media. Given the widespread public perception that politics lacks civility and the argument that the media are to blame for this problem, uses-and-gratifications theory, active-audience theory, and research on selective exposure suggest that certain political coverage appeals to people who have a taste for argument and incivility. Those who do not like this conflict will turn away from media coverage of politics (per the *tune-in hypothesis*) or turn to a few select platforms or outlets. Given the distinctions between types of media laid out here, I expect conflict-avoidant individuals to prefer low-conflict media formats, while the conflict-approaching turn to high-conflict programming.

Media-choice hypothesis: Conflict-approaching individuals will report preferences for high-conflict sources, such as Internet-only sources and cable television. Conflict-avoidant individuals will report preferences for media outlets that could be perceived as more civil—specifically, network television and newspapers.

SEEKING OUT INCIVILITY

Given this understanding of selective exposure to incivility, the conflict-avoidant have two exit points on their path to learning about politics: they can choose not to tune in to politics in the first place, or they can tune in but select specific outlets or platforms on which they are less likely to experience vitriolic language. On the one hand, this sounds great—only those people who can tolerate incivility will be frequently exposed to it—but disparities in media consumption have been shown to exacerbate inequalities in political knowledge and electoral turnout (Prior 2007). When people decide not to listen to political radio or catch the evening news, they learn less about what is going on in politics and are far from the ideal democratically engaged citizens. On the other hand, those who persist in tuning in to politics are not exposed solely to the types of information best suited to learning about politics. In some cases, they are exposed to the very thing they were trying to avoid, and this exposure changes the way they look for and interpret future information. Once individual feel anxious, they tend to seek out and remember threatening information about that policy at the expense of other issues, thereby applying an unbalanced set of considerations to their evaluation of a policy or political situation (Albertson and Gadarian 2015). Reading an article that makes one anxious about immigration, for example, will lead to additional search for information about the threats posed by immigration. It stands to reason that in the face of incivility, those who are content to experience conflict will take a different approach to processing information than those who want to avoid it.

To assess these divergent approaches, scholars have focused on information processing in the absence of choice. In other words, once individuals are exposed to incivility, how does this change what they learn or what information they seek out next? Research suggests that incivility plays a role in one's ability to find and recall political messages. Minich, Mendoza, and Brown (2018) have found that when an argument is framed civilly, participants are more likely to click on subsequent links to news stories. While civility appears to keep people engaged with news longer, studies of its effects on recall are mixed. In comparison with those who watched a civil campaign ad, Brooks and Geer (2007) found a small, not statistically significant decrease in factual recall among those who were exposed to an uncivil ad. However, Mutz (2015) found that incivility increased attention to content, substantially increasing individuals' recall of issue arguments. Incivility frames political material in a way that is—for some people—more entertaining (Jasper 1998; Lepper 1994; Mutz 2015). Clearly, then, framing political information in an uncivil manner changes the way in which individuals seek out or avoid additional political news.

When given the choice, the conflict-avoidant are expected to turn away from incivility and the conflict-approaching to move toward it. But once both groups have been exposed to uncivil political news, research in political psychology and communication suggests that their behavior will run counter to our expectations and intuitions. Rather than turning away from incivility, the conflict-avoidant will lean in, seeking out more of the very thing that makes them uncomfortable. This biased information processing could stem in part from the anxiety the conflict-avoidant feel as a result of incivility. Just as the individual who is worried about immigration cannot stop reading news about the threat posed by immigrants, the conflict-avoidant consumer cannot stop watching people shout at one another and use derogatory language.

Alternatively, this tendency could be a result of the linkage between conflict-avoidance and the Big Five trait agreeableness. As discussed in chapter 2, conflict-avoidant individuals are more likely to score highly on agreeableness, and therefore to be naturally good-natured and cooperative. Agreeable individuals are susceptible to demand effects: they continue to do things not because they enjoy them, but because the tasks are expected or because they will improve social harmony. They may see exposure to political incivility as the expected result of turning on the news, and therefore continue to seek it out because that is what is expected of them as political news consumers. The studies presented here cannot fully explore which of these mechanisms most likely shapes the relationship between conflict-avoidance, incivility, and information search. Instead, I focus on the primary and somewhat counterintuitive hypothesis that the conflict-avoidant will search for more incivility after being exposed to it in political media.

A different body of research helps us understand why the conflict-approaching, faced with incivility, might engage in a type of satisficing behavior, essentially saying "OK, that's enough, I can turn to other things now." Mood-management theory suggests that people turn to media to regulate their broader emotional state. Individuals who are in a good mood are less concerned about whether the media they are about to consume have a positive or negative tone, whereas those who are in a bad mood look for media that will improve it (Knobloch-Westerwick 2006). For example, Knobloch (2003) finds that people experiencing positive affective states spend more time on positive web content than those with mediocre moods, but less time with the same content than those in negative moods. In the previous chapter, I demonstrated that the conflict-approaching are more likely to experience positive emotions in the face of incivility than their conflict-avoidant peers. To these individuals, uncivil coverage of politics is perceived as positive content; it is something they enjoy spending time viewing. This is not to say they dislike civil political news, but because they are already in a good mood in the wake of uncivil political media, they will put less effort into seeking out media options that will maintain that mood. Sufficiently entertained by the uncivil news they have been exposed to, the conflict-approaching look at less incivility and less political news because they have already met their media needs.

Information-search hypothesis: The conflict-avoidant will be more likely to seek out uncivil media clips after being exposed to incivility. The conflict-approaching will turn to civil news after being exposed to incivility.

TESTING THE EFFECTS OF CHOICE

To test the first two hypotheses—that citizens seek to expose themselves to uncivil media only to the extent that their conflict orientation allows—I use data from Project Implicit and the first Mechanical Turk (MTurk) study. Each survey asks a set of questions from the Conflict Communication Scale and invites participants to report their typical media consumption and political participation in the past year (see appendix A for specific survey questions).

The two sets of studies take different approaches to measuring patterns of media use. Project Implicit focuses on daily consumption patterns. I asked participants, "During a typical week, how frequently do you watch/ read/listen to . . . network television/cable television/radio/ Internet/ newspaper?" Participants were asked to select from a range of zero to seven days. I use this measure to estimate the amount of time spent tuning in to political news, constructing an average of the number of days a week that participants consumed any of the five types of news. A lower average amount of weekly consumption of any news suggests that participants were choosing other activities or entertainment over political information. This measure offers a general understanding of the extent to which individuals are selecting whether or not to consume political information, in addition to providing comparative consumption statistics for different types of media.

Frequency measures like those used in the Project Implicit study are sometimes challenged as an effective measurement technique because they are difficult for individuals to report correctly (Price 1993; Schwarz and Oyserman 2001). The belief is that these self-reporting measures lead to inflated reports of media usage. Dilliplane, Goldman and Mutz (2013) argue that rather than focusing on the frequency of study participants' media consumption, as in the Project Implicit study, researchers should ask participants to select their regularly viewed programs from a list. The program-list approach reduces the cognitive burden on participants and is found to provide a more reliable estimate of actual media consumption (Dilliplane et al. 2013). Therefore, in MTurk Study 1, I asked participants to respond to the question "Which of the following is your main source of political news and information?" Participants chose among eight options: Internet-only sources, newspapers, network television, cable television, radio, social media such as Facebook and Twitter, talking with others, or saying they did not really follow political news.[3] They were then asked to report their second major source of political news and information. Although these questions are not an entirely accurate reflection of Dilliplane et al.'s program-list strategy, or of the choice environment in which participants select where to get their political news, it does reduce concerns about overreporting and encourages them to choose their preferred news source. Responses to this question shed light on whether conflict-avoidant and conflict-approaching individuals prefer different types of media as their primary source of political information.

Table 4.2 displays descriptive statistics for both methods of measuring media consumption. Across both sets of studies, the Internet is turned to most frequently as the preferred media source—an average of 4.5 days a week, and the first choice of 35.2 percent of the MTurk sample.[4] Cable and network television are used at relatively similar frequencies (both are watched 2.9 days a week, on average) and are the most-preferred source

TABLE 4.2 MEDIA CONSUMPTION HABITS OF THE SAMPLES

	AVERAGE NUMBER OF DAYS PER WEEK PARTICIPANTS REPORTED USE	PERCENT REPORTING MEDIUM AS FIRST-CHOICE OUTLET
Internet sources	4.5	35.2
Newspaper	1.8	19.6
Network television	2.9	12.3
Cable television	2.9	16.8
Radio	2.7	5.7
Social media such as Facebook and Twitter	—	4.7
Talking with others	—	3.1
Don't really follow political news	—	2.7

Sources: Average number of days consumed—Project Implicit. Percent reporting medium as first-choice outlet—Mechanical Turk Study 1. Participants in the PI study were not asked how frequently they used social media or talked to others about politics.

of a similar percentage of participants (16.8 percent report a preference for cable television and 12.3 percent for network television). Radio ranks next, with Project Implicit participants tuning in around 2.7 days a week and only 5.7 percent of the participants in MTurk Study 1 reporting that radio is their preferred source for political information. The additional media choices offered to Mechanical Turk respondents—social media, talking to others, and not following political news—were collectively the preferred outlets of just over 10 percent of the sample.

The major discrepancy across the two measurement strategies is in the prevalence of newspaper use and the number of individuals reporting that newspapers are their preferred source of news. Project Implicit participants read newspapers only an average of 1.8 days a week, making them the least used of the five sources. However, almost 20 percent of MTurk users reported that newspapers were their preferred news source, making it the second most popular media source after the Internet. This disparity likely stems from differences in the question wording. In Project Implicit, participants were asked about how frequently they read print newspapers. Mechanical Turk participants, on the other hand, were asked specifically to report their use of newspaper websites as part of the newspaper category, rather than as an Internet source. Therefore, people who visit newspaper websites were captured as using the Internet in the Project Implicit sample but as reading newspapers in MTurk Study 1.

CHOOSING POLITICS AND CHOOSING A SOURCE

According to the *tune-in hypothesis*, individuals first make a choice about whether to tune in to politics or do something else. This choice is influenced by a given individual's conflict orientation. The conflict-avoidant should spend less time consuming political news than their conflict-approaching peers.

The Project Implicit study asks about how many days a week participants use different types of media, so we can use that question to examine whether the conflict-approaching spend more time watching, listening to, or reading political news. Looking first at the results of bivariate linear regression[5] of media consumption on conflict orientation, it is clear that those individuals who are more comfortable with conflict are likely to consume all forms of media with greater frequency. A one-unit increase in conflict orientation (or a one-unit shift toward a conflict-approaching inclination) results in a very small increase in the number of days an individual reports consuming each type of media. As figure 4.1 shows, these small increases compound rapidly and lead the most conflict-approaching individuals to consume many forms of media one full day more frequently than their most conflict-avoidant counterparts. Each of these differences is statistically significant, with the exception of the two television categories.

These bivariate analyses offer support for my claim that people who are more comfortable with conflict choose to consume more political news; the regression coefficients are in the expected directions even when they fail to approach statistical significance. However, this analysis uses observational data and therefore requires the introduction of controls to increase our confidence that it is truly conflict orientation that is shaping these preferences and not some unobserved characteristic that is correlated with both conflict orientation and media preferences. In chapter 2, I established that conflict orientation is tied to a range of demographic and political characteristics that also are likely to affect the frequency with which one consumes political media; once I control for these demographic characteristics—interest, ideology, party identification and strength, age, gender, personality, and education level—conflict orientation's effects on the frequency with which individuals are exposed to political media and their reported preference for particular sources disappear (see table 4.3). This could suggest that conflict orientation is not guiding political behavior, at least in the context of media consumption, or that the effects of conflict orientation are mediated by these demographic characteristics.

For example, political interest is moderately correlated with conflict orientation and is likely to influence how regularly we look at political media.[6] It is possible that conflict orientation will play a different role in the media habits of the extremely politically interested than it would for those not

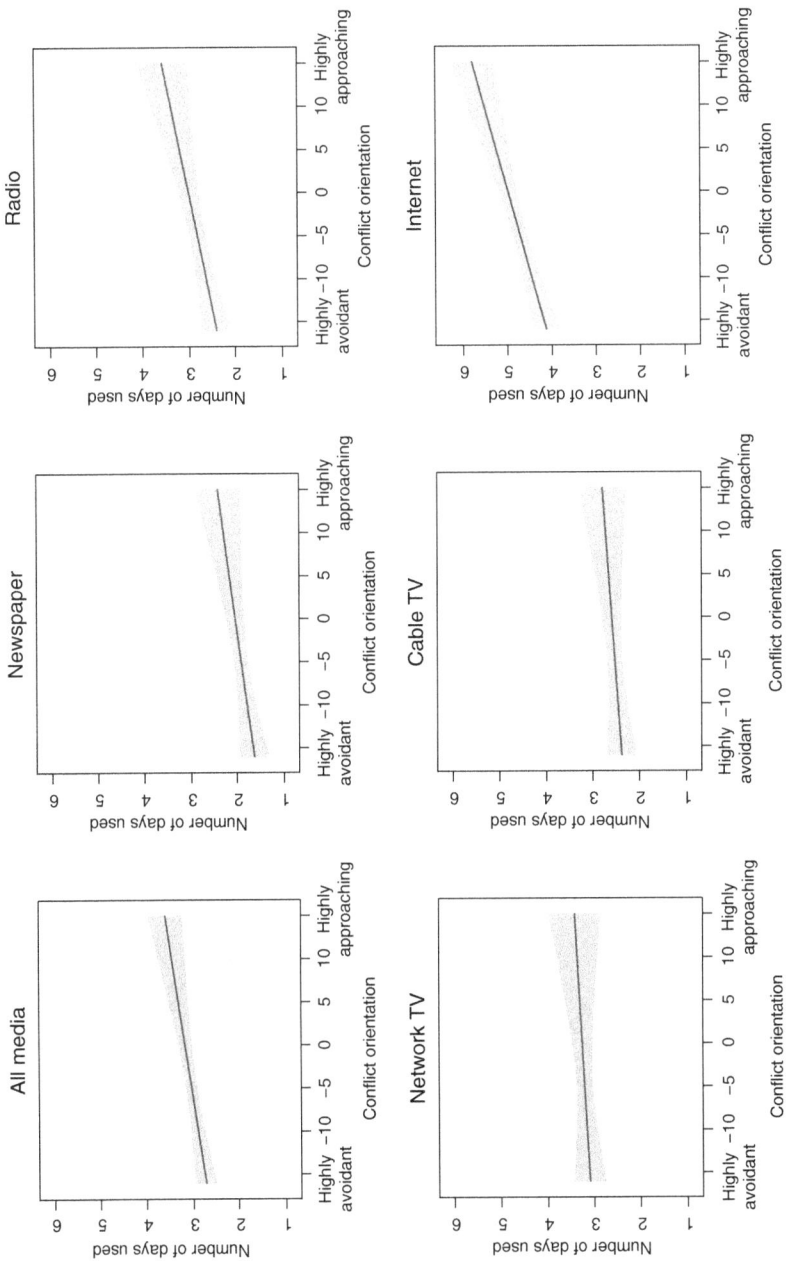

FIGURE 4.1 Average frequency of media use, by conflict orientation.

Note: Linear predictions derived from bivariate regressions of media use on conflict orientation. Shaded areas represent 95% confidence intervals.

Source: Project Implicit.

TABLE 4.3 REGRESSION OF CONFLICT ORIENTATION ON MEDIA CONSUMPTION, CONTROLLING FOR DEMOGRAPHIC INFLUENCES

	AVERAGE WEEKLY USE	NEWSPAPER	NETWORK TV	CABLE TV	RADIO	INTERNET
Conflict orientation	0.01	0.01	−0.0008	0.009	0.02	0.02
	(0.009)	(0.014)	(0.015)	(0.013)	(0.014)	(0.013)
Political interest	0.58**	0.40**	0.59**	0.62**	0.44**	0.83**
	(0.047)	(0.074)	(0.080)	(0.072)	(0.079)	(0.070)
Party ID	−037**	−0.51*	−0.08	−0.46*	−0.23	−0.57**
	(0.134)	(0.212)	(0.229)	(0.206)	(0.226)	(0.200)
Party strength	−0.11	−0.20	−0.33	−0.11	0.06	0.06
	(0.102)	(0.161)	(0.174)	(0.157)	(0.172)	(0.152)
Age	0.04**	0.04**	0.06**	0.06**	0.05**	0.01*
	(0.004)	(0.006)	(0.006)	(0.006)	(0.006)	(0.005)
Education	0.03	0.09**	−0.08*	−0.09**	0.10**	0.10**
	(0.021)	(0.033)	(0.035)	(0.032)	(0.035)	(0.031)
Hispanic	0.22	−0.19	0.85**	0.77**	0.20	−0.50*
	(0.163)	(0.257)	(0.277)	(0.249)	(0.273)	(0.243)
Black	0.55**	0.05	1.48**	0.88**	0.48	−0.15
	(0.167)	(0.263)	(0.284)	(0.255)	(0.280)	(0.249)
Extraversion	0.02	0.01	0.04	0.02	0.03	−0.03
	(0.015)	(0.024)	(0.025)	(0.023)	(0.025)	(0.022)
Agreeableness	0.008	−0.02	0.04	0.02	0.003	0.02
	(0.022)	(0.035)	(0.038)	(0.034)	(0.037)	(0.033)
Conscientiousness	0.06**	0.07**	0.09**	0.10**	0.05	−0.03
	(0.016)	(0.028)	(0.030)	(0.027)	(0.030)	(0.027)
Emotional stability	0.02	0.001	0.07*	0.004	0.0002	0.004
	(0.018)	(0.028)	(0.030)	(0.027)	(0.029)	(0.026)
Openness	−0.03	0.003	−0.11**	−0.09*	0.02	0.03
	(0.022)	(0.035)	(0.038)	(0.034)	(0.037)	(0.033)
Constant	−0.73**	−1.37**	−0.69**	−1.23**	−1.31**	0.92**
	(0.195)	(0.309)	(0.333)	(0.300)	(0.328)	(0.292)
R^2	0.18	0.17	0.24	0.27	0.21	0.27
N	993	993	992	992	993	993

Source: Project Implicit.

Note: Cell entries are OLS regression coefficients with standard errors in parentheses.

*$p < 0.05$, **$p < 0.01$

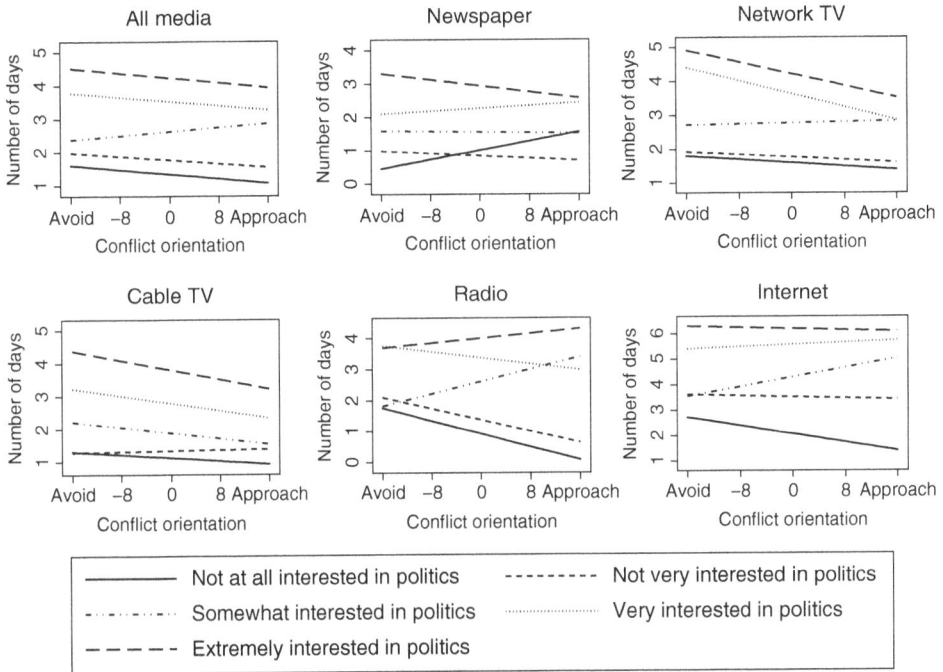

FIGURE 4.2 Media use changes with conflict orientation and political interest.

Note: Figures represent linear predictions from a multivariate regression that includes an interaction between interest and conflict orientation.

Source: Project Implicit.

at all politically interested. Figure 4.2 displays the results of a regression of the frequency of media consumption on conflict orientation, political interest, and the interaction between the two.[7] The figure demonstrates that the effects of conflict orientation on the frequency of media consumption change at different levels of political interest and across types of media. While there is no clear pattern across all types of media, conflict orientation influences consumption habits differently for those with different levels of political interest. In many cases, those who are very or extremely politically interested (the top two lines on each graph) look different from those who are not at all or somewhat interested in politics.

Looking first at the frequency with which individuals at various levels of political interest report weekly consumption of any form of media, those who are somewhat interested in politics stand out as having conflict orientation shape their consumption. Somewhat-interested individuals who are the most conflict-avoidant report consuming political media on any platform 2.5 days a week on average, while the most conflict-approaching participants who are somewhat interested in politics report exposure to political media close to three days a week. The same pattern is true for the frequency with which the somewhat politically interested tune in to radio and Internet media. Those at the most approaching end of the spectrum report using the radio or Internet one full day more than their conflict-avoidant peers.[8]

Ultimately, the evidence suggests that conflict orientation plays a role in the decision to tune in to political media, but that it plays a much smaller role than other relevant characteristics, such as one's interest in politics. Those who are interested in politics are more likely to spend their time consuming the news. But once they make that choice, they are faced with an array of outlets across many media platforms. The *media-choice hypothesis* proposes that conflict orientation also shapes behavior at this second decision point. If conflict-avoidant individuals know that they are more likely to be exposed to disagreement, shouting, and nasty talk on cable news than they are when reading a newspaper, they will turn to the newspaper. Therefore, we now turn to the analysis of Mechanical Turk Study 1, which asked people which types of media they preferred, rather than how frequently they watched each.

When media consumption is measured as a preference for a particular type of media, rather than the frequency with which individuals consume each type, the results more accurately reflect my hypotheses. As figure 4.3 shows, conflict-approaching individuals are more likely to list cable television, Internet-only sources like the *Huffington Post*, or cable television as their top source for political news. Conversely, they are less likely than their conflict-avoidant counterparts to state that network television or social media are their preferred news source. Participants' preferences for newspapers did not follow the hypothesized pattern.

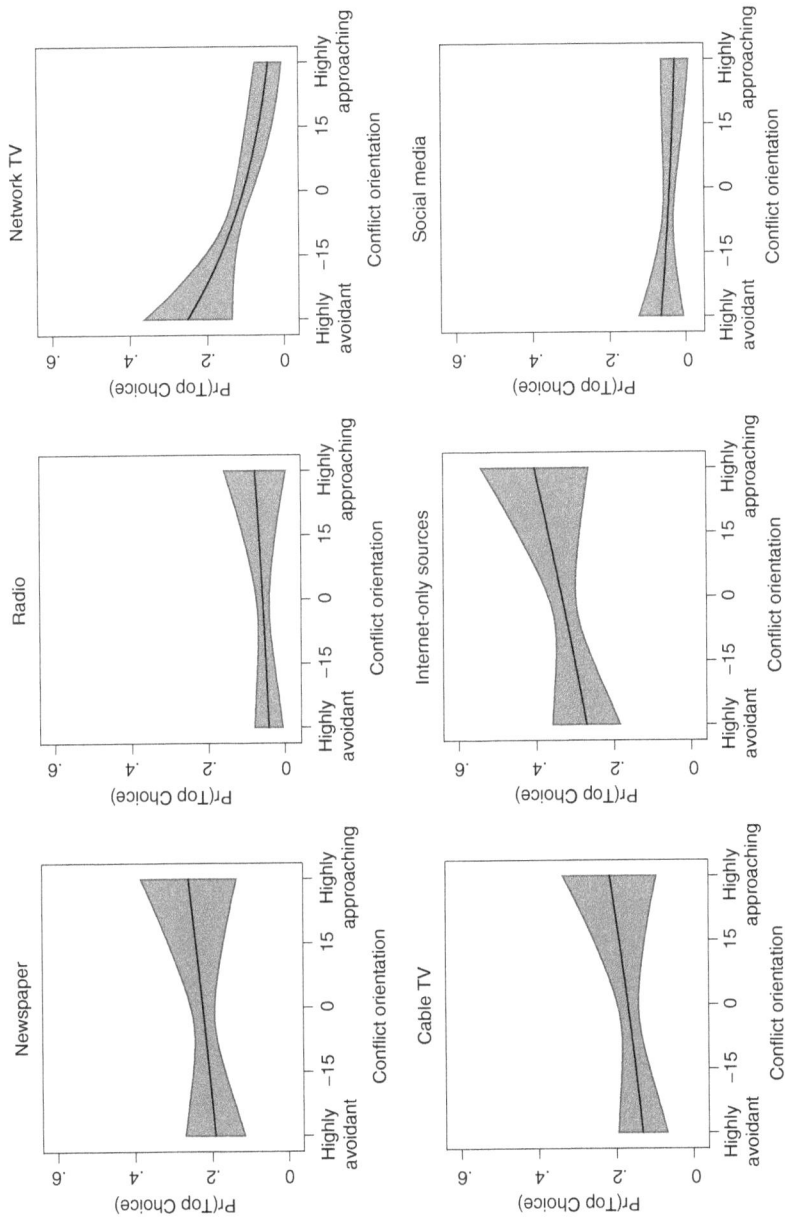

FIGURE 4.3 Probability of selecting each type of media as one's preferred source.

Note: Participants were asked to name their preferred source of political information. Each figure represents the predicted probability of selecting a given medium as one's first choice, given conflict orientation. Predicted probabilities were calculated from a bivariate logistic regression.

Source: Mechanical Turk Study 1.

I expected that conflict-avoidant individuals would express a greater preference for newspapers than the conflict-approaching, but the relationship appears to run in the other direction, with the conflict-approaching indicating a greater probability of choosing hard-copy newspapers as their preferred news source.

Although these findings support my overall expectations, it is important to take them with some caution. Only one relationship is statistically significant: that between conflict orientation and the preference for network television. Here, the most conflict-avoidant participants have about a 25 percent chance of selecting low-conflict network TV as their favorite source of political news, while the most conflict-approaching choose network television only about 5 percent of the time. In some cases, small sample sizes make statistical accuracy difficult. As shown in table 4.2, 35 percent of participants reported that the Internet was their preferred source, and the remaining 65 percent spread themselves across the other seven media options. Once these groups are broken down by conflict orientation, there are only a few individuals in each category, leading to high standard errors in the analysis.

In an attempt to overcome this sampling problem, I analyzed the data from MTurk Study 1 again, this time with individuals placed in one of three categories based on their CCS scores. Following Mutz (2015), I divide the CCS into equal thirds. Those in the lowest third are conflict-avoidant, the middle is considered conflict-ambivalent, and the highest third are conflict-approaching. I then compare the average probability of choosing each news source for those who are highly avoidant versus highly approaching. Looking at conflict orientation in this way, Bonferroni estimates from a series of one-way ANOVAs suggest that the conflict-avoidant and conflict-approaching have different preferences for network television and social media. About 3.7 percent more conflict-avoidant than conflict-approaching individuals prefer network television ($F(918) = 4.81, p = 0.008$), while the conflict-avoidant are about 5 percent more likely to prefer social media ($F(918) = 2.63, p = 0.072$). These results lend further support to the initial bivariate estimates, and offer weak evidence that conflict orientation drives individuals' preferences for particular media platforms.

Ultimately, these findings offer only weak support for my expectations that conflict orientation guides individuals in two key decisions: whether to consume political media and, if so, what media platforms to turn to. Each set of measures has its own weaknesses and is a relatively blunt measure for assessing individuals' specific media choices at the program level. Furthermore, neither directly assesses individuals' choices in relation to their exposure to incivility, instead relying on categorization of platforms as more or less uncivil. Therefore, the next section focuses on the information-search hypothesis, examining how individuals' media consumption and information-searching behavior change when they are exposed to political incivility.

SELECTIVE EXPOSURE AND THE SEARCH FOR INFORMATION

Evidence from the observational data is mixed about the extent to which conflict orientation guides individuals' choice to consume political news or their choice of media platforms. However, the third hypothesis proposes that conflict orientation's influence on information-search habits is activated upon exposure to political incivility. Conflict-approaching individuals will be satisfied by this initial experience with incivility and seek out less news and less uncivil news than they would if they watched a civil political clip first. The conflict-avoidant, on the other hand, will continue to look for information about politics and, ironically, will be drawn to incivility regardless of whether they are looking at politics or entertainment.

Mechanical Turk Study 2 was designed to evaluate this hypothesis. The experiment assessed media choice in the style of Arceneaux and Johnson (2013). After participants reported their preferences for news, entertainment, civil media, and uncivil media, they were asked to make a choice between four headlines that varied on each of the two dimensions— civility and news/entertainment. The control group made this choice without forced exposure to any additional media; the treatment groups were first asked to watch either a civil or an uncivil video clip. This setup allows us not only to see how conflict orientation shapes media choice in the absence of prior exposure, but also how prior preferences for certain types of news, combined with exposure to incivility or civility, might moderate the effects of conflict orientation on participants' choices.

The lack of exposure to either a civil or an uncivil interaction in the control condition allows us to determine what effects stem from exposure to uncivil political news and what come simply from being exposed to political news at all. Participants assigned to a treatment condition were shown either the civil or uncivil CSPAN clip of coverage of recent congressional hearings about Planned Parenthood described in chapter 3. After exposure to the treatment condition, the subjects indicated how civil and informative each clip was on a scale from 0 to 4, where 0 indicated "not at all" and 4 signified "extremely." Participants' assessments of these two characteristics were used as a manipulation check;[9] a two-sample t-test suggests that participants found the civil treatment to be significantly more civil ($\overline{x} = 2.9$, sd $= 0.99$).

After the subjects had answered these questions (or in the case of the control group, immediately after completing the pretest questionnaire), they were given the option to watch more clips related to politics and entertainment. If they chose to watch a clip, viewers were given the choice to continue watching additional clips or finish this section. There were a total of five clips to watch, each lasting approximately one minute: two political news clips and three reality television clips. Both types of clips had at least one civil and one uncivil option. Each clip was titled so as to indicate whether it depicted conflict, as well as the subject matter. As table 4.4 shows, phrases such as "activists feud" and "accuses teammates of lying, double-crossing" were used to indicate conflict and incivility, whereas phrases such as "Poll: Americans want a hearing for next justice" or "Contestants reflect on their success" were used to indicate civility and a lack of conflict. The uncivil political news clip featured two commentators arguing rudely and talking over one another. The uncivil reality television clip depicted two members of a team interrupting one another and accusing one another of

TABLE 4.4 HEADLINES PARTICIPANTS COULD CHOOSE TO WATCH

CATEGORY		HEADLINE
Political	Civil	CNN: "Poll: Americans want a hearing for next justice"
	Uncivil	CNN: "GOP activists feud over Trump's potential damage to the party"
Entertainment	Civil	*The Amazing Race*: "Contestants reflect on their success in plate-spinning"
	Civil	*Master Chef*: "Chef and judge disagree about pasta dish"
	Uncivil	*Survivor*: "Sierra accuses teammates of lying, double-crossing her"

lying and name-calling. The civil political news clip featured a commentator reporting on a poll. The civil reality television clip showed two members of a team complimenting one another and acting in a jovial manner. Because each clip was explicitly titled and subjects were allowed to select the clip of their choice (as well as when to finish this section), we were able to monitor their search habits.

When evaluating the choices participants made to engage with the five headlines, I looked for three key measures: how many headlines participants clicked on, whether those headlines were civil or uncivil, and how long participants spent watching the videos associated with each headline. Across the three conditions, on average, participants clicked on about two headlines, with some selecting all five (3 percent) and others ignoring them entirely (24.5 percent) and moving on to the next section of the experiment ($\bar{x} = 1.91$, sd $= 1.13$). Those who did choose to watch clips overwhelmingly selected headlines that were civil (80 percent of clips selected were civil) and about entertainment topics (75 percent). They spent a little over a minute on the pages containing the videos associated with each headline

($\bar{x} = 67.7$, sd $= 68.5$ *seconds*). Even though people were more likely to select civil videos overall, the most popular single selection was the CNN piece about the feud between GOP activists, which was viewed by 51.7 percent of those who chose to view at least one clip, followed by the civil clip from *Master Chef*, which was seen by 39.7 percent of participants who chose to engage with the headlines. The least popular video was the clip from *Survivor*, which was viewed by 17.6 percent of participants.

Having described the contours of the experiment, I can now assess the extent to which conflict orientation, prior media preferences, and exposure to incivility shaped individuals' search for additional information. Before examining the effects of conflict orientation and individual preferences for civil or uncivil media, it is worth noting that the two are related. A one-tailed, two-sample t-test demonstrates that participants who report preferences for uncivil political and entertainment television have, on average, a higher score on the conflict communication scale (mean $= -1.63$, sd $= 0.27$) than those who prefer civil news (mean $= -2.36$, sd $= 0.45$, $p = 0.075$). This relationship lends additional support to the two hypotheses presented earlier: conflict orientation shapes the kinds of media people prefer, and those who like conflict are also more likely to prefer shows that introduce incivility and disagreement.

That being said, preferences for civil or uncivil news play less of a role in an individual's decision to search for information or select uncivil clips than does conflict orientation. We see this first when looking at how many videos participants chose to watch. Individuals' preference for incivility and the match between their preferencs and the level of civility in the treatment both played a statistically insignificant role in the decision to click more articles. However, conflict orientation did play a significant role, both on its own and in conjunction with the treatments. As you can see in figure 4.4, conflict-avoidant participants, on average, clicked on about two stories after being exposed to either treatment. The conflict-approaching behaved a little differently. Those who saw the civil condition also clicked on two or more articles, on average, but those who watched an uncivil clip first were less likely to click, averaging only one additional article after the treatment.

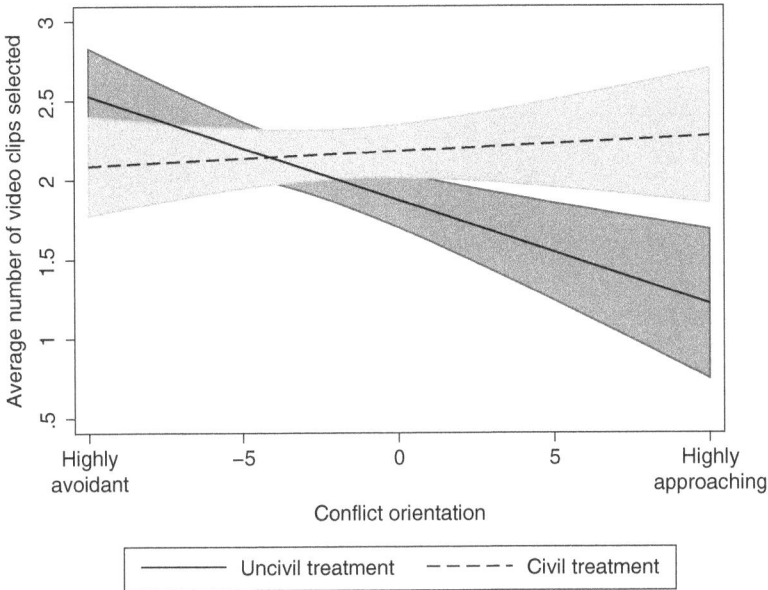

FIGURE 4.4 Incivility reduces information search among the conflict-approaching.

Note: Linear predictions derived from regression of the interaction of conflict orientation and treatment assignment, controlling for demographic and political variables.

Source: Mechanical Turk Study 2.

We see the same pattern if we look at how much time participants allocated to watching the videos. The graph on the left side of figure 4.5 displays the probability that an individual would spend *any* time watching a selection of videos from the options presented. As you can see, the conflict-avoidant are highly likely to spend time watching additional clips, regardless of whether they were first exposed to civil or uncivil political news. The conflict-approaching are also very likely to devote a non-zero amount of time to watching additional videos after watching a civil clip, but this tendency drops dramatically if they watch an uncivil clip first. A conflict-approaching individual who watched an uncivil clip had only about a 30 percent probability of allocating time to watching more clips. The same pattern plays out when we look at the right side of the graph, which

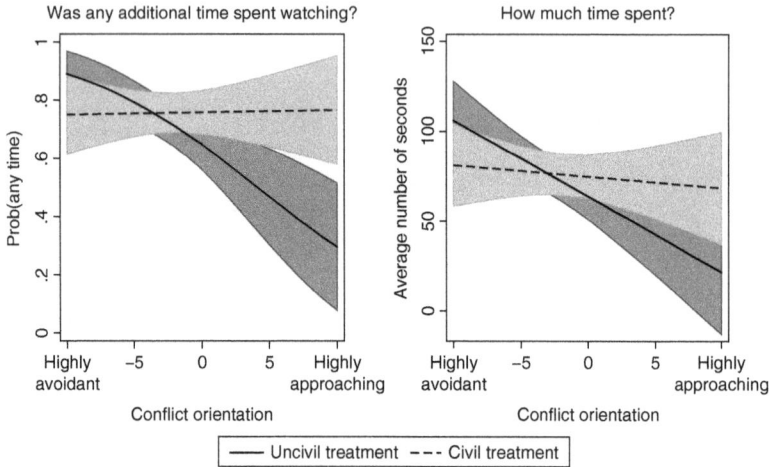

FIGURE 4.5 Incivility reduces time spent watching videos by conflict-approaching.

Note: The figure on the left presents results from a logistic regression, while the right-hand figure displays the results of a OLS model. Both evaluate the effects of conflict orientation and treatment assignment, controlling for demographic and political variables.

Source: Mechanical Turk Study 2.

estimates the average number of seconds spent watching across treatments and conflict orientations. The conflict-avoidant spend about 75–110 seconds watching clips, regardless of whether they saw civility or incivility first. The conflict-approaching spend less time watching once they have already been exposed to incivility; on average, they spend just under a minute less time reading in the wake of watching an uncivil clip.

We might look at these data as evidence that in this case, exposure to incivility is having a negative impact on the conflict-approaching, but not on the conflict-avoidant. After all, more exposure to information and increased media consumption make people better democratic citizens (Dahl 1967; Downs 1957; Lupia and McCubbins 1998). However, as Albertson and Gadarian (2015) show, not all information-searching habits are normatively positive. When individuals are anxious, for example, they are more likely to look for information about the threat, place greater trust in government "experts," and support protective policies.

Therefore, we might expect the conflict-avoidant—who we know are more anxious once exposed to incivility—to spend more time than the conflict-approaching looking at additional clips because of their feelings of anxiety. The conflict-approaching are not only looking for less information once exposed to incivility, but they are also engaging in different search patterns when they do choose to look at video clips.

Given this relationship between anxiety and a focus on threatening material, I am interested in two patterns of information search. First, are participants seeking out the uncivil clips when they are given the option to watch additional videos? The conflict-avoidant may be watching more clips than the conflict-approaching and gravitating toward incivility more frequently. Results from a multinomial logit model suggest this is the case. Figure 4.6 displays the predicted probability of choosing either only

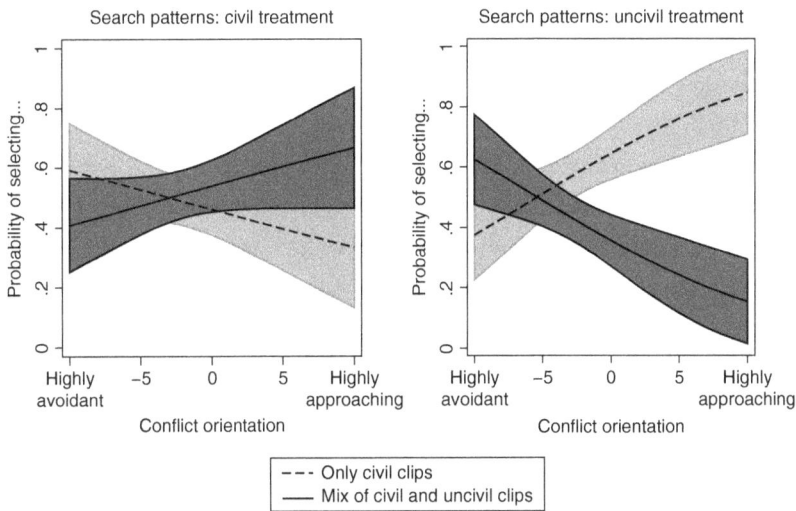

FIGURE 4.6 Participants search for different types of articles if they see incivility first.

Note: Figures represent predicted probabilities of selecting civil or uncivil articles across conflict orientations after viewing a particular treatment, controlling for demographic and political variables.

Source: Mechanical Turk Study 2.

civil videos or a mix of civil and uncivil clips, given the treatment and an individual's conflict orientation. On the one hand, the conflict-approaching seem to move away from incivility after they have been exposed to it once. When participants are assigned to the civil treatment, the conflict-approaching have a 70 percent probability of looking at a mix of civil and uncivil videos, while the avoidant have a 60 percent chance of gravitating toward the civil clips. Conflict-approaching participants exposed to the uncivil treatment, however, are far more likely to seek out only civil videos when they get to choose what to read, with an 80 percent probability of choosing only civil clips, as opposed to only 15 percent likelihood of choosing a mix. In other words, once the conflict-approaching have been exposed to incivility once, they appear to move on. If they only see civility in the treatment clip, they are more likely to seek out incivility when given the choice. In contrast, conflict-avoidant individuals who are exposed to incivility continue to watch uncivil video clips, as we would expect from individuals responding to an anxiety-inducing stimulus. This decision to continue to seek out incivility, as we will see in the next chapter, has further effects on the conflict-avoidant individuals' decisions about participating in and talking about politics.

In addition to examining individuals' search for incivility, I was interested in whether participants sought out political or entertainment clips. Here, the predicted probabilities (see figure 4.7) derived from the multinomial logit model suggest that civility makes the conflict-approaching more likely to choose to watch political videos. After watching a civil political clip, the conflict-avoidant are more likely to choose entertainment videos, while the conflict-approaching seek out a mix of entertainment and politics (only one participant in the entire sample chose only political videos). Once they have been exposed to political incivility, there is no statistical difference in conflict-avoidant individuals' likelihood of choosing politics or entertainment—they have a 50–50 probability of selecting a political clip. However, the conflict-approaching are more likely to turn solely to entertainment, choosing a mix of political and entertainment about 65 percent of the time.

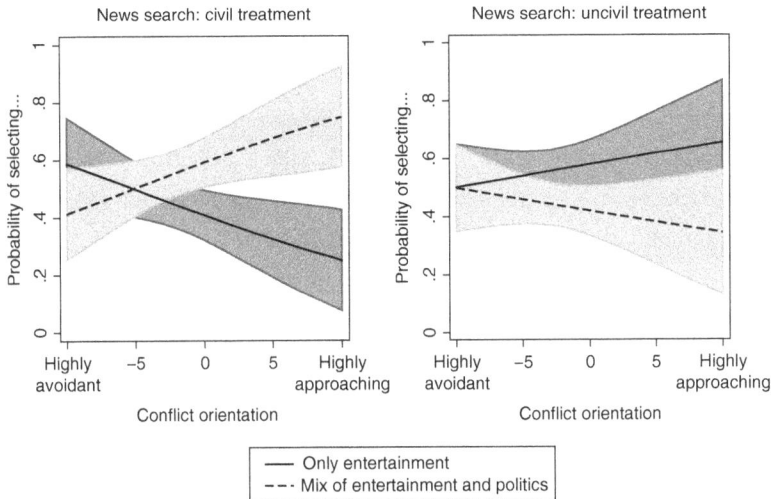

FIGURE 4.7 Conflict-approaching participants search for a mix of entertainment and politics after civil treatment.

Note: Figures represent predicted probabilities of selecting political or entertainment articles across conflict orientations after viewing a particular treatment, controlling for demographic and political variables.

Source: Mechanical Turk Study 2.

Together, these two sets of results present some challenges for our assumptions about how individuals seek out political information. Political science has long accepted that individuals are suboptimal information-seekers who use shortcuts and heuristics to make political decisions (Converse 1964; Lupia 1994). The findings here suggest that the tone of political communication plays a role in an individual's decision-making process: if political information is conveyed in an uncivil manner, it can lead to a focus on that incivility among some people and a decision to turn to entertainment among others. For the conflict-approaching, the choice to select civil video clips in the wake of exposure to incivility is encouraging, while the decision to avoid political news runs contrary to what we might hope for in encouraging democratic citizenship.

THE MEDIATING ROLE OF EMOTIONS

In explaining the effects described, I hypothesized that the relationships between conflict orientation, exposure to incivility, and information search habits were at least partly a result of the differing emotions individuals felt upon watching the uncivil video clip. Mechanical Turk Study 2 lets me test the role of each of these emotions by using Baron and Kenny's (1986) approach to mediation models. The first step in their procedure is to demonstrate that the initial variable—in this case, the interaction between conflict orientation and incivility—has an impact on the outcome: information search habits.[10] The findings in the previous pages demonstrate that this is the case. The second step requires demonstrating that the initial variable correlates with the mediator: emotion. Chapter 3 demonstrates that conflict orientation and incivility interact such that conflict-avoidant individuals experience negative emotions in the face of incivility and conflict-approaching individuals experience positive emotions.

The final two steps require the establishment of a correlation between the mediator variable, the various emotional responses, and the outcome variable, holding the initial variable constant. At this stage, the mediation analysis breaks down. Across all five emotional reactions (anxiety, disgust, anger, enthusiasm, and amusement) and the three outcomes of interest, no emotional response has a statistically significant impact on the number of videos participants clicked after exposure to the treatment, nor on the amount of time they spent reading those articles or on the proportion of articles that were uncivil or political. In short, there is minimal evidence that any single emotional response can explain why the interaction between conflict orientation and incivility shapes individuals' search for political information.

However, this is not to say that emotions play no mediating role. As I suggested earlier in this chapter, individuals' overall mood, rather than specific emotions, may also play a role in shifting their approach to consuming information. Therefore, I ran the mediation models a second time, using a dummy variable for "positive mood" if a participant had reported any of the three positive emotions and another, "negative mood," if a participant had indicated experiencing anxiety, disgust, or anger. The interaction between conflict orientation and incivility has no effect on the negative mood variable; there is only a direct effect of incivility on participants' experience of negative emotions. Negative mood does not appear to moderate the relationship between incivility, conflict orientation, and information search.

Positive mood, in contrast, does have a mediating effect on the relationship between incivility, conflict orientation, and individuals' decision to seek out information. Those individuals who were in a positive mood were slightly less likely to seek out information than their peers who did not report positive emotional reactions to the same treatments. Figure 4.8

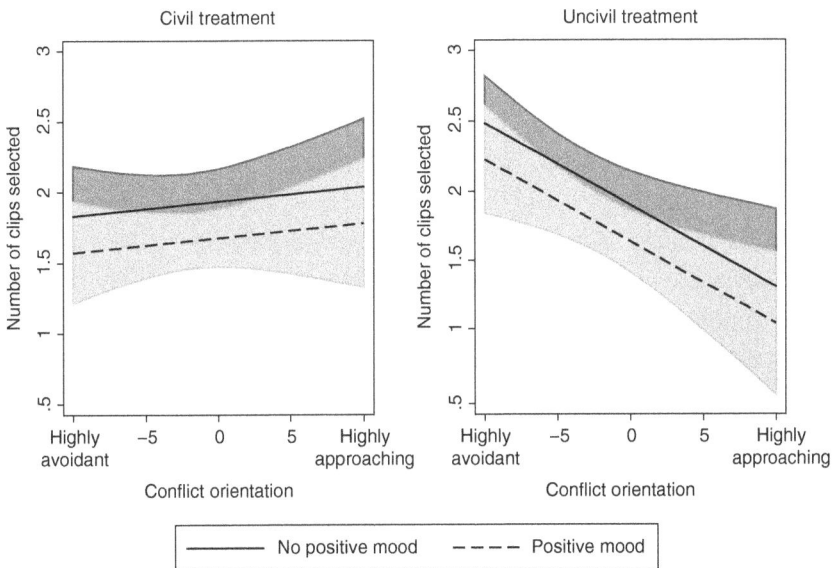

FIGURE 4.8 Positive mood mediates the join effect of incivility and conflict orientation.

Note: Linear predictions derived from regression of the interaction of conflict orientation and treatment assignment and reported positive mood.

Source: Mechanical Turk Study 2.

displays the results of the final regression models, including positive mood as a mediator. The effect of positive mood is small—reducing information search by about half a video clip—but offers support for the expectations derived from mood-management theory. Positive mood leads to less information search, explaining a portion of the relationship between conflict orientation, incivility, and information search.

* * *

Previous research shows that individuals are active consumers of media content, particularly in today's choice-filled environment. Americans can choose to watch the nightly news or scroll through the *New York Times* app, or step away from politics altogether and turn on *The Bachelor*. These choices are shaped by their interest in politics, their mood, and the emotions they experience as a result of exposure to certain information. My results are consistent with this work and build upon it, demonstrating that the choices we make about our media environment are also shaped by our orientation toward conflict. The conflict-approaching spend more time using media to learn about politics. The positive affect they feel when watching incivility leaves them with a sense of satisfaction that leads them to subsequently seek out fewer uncivil video clips than when they watch civil news. However, this same civil news encourages them to keep learning about politics; in the civil condition, the conflict-approaching are more likely to incorporate political videos into what they watch. To summarize: in the face of incivility, the conflict-approaching can step back and say "we're good, we don't need more nastiness," while still engaging with media content. In the face of civility, they are more likely to seek out political information.

The conflict-avoidant, in contrast, face an uphill battle in their quest to learn about politics. They begin by being less interested in politics, and therefore spend fewer days of the week tuning in to political news. When exposed to political news, they make a decision to further engage, but they are just as likely—if not more likely—to seek out entertainment content than a mix of politics and entertainment. What is more, they are likely to engage with new clips that are also uncivil, consistent with research suggesting that anxiety leads individuals to pay more attention to perceived threats. However, anxiety does not serve a mediating role, according to this data set, raising the possibility of other explanations for the somewhat counterintuitive finding that when we are conflict-avoidant, we actually search for more rude and nasty conversations. In the context of this experiment, the conflict-approaching are not behaving as the ideal citizen when it comes to the search for political information. The conflict-avoidant are even further disadvantaged and discouraged by the political system.

5

MIMICRY AND TEMPER TANTRUMS

Political Discussion and Engagement

At this point, and I cannot believe I am about to do this, I would like to address the Internet commenters out there directly. Good evening, monsters. This may be the moment you've spent your whole lives training for . . . for once in your life, we need you to channel that anger, that badly spelled bile that you normally reserve for unforgivable attacks on actresses you seem to think have put on weight, or politicians that you disagree with. We need you to get out there and, for once in your life, focus your indiscriminate rage in a useful direction. Seize your moment, my lovely trolls, turn on caps lock, and fly my pretties! Fly! Fly!

—JOHN OLIVER, *LAST WEEK TONIGHT*, JUNE 1, 2014

I N 2014, THE Federal Communications Commission opened public comments on the issue of "net neutrality," which prevented Internet service providers like Comcast from prioritizing certain types of web content over others. In an attempt to draw attention to the issue, comedian John Oliver spent thirteen minutes of his HBO show *Last Week Tonight* explaining net neutrality and encouraging his viewers to leave public comments for the government agency. In the subsequent days, the FCC received more than 45,000 new comments on net neutrality, and the online system experienced technical difficulties as a result of heavy traffic (McDonald 2014). As the net neutrality debate heated up again in May 2017, Oliver again argued against a plan to roll back net neutrality measures, and again the FCC received an influx of public comments—150,000 in a few days, or five times as many as it had received in the thirty days before Oliver's plea (Breland 2017).

On its face, Oliver's war with the FCC over net neutrality seems to be a story about the ways in which political behavior can be influenced by celebrities and tastemakers. Implicit in Oliver's call to action, as highlighted in the epigraph to this chapter, are questions about the connection between political incivility and participation. His expectation is that if enough people "focus [their] indiscriminate rage in a useful direction," the FCC will change its position on net neutrality. Citizens' participation in political discourse, specifically uncivil political discourse, will lead to their preferred policy outcome.

The deliberative democrat is swift to counter Oliver's expectation: incivility diminishes our respect for one another and our political institutions, thereby making political discussion and compromise difficult (Ferree et al. 2002; Gastil 2008; Gutmann and Thompson 1996). Theorists who emphasize the importance of participation to the democratic polity take a rosier view, pointing to the relationship between incivility and political participation. As Almond and Verba argue in *The Civic Culture* (1963), the most stable political systems are those that have relatively high levels of both tolerance and participation, blending the priorities of the two theoretical camps. In their ideal "mixed" society, the amount of engagement is important—democratic republicanism requires that citizens make their preferences known to elected officials through voting, protests, letters, etc.—but so is the quality of that engagement. However, my investigation into the role that conflict orientation plays in shaping political behavior suggests that these two approaches are not blending as well as we might hope. The conflict-approaching are more likely to participate in a range of political activities, and their commentary on political news mimics what they see in the media. If individuals are exposed to incivility, they will be more likely to use it in their own political conversations.

These patterns suggest that if the contemporary political environment truly is riddled with greater incivility, conflict orientation becomes a resource citizens must use to successfully navigate their political world. Those who are conflict-approaching have greater capital when entering the political arena, ultimately making them more likely to participate in political activities that demand an ability to handle disagreement and incivility. In this chapter, I test the *participation-quality* and *participation-quantity hypotheses* by investigating this relationship between incivility, conflict orientation, and participation. First, I examine the correlation between conflict orientation and different forms of political participation. When a political activity opens individuals up to incivility and conflict, the conflict-approaching are more likely to engage than the conflict-avoidant. Then, focusing on political discussion, I explore how the presence of incivility changes both the likelihood of engaging in online political discussion and the content of that discussion. Across three studies, the results indicate that a more uncivil political landscape not only leads certain types of people to participate more than others, but also changes the way in which they participate, further raising the barrier to entry and reinforcing preexisting inequalities in engagement.

SHAPING POLITICAL ACTIVITY

Year after year, survey respondents report voting in recent elections at high rates, but demonstrate much lower engagement with other forms of political participation such as protest, campaign work, contacting elected officials, or engaging in interpersonal political discussion. In their quest to explain this variation across political activities, as well as why citizens participate in politics more broadly, Brady, Verba and Schlozman (1995) shift the question, asking why people do not take part in politics. They write:

> Three answers immediately suggest themselves: because they can't, because they don't want to, or because nobody asked. "They can't" suggests a paucity of necessary *resources*. . . . "They don't want to" focuses on the absence of psychological *engagement* with politics—a lack of interest in politics, minimal concern with public issues, a sense that activity makes no difference. . . . "Nobody asked" implies isolation from the *recruitment networks* through which citizens are mobilized to politics. (271)

They go on to demonstrate that three political resources—civic skills, money, and free time—shape individuals' likelihood of participating in different political activities and that these resources, in turn, are linked to demographic and socioeconomic characteristics of individuals. At first glance, conflict orientation does not seem to have much in common with these resources. I have been making the case throughout this book that it is a psychological trait, but it does not quite fall into the category of Brady, Verba and Schlozman's second explanation, psychological engagement. Conflict orientation is distinct from efficacy or political interest. Individuals may want to participate in politics but feel they cannot because they do not have the tolerance for disagreement, negativity, or vitriol that they perceive is needed to engage. From this perspective, conflict orientation is a resource, just like money or civic skills.

This resource helps citizens navigate some political activities better than others. Research on political behavior tends to focus on a standard set of political activities; since the 1950s, the American National Election Study has asked citizens if they voted, attended political meetings, rallies, or speeches, wore a campaign button or put a sign in front of their house, or talked to anyone to show them why they should vote. More recently, they have included questions about donations to political causes and online discussion of political issues. As Ulbig and Funk (1999) explain, certain participatory acts are more likely to expose an individual to conflict. Specifically, activities that require public expression of one's beliefs are more likely to elicit interpersonal disagreement (Verba and Nie 1972; Milbrath 1965), as are those that provide more opportunity for far-reaching change (Verba and Nie 1972). Given these two dimensions, they argue that protest represents a high-conflict political activity, campaign support and discussion of politics reflect a medium likelihood of exposure to conflict, and voting and contacting officials are low-conflict activities (Ulbig and Funk 1999).

Following Ulbig and Funk, I categorize different types of political engagement into high-conflict, midrange, and low-conflict activities (see table 5.1). In many cases, my classification mirrors theirs; however, in addition to looking at protest, voting, and contacting officials, I break political discussion into two separate acts: commenting on political blogs and

TABLE 5.1 CATEGORIZATION OF POLITICAL ACTIVITIES
BY EXPOSURE TO CONFLICT

HIGH-CONFLICT	MIDRANGE	LOW-CONFLICT
Commenting on political blogs	Contacting government officials	Donating money
Persuading others to vote	Wearing a campaign button	Voting
Attending a political protest	Putting up a political sign	
Attending a local meeting	Working for a candidate	

persuading others to vote. I also differentiate between types of campaign work: donating money, wearing a campaign button, putting up a political sign, working for a candidate, and attending a local meeting.

The assessment of conflict in political activities is in part a function of the public or private nature of the participation. Donating money and voting are the sole low-conflict activities because they are the only means of engaging in politics privately, without interacting with another person. Unless you tell friends and family how you voted or that you donated money, these decisions remain relatively anonymous and are unlikely to provoke conflict. Most of the campaign activities are classified as midrange; one's opinion is no longer anonymous and is publicly exposed, but not necessarily in a venue that invites discussion or uncivil reactions. For example, if you put a political sign in your front yard, your neighbors will all know for whom you voted, but unless they happen to be walking their dog while you are out mowing the lawn, you are unlikely to experience interpersonal conflict as a direct effect of the yard sign. Similarly, if you work for a candidate, whether by going door to door, phone-banking, or participating in other Get Out the Vote efforts, you are likely calling undecided voters or the candidate's base—individuals who are less likely to challenge your support for that candidate. High-conflict activities are those in which one has the opportunity to voice one's own opinion and where others can respond. These can be situations in which individuals are or are not anonymous, but where they are likely to receive pushback on their views. Protests are designed to instigate conflict between opposing sides. Even if the majority of protestors are in agreement about an issue, an individual in attendance is more likely to hear disagreement, frequently expressed through name-calling or other forms of incivility. Similarly, participating in the comments section of a blog or news article or persuading others to vote signals a clear intention to discuss political opinions with others who might disagree and opens one up to challenges and offensive statements.

To summarize, people's conflict orientation will affect their decision to participate in political activities where they are more likely to be exposed to conflict. Here, conflict does not mean just incivility, but incorporates a wider definition that captures disagreement as well as incivility. When presented with an uncivil political environment, individuals who enjoy conflict will engage. Conversely, more conflict-avoidant individuals possess less of this resource in the political realm. They shy away from activities that could force them to experience incivility and disagreement. The conflict-avoidant take steps to reduce their exposure to conflict, while the conflict-approaching hunt for it.

Participation-quantity hypothesis: The conflict-approaching will be more likely to participate in high-conflict activities, but there will be no difference in participation in low-conflict activities across conflict orientations.

As the high-conflict participatory acts center around public expression of one's opinion, it seems important to further investigate the role of incivility in this domain, disentangling it from disagreement. Many scholars in the realm of political psychology and communication have found that individuals are intimidated by the prospect of engaging in public political conversation. Hayes, Scheufele, and Huge (2006) argue that political engagement, including discussing our own opinions, risks upsetting delicate interpersonal relationships. The fear of upsetting or excluding others is why etiquette experts recommend avoiding political conversation; Anna Post of the Emily Post Institute emphasizes respect and the use of civil language as means of keeping the peace (Grinberg 2011). Participants in Conover, Searing, and Crewe's (2002) focus groups reported fears of looking uneducated, facing social rejection or isolation, and encouraging social conflict when faced with the prospect of political conversation. Those who do enjoy political discussion tend to share particular personality traits (Gerber et al. 2012; Testa, Hibbing, and Ritchie 2014) or seek out discussion forums that provide connections to like-minded others in an "imagined community" (Berry and Sobeiraj 2014). Experiencing both enjoyment and displeasure while having a political conversation depends on the characteristics of the environment and the individual.

Increasingly, Americans report that they are talking about politics not only with their friends and family in face-to-face discussion, but with a wider network of acquaintances and strangers on the Internet. According to a Pew report on the political environment on social media, approximately one-third of American adults use social networking sites such as Facebook and Twitter to engage in political conversations (Duggan and Smith 2016). Furthermore, the Internet serves as a venue for citizens to directly engage with their elected officials and political candidates. All serious presidential candidates (and the vast majority of congressional candidates and candidates for state offices like governor) have Facebook accounts and Twitter pages. A focus on the qualitative and quantitative effects of online incivility is particularly warranted as the Internet becomes an increasingly important space for citizen-to-citizen and citizen-to-leader communication about politics.

In general, incivility influences individuals' willingness to engage in political conversation, but this is particularly true online. According to Duggan and Smith (2016), 40 percent of those who engage in political conversations on social media agree strongly with the statement that "social media are places where people say things while discussing politics that they would never say in person (an additional 44 percent feel that this statement describes social media somewhat well)." Attributes of online comment sections, discussion forums, and social networking sites, such as anonymity and a sense of disinhibition, facilitate the use of incivility (Santana 2014; Suler 2004). The presence of incivility, in turn, has mixed effects on users' participation in online commentary or deliberation. In one study, people who were exposed to civil discussion reported greater willingness to participate in political discussion than those exposed to uncivil discussion (Han and Brazeal 2015). People exposed to online incivility are also less likely to believe that deliberation in public discourse can resolve political problems (Hwang, Kim, and Huh 2014). Other studies have found that uncivil discussion does not affect respondents' intent to participate in discussion; if anything, it increases participatory intent (Borah 2014; Ng and Detenber 2006). One possible explanation for these divergent findings stems from the role of conflict orientation. Per the participation-quantity hypothesis, the conflict-avoidant are less likely to comment on a blog post, protest, or engage in political discussion because those types of activities invite conflict. When they are confronted by incivility, then, they will also be less likely to participate.

> *Political-discussion hypothesis:* When the conflict-avoidant are faced with incivility, they will be less likely to participate in online discussion. When the conflict-approaching are faced with incivility, they will be more likely to participate.

SHAPING THE QUALITY OF POLITICAL ENGAGEMENT

Scholars concerned about the effects of incivility on discussion are worried not only that incivility reduces individuals' willingness to talk about politics, but also that incivility changes the quality of the conversation. As discussed in chapter 4, a wealth of research suggests that incivility is particularly present in online political discourse, as attributes of the platform facilitate its use. Anonymity, reduced self-regulation, and reduced self-awareness lead to depersonalized messages that in turn encourage more assertive and uninhibited responses (Kiesler, Siegel, and McGuire 1984; Anderson et al. 2014). In other words, the normative expectations about nonverbal behavior and respectful tone that hold for face-to-face communication break down online, reducing the quality of political discussion.

Furthermore, incivility begets incivility in political conversation because humans learn appropriate behavior by observing their surroundings.

Drawing on both cognitive and behavioral strands of psychological research, Bandura (1977, 2002) argues that we watch others' interactions with their environments and, based on the positive or negative outcomes of those interactions, adapt our own behavior. This sort of modeling behavior is evident in investigations into the effects of incivility on group dynamics and political conversation, particularly conversation occurring on the Internet. In real-time online discussions, individuals mimic the overall tone of the group; a negative overall tenor to a conversation will lead certain people to use negative language in their own comments (Price, Nir, and Cappella 2006). Similarly, Gervais (2011, 2015) has found that incivility both on television talk shows and in online discussion forums leads viewers or participants to be more uncivil in their own comments and discussion of issues. Taking a more positive approach, Han and Brazeal (2015) found that people exposed to civil discussion demonstrate more civil discourse in their own comments. Applying social-learning theory to an online environment rife with incivility, it seems probable that those who are more likely to comment online—the conflict-approaching—will also be more likely to use incivility in their comments.

Participation-quality hypothesis: Conflict-approaching individuals who are exposed to incivility will be more likely to use incivility in their own online comments.

MAKING DECISIONS: CHOOSING POLITICAL ACTIVITIES

Participants in three of the studies describe in chapter 1 were asked to report whether they had engaged in a range of political activities in the past year and whether they had voted in the last presidential election.[1] Activities in which participants could report participating included attending local political meetings (such as school board or city council); going to a political speech, march, rally, or demonstration; trying to persuade someone to vote;

putting up a political sign (such as a lawn sign or bumper sticker); working for a candidate or campaign; wearing a campaign button or sticker; phoning, emailing, writing to, or visiting a government official to express their views on a public issue; commenting on political blogs or online forums (not surveys); and donating money to a candidate, campaign, or political organization. As discussed earlier and displayed in table 5.1, I categorize each of these activities as high-conflict, midrange, or low-conflict based on the likelihood that individuals participating in each will encounter disagreement or incivility and have to respond or defend their own viewpoint.

As is frequently the case with political participation, the vast majority of participants reported having voted in the previous election (approximately 71 percent of Project Implicit participants and almost 88 percent of Mechanical Turk participants), but far fewer people reported engagement in more resource-intensive activities like attending a meeting or working for a candidate. As table 5.2 shows, commenting on blogs, contacting

TABLE 5.2 POLITICAL PARTICIPATION ACROSS SAMPLES

		PERCENTAGE PARTICIPATING IN THE PAST YEAR (PROJECT IMPLICIT)	PERCENTAGE PARTICIPATING IN THE PAST YEAR (MTURK STUDY 1)
High-conflict	Commented on political blogs	18.6	28.1
	Persuaded others to vote	27.7	38.0
	Contacted government official	22.2	19.3
	Attended political protest	13.5	9.5
Midrange	Attended local meeting	13.4	9.0
	Wore a campaign button	12.1	13.2
	Put up political sign	11.3	13.1
	Worked for a candidate	4.8	4.6
Low-conflict	Donated money	13.2	11.5
	Voted	70.8	87.7

government officials, and persuading others to vote are the most popular forms of more active engagement; between 19 and 38 percent of participants reported engaging in these activities in the past year. These high-conflict activities are also potentially the most interesting for an investigation into the effects of conflict orientation, as they all require interpersonal communication. Engagement in other participatory activities, most of which require an investment of time or money, hovers at 15 percent or lower. Working for a candidate is the least frequent form of political engagement, with less than 5 percent participation across both samples, but is also arguably the most time- and knowledge-intensive activity.

RESULTS: POLITICAL PARTICIPATION

The participation-quantity hypothesis asserts that citizens make decisions about political participation on the basis of the potential for exposure to incivility. If they enjoy conflict, they will be more likely to participate in high-conflict and midrange political activities than those who have an aversion to conflict. The data provide evidence of conflict orientation's ability to shape participation in different political activities, particularly activities that present the possibility of uncivil or confrontational discussion.

Figure 5.1 displays the bivariate relationships between participatory acts and conflict orientation in the Project Implicit sample.[2] From these graphs, it is clear that more conflict-approaching individuals are more likely to participate in most political activities. The one exception to this pattern is the likelihood of voting, which is uniform across conflict orientation; regardless of conflict orientation, there was about a 70 percent chance that a participant reported voting in the last presidential election. Beyond voting, the relationship between conflict orientation and participation is statistically significant and positive, although the size of this effect varies from activity to activity. In line with my hypothesis, the effects of conflict orientation are larger for the activities categorized as high-conflict. The likelihood of attending a protest, contacting one's

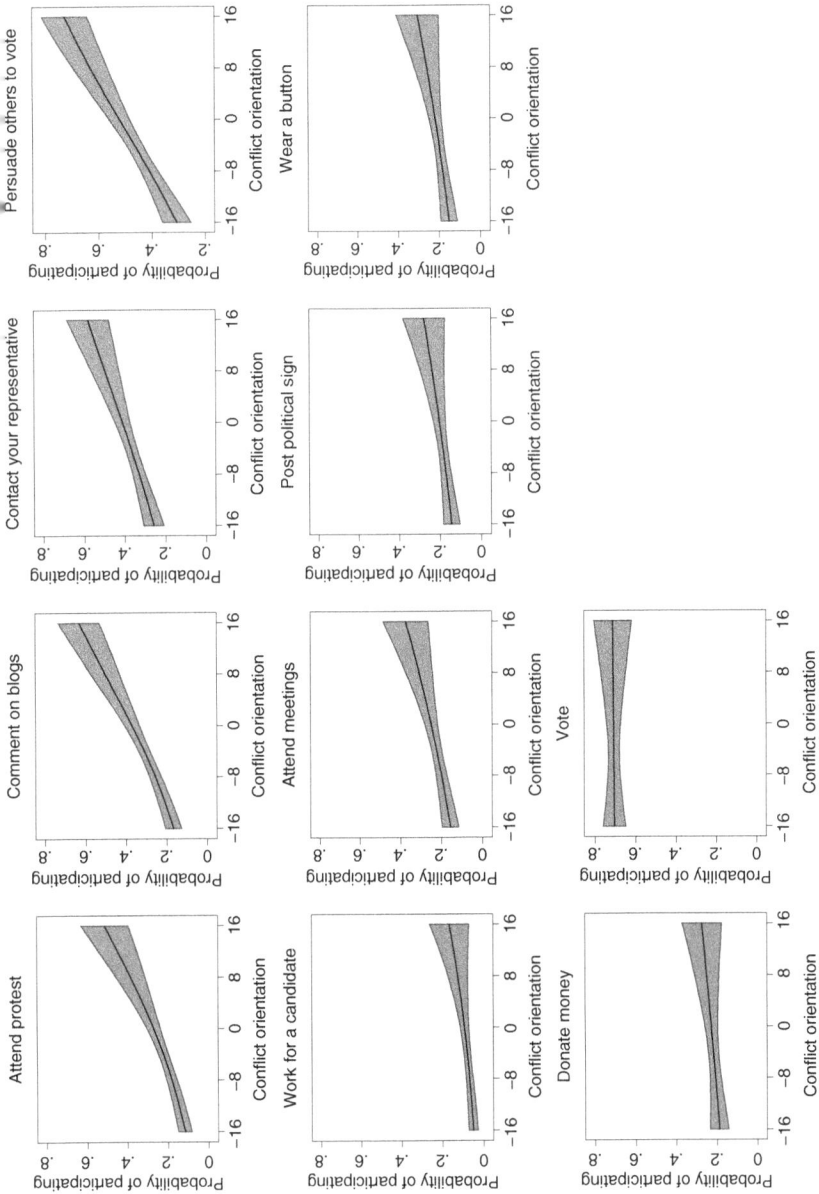

FIGURE 5.1 Bivariate analyses suggest conflict-approaching individuals are more likely to participate in political activities.

Note: Probabilities are reported from bivariate logistic regressions of each participatory activity on conflict orientation. Lower values on the conflict orientation scale represent more conflict avoidance; higher numbers equal more conflict approaching tendencies. Shaded areas represent 95% confidence intervals.

Source: Project Implicit.

representative, persuading others to vote, and commenting on blogs shifts significantly from the most conflict-avoidant (20 to 30 percent chance of reporting participation in the past year) to the most conflict-approaching (50 to 75 percent probability). The midrange or low-conflict activities exhibit, at most, a 30 percent change from one extreme of the Conflict Communication Scale to the other. Conflict-avoidant individuals report a 5 to 20 percent likelihood of engaging in politics by working for a candidate, attending a meeting, posting a political sign, or wearing a button, while their conflict-approaching peers report a 15 to 35 percent probability of engaging in these activities.

As with the investigation into patterns of media consumption, this analysis incorporated other participant characteristics that are known to influence political participation. Once I factor in the effects of these demographic and political variables on an individual's participation, the story of conflict orientation's role in participation is slightly different. As figure 5.2 shows, conflict orientation still plays a statistically significant role in citizens' reporting that they had attended a protest, contacted their representative, commented on blogs, or persuaded others to vote: conflict-approaching participants are more likely than those who are conflict-avoidant to participate in each of these activities. However, conflict-approaching individuals are no more likely to participate in the midrange or low-conflict activities— working for a candidate, attending a meeting, posting a sign, or wearing a button—than the conflict-avoidant participants.

These differences in likelihood of participation are more pronounced for those who are more interested in politics.[3] Looking exclusively at the four forms of participation that are statistically significant when controlling for demographic and political characteristics (commenting on blogs, protesting, calling a representative, and persuading others), it is clear that political interest plays a major role in getting people to engage in these activities (figure 5.3). Being conflict-approaching further increases the proclivity to participate if an individual is already interested in politics. Survey respondents who reported that they were not at all interested in politics show minimal change in their probability of participating across the CCS. The slope of each predicted probability line increases with the

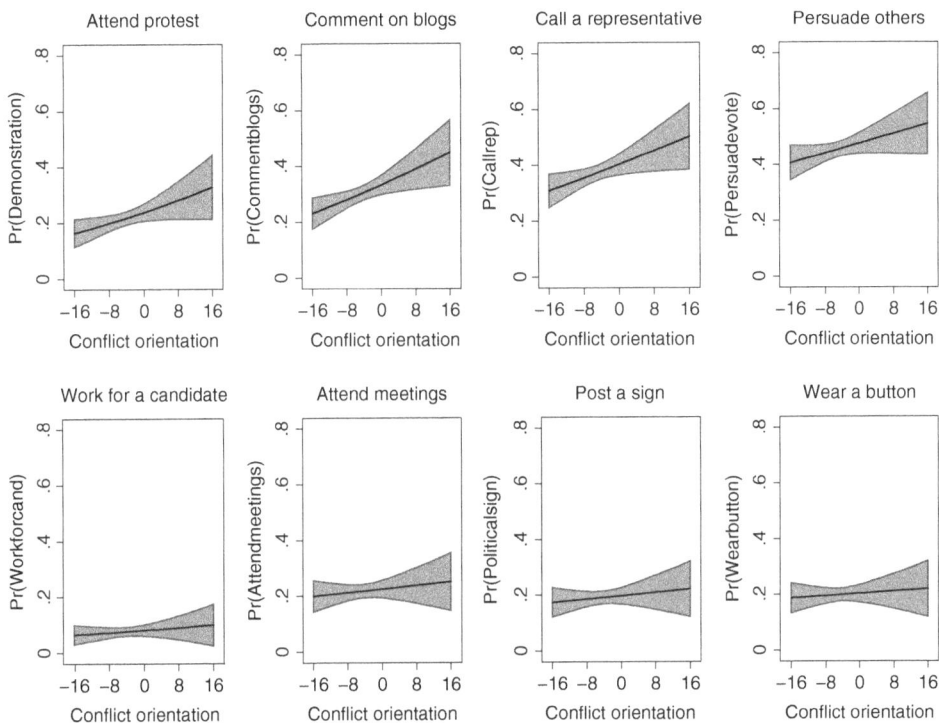

FIGURE 5.2 Controlling for other characteristics, conflict-approaching more likely to participate in high-conflict activities.

Note: Probabilities are reported from multivariate logistic regressions of conflict orientation, controlling for personality, gender, age, education, race, ethnicity, party identification, party strength, and political interest. Lower values on the conflict orientation scale represent more conflict avoidance; higher numbers equal more conflict approaching tendencies.

Source: Project Implicit.

increase in political interest; very and extremely interested participants who are conflict-avoidant are about 20 percent less likely to participate in any activity than those who are somewhat interested or less so.

To summarize, the participatory findings presented here demonstrate that there is a direct relationship between political engagement and conflict orientation. Conflict-approaching individuals are more likely to report having participated in high-conflict activities—that is, activities in which they are more likely to be exposed to disagreement or incivility—than their

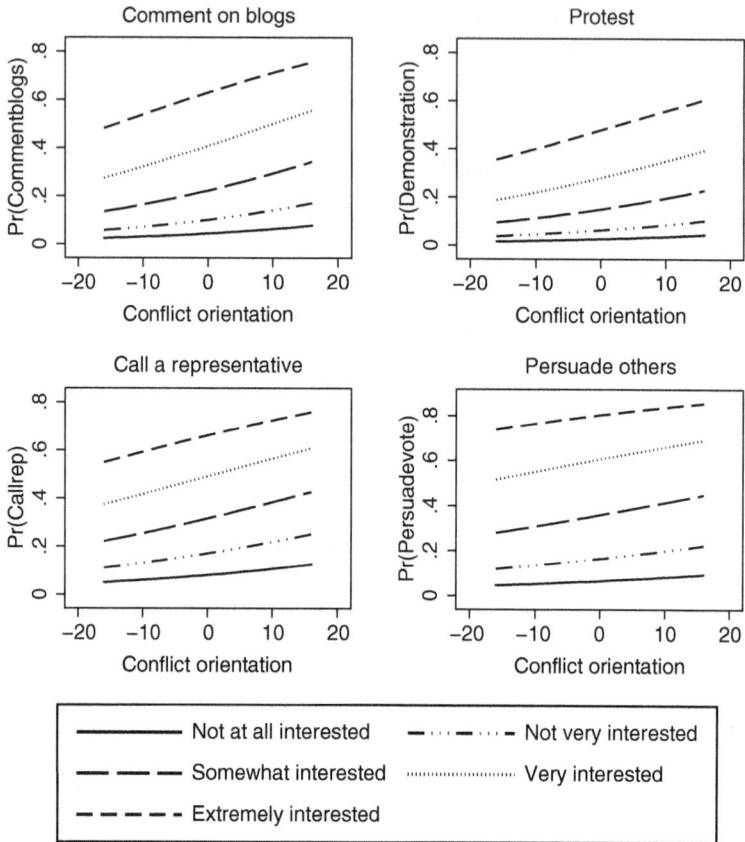

FIGURE 5.3 Effects of conflict orientation at different levels of political interest.

Note: Figures represent linear predictions from a multivariate regression that includes an interaction between interest and conflict orientation.

Source: Project Implicit.

conflict-avoidant peers. This is particularly true for people who are also interested in politics. The effect of conflict orientation is stronger for the extremely interested than it is for those who are not at all interested. One's predisposition toward conflict does not appear to play a part in the decision to engage in the midlevel to low-conflict forms of political participation. For these activities—wearing a button, working for a candidate, donating money, and perhaps most important, voting—the conflict-avoidant are just as likely to participate as the conflict-approaching.

Over each set of results, there is a consistent finding: the conflict-approaching are more likely to participate in three of the high-conflict activities: protest, commenting on a blog, and persuading others. However, these results are purely observational. It is impossible to tell whether it is the conflict inherent in these activities or something else that is driving the decision to participate. The GfK experiment offers some insight into the causal role that incivility plays in leading individuals to comment on or share civil and uncivil video clips.

As discussed in chapter 3, participants in the GfK study were shown one of four video clips that varied on two dimensions: politics/entertainment and civil/uncivil. The entertainment clips were edited from an episode of *Master Chef*; the political clips were from CSPAN coverage of a congressional hearing concerning Planned Parenthood. After watching their assigned video, respondents were given the opportunity to comment on the clip and were asked whether they would share the story with friends on social media, and if so, what their own commentary on the piece would be. In response, 63 percent of respondents commented on the clip they had watched, with a high of 68.6 percent for those who had watched the civil Planned Parenthood clip and the lowest frequency of comments from those who had watched the civil *Master Chef* clip. Only 6 percent of the total sample reported interest in sharing the story, with a similar distribution across the four videos, varying from 4.8 percent (the civil *Master Chef* clip) to 7.6 percent (the civil Planned Parenthood clip).

While it is important to acknowledge that there are distinctions across the four treatments, the primary question is whether incivility—manifested in political or entertainment discourse—affects the likelihood of participating in conversation about the issues presented. Therefore, I collapsed the treatments along the civility/incivility dimension to explore whether the tone of the clip affected individuals' likelihood of commenting on or sharing the clip. A two-sample test of proportions suggests that there is no difference between individuals' likelihood of commenting on the civil and uncivil video clips (civil = 62.2 percent, uncivil= 64.0 percent, one-tailed p = 0.16). However, there is a difference in the proportion of individuals who were willing to share the story with their friends on social media.[4] Whereas 7.4 percent of people reported an interest in sharing the uncivil clips, only 5.2 percent of those who saw a civil clip were interested in sharing the story (one-tailed, p = 0.006). In other words, participants were no more likely to comment on a clip that was uncivil, but they were more likely to (hypothetically) share that uncivil clip with their social networks.

Finally, we can investigate the role that conflict orientation plays in moderating the effects of incivility on commenting on or sharing these video clips. The *political-discussion hypothesis* suggests that the conflict-approaching will be more likely to engage when a story is uncivil, while the conflict-avoidant will be less likely to comment on or share the same story. Results from a logistic regression suggest that both incivility and conflict orientation do shape the likelihood of sharing a story, but not in the interactive way I predicted (see appendix B for full regression results). Instead, people across all conflict orientations are more likely to share the uncivil story than the civil story. At the same time, conflict-approaching respondents also reported being more likely to share than their conflict-avoidant counterparts. This relationship is depicted graphically in figure 5.4.

As you can see from the graph, the highly avoidant are very unlikely to express interest in sharing any video clips, regardless of whether they are civil or uncivil. The most conflict-avoidant people have a 2 percent probability of sharing the civil clip and a 3 percent probability of sharing the uncivil clip. On the opposite side of the graph, we can see both that the gap has widened slightly between the likelihood of sharing the civil and uncivil clips (although this is clearly not statistically significant) and that the most conflict-approaching respondents are more willing to consider sharing. The highly conflict-approaching have a 16 percent likelihood of sharing a civil clip and a 20 percent likelihood of reporting interest in sharing the uncivil clip.

While these results do not depict a clear interactive effect, they nevertheless demonstrate the importance of considering incivility and conflict orientation simultaneously. The conflict-approaching are the ones doing the

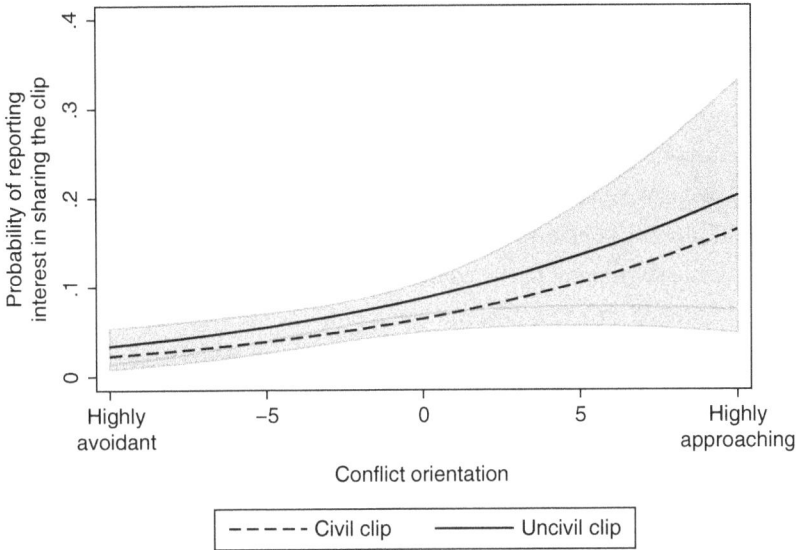

FIGURE 5.4 Conflict-approaching more likely to share incivility.
Source: GfK.

sharing on social media, and they are sharing civil and uncivil video clips at roughly equivalent rates. However, if the conflict-approaching are more frequent posters of content, we also have to consider how their reactions to that content might shape the quality of conversation.

MAKING BETTER CONVERSATION?

From a normative perspective, it matters little that conflict-approaching individuals are more likely to participate in high-conflict activities if their participation is reinforcing the link between political expression and uncivil discourse. Citizens might be participating, but they are participating in a manner that is detrimental to political discourse premised on mutual respect and focused on bridging lines of difference. Therefore, we must not only investigate whether the conflict-approaching are participating in politics, and specifically political conversation, more than their conflict-avoidant peers, but also assess the quality of that participation. Are those who choose to comment on political news doing so in a civil manner?

Participants in the GfK study were asked to offer comments or ask questions about the video they had watched as if they were making a comment on YouTube or a similar social media site. In response, 63 percent of participants wrote something in the comment box, although 15.5 percent of those explicitly stated that they had "no comment," included gibberish ("ffffff"), or expressed confusion about what they were being asked to do ("I do not understand"). Still, 54 percent of the comments fell into at least one of the other four categories used in the coding scheme; they engaged in meta-communication around the televised conversation, used incivility in their response, offered an opinion about the issues discussed, or asked questions about the content.

The two most prevalent types of responses were those that offered an opinion about the content and those that commented on the tenor of the conversation in the clip (see table 5.3). Over 24 percent of those who made comments engaged in a form of metacommunication, calling attention to the manner in which the interaction in the video took place rather than to the content of the exchange. Many of these comments focused on the specific exchange the participant had just viewed, as in this comment about the back-and-forth between Jim Jordan and Cecile Richards:

> Rep. Jim Jordan interrupts way too often and does not allow the other party to speak a full thought or comment. It sounded more like one party (Jim) shutting down another party (Cecile) versus really trying to hear or understand that other party's comment. It was not a civil disagreement or argument, instead it was an aggressive, emotional shut-down, which I found to be inappropriate and unprofessional. (participant 759)

Another participant also called Jordan out for his tone and behavior, stating, "The jerk Ohio representative is obviously on a witch hunt. He is hitting the PP president with constant argumentative comments and

TABLE 5.3 FREQUENCY OF CERTAIN TYPES OF COMMENTS

	PERCENT OF COMMENTS
No comment/gibberish	8.1
Confusion about task	7.5
Metacommunication	24.4
Offers opinion	21.9
Wants to learn more	5.6
Uses incivility	9.1

expecting her to answer . . . this is an obvious one-sided questioning which the representative wants to make sure comes out his way" (participant 3667). Each of these participants felt that Jordan was bullying Richards rather than engaging in an open conversation about the allegations levied at Planned Parenthood.

Other comments drew on the tenor of the media clip to make a generalization about the negative tone of political conversation or reality television. One participant noted, "This is the problem with our nation we can not be civil at anything even cooking" (participant 1432). This dismay at the lack of civility in reality-television programming was echoed by another participant, who thought the judge could have been less critical of the dish he tasted: "My general comment about reality shows is that in general I really . . . dislike them because I think they encourage rudeness, confrontation, major self-promoting, and a loss of civility" (participant 1227). In the political realm, participants who watched the uncivil exchange between Jim Jordan and Cecile Richards saw it as typical of contemporary political discourse. "It seems like all politics is anymore is people arguing," wrote one participant (1056). Another added, "As usual, congress people are discourtious, impolite . . . if I were the congressmans constittuant [*sic*], I may choose to not vote for him" (participant 2117). Many viewers perceived the actions and tones used as emblematic of a larger group, and for some, that tone shaped their hypothetical reactions to the clips.

While many participants assigned to watch the uncivil clips referenced the argumentative or negative tone of the congressional exchange, participants who viewed the civil treatments recognized the civility or respect with which the representative and the *Master Chef* judge engaged. After watching the *Master Chef* clip, one participant noted that Lydia gave "good constructive feedback," while another commented, "It seemed like she gave pretty kind constructive criticism, and from her perspective it would have been easy to be rude and condescending, but I think she at least turned the meal down in an understanding and educative manner" (participant 2909). Of those who watched the political clips, one participant noted that Representative Cummings was "respectful, logical, and well-spoken. I appreciated that." Others said that Cummings's calm demeanor "made me listen" (participant 2969). In other words, participants were aware of the civility or incivility of the televised individuals and acknowledged that the language used had an impact on their willingness to keep watching and their openness to the speaker's critiques.

Finally, others made a clear connection between the tone of the clip they had watched and their own media consumption habits, providing qualitative evidence for the arguments made in chapter 4. One participant acknowledged how difficult it was to keep watching even the thirty-second clip in the experiment:

> I almost hit the pause button but thought I'd stick it out because it wasn't very long. It is this type of stuff (people bickering and being rude to each other and there is always one who is more domineering over the other) that when I see it I quit watching. No matter the topic, I'll turn it off or skip over it. (participant 2151)

Similarly, another participant suggested the exchange between Jordan and Richards was representative of "typical bureaucrats. Congressman asking, loudly, talking over another person, not letting the other person say anything. While the woman supposedly there to answer questions deflects them and tries to make her written statement instead of answering the question. Which is why I don't watch that kind of "news" or programming" (participant 3700). Several participants were turned off by the tone of the *Master Chef* clips as well. As one participant wrote, "I [hate] shows that constantly put people down and I don't watch them!" (participant 2852). Incivility turns certain people away from political information and discussion.

Others, however, were drawn into the video debate enough to offer their own opinion about the contested issue. Of those who commented, 22 percent engaged with the content, and the vast majority of these comments (91 percent) were civil. Among those who watched the *Master Chef* videos, many opinions fell into two categories: they expressed a commitment either to classic dishes or to a willingness to try new things. For example, one participant noted, "I agree completely [with the judge]. I cook with friends who add this and that and this and that. The final result is muddled. I love the classics and then tweeking [*sic*] the classics. No more" (participant 863). Another disagreed, arguing that the judge could have tried to balance her critique with the recommendation that "he might want to try a new or different spice next time. Especially with cooking (which I'm not a cook) if people never tried anything different we'd all be eating plain hamburgers. How boring!" (participant 1632). Particularly in the civil condition, respondents felt they could offer their own critique of the contestant's dish.

For those who viewed the CSPAN clips, opinions spoke to three overarching themes: abortion policy and Planned Parenthood generally, the alleged video that was the specific topic of the congressional hearing,[5] and Representative Cummings's commentary in the civil clip about respecting the rule of law. As we might expect from public opinion research into American opinions on abortion (e.g., Press and Cole 1999), participants' opinions varied in their direction and intensity. Some participants, like this one, acknowledged that Planned Parenthood provides a wide range of services for young women:

> Planned parenthood is important for all ages. As a young adult, I find it important to be prepared for parenting. Some people may not have the ability to wait years and years to have a child. People get older.

People may not be financially stable enough to have a child then they may feel having a child without planning is a priority because of their age and time clock. That's why Mr. Cummings broadcast was important for everyone view. Parents' decision to have a child may not have always have been planned it's more of a surprise or spontaneous timing situation. That doesn't mean that people aren't prepared, but with training before pregnancy people can be prepared in classes like home ec and parenting classes. It is very important to have planned parenthood classes (participant 2281).

Others argued that the government should not be supporting Planned Parenthood because that support amounted to the implicit sanctioning of infanticide. Participant 3274 wrote, "Planned parenthood is nothing but a government funded murder facility. This man [Rep. Cumming] says he must uphold the law which includes child abuse laws. Child abuse in the U.S. is such a terrible crime but murdering babies before they're born is perfectly legal. What a joke." In both the civil and uncivil conditions, participants expressed support for and opposition to Planned Parenthood, legalized abortion, and the government's role in funding the organization's services (even, in some cases, while acknowledging that the government was not funding abortion services specifically).

Beyond attitudes about abortion and government provision of health services, people also engaged around ideas of institutional legitimacy and the importance of rule of law. In the civil CSPAN clip, Elijah Cummings argues, "You are doing what is within the bounds of the law, and you know, there are a lot of things I don't like, a lot of laws I don't like, but I still live in the United States of America and there's a system of government, and I as a lawyer and a member of Congress I'm sworn to uphold those laws. Now, I might want to change them, I'll do everything in my power to change the ones I don't like, but in the meantime, that's where I am." Many participants agreed with him and demonstrated a more nuanced understanding of representation and political activism in the United States. One participant stated, "I agree with his comments. There are laws that I personally do not like but I will abide by them while I work at trying to have them changed" (participant 501). Another noted that Cummings's argument stands in stark contrast to discriminatory laws against African Americans throughout U.S. history: " 'Its the Law, Its the law' he repeats—it was also 'the Law' in Nazi Germany to send Jews to gas chambers—it was also 'the law' in our own antebellum south to keep black people in slavery. There is a LAW far above Elijah Cummings and a God to whom he and his fellow baby murderers will answer" (participant 1225).

Still others tied Cummings's argument to concerns about Congress's representation of citizens over special interests and major donors. One participant wrote:

> I agree with Mr. Cummings. If we don't agree with a law, then it is up to us to change it. As long as something is law, it has to be obeyed and enforced, otherwise what is the point of government? The problem in today's government is special interest groups using their money and influence to push legislation through that is usually not in tune with the will of the people. This is the reason behind the unrest in this country. We are not being represented, therefore, we have no real power over our own lives. (Participant 1471)

Similarly, another participant agreed that Representative Cummings was correct and that we did not have the right to disobey the majority's decision. "However, in saying that," he wrote, "I believe that many members of congress do not represent the views of their constituents but simply that of their donors . . . many of whom do not live in their districts" (participant 767). These participants saw an opportunity to discuss not only policy outcomes, but also overarching political principles.

Some participants combined all three themes in their response and offered their opinion about each level of the policy debate—Planned Parenthood generally, the video's contents specifically, and the overarching principle of rule of law. One participant in the civil condition teetered on the brink of civility in his own response, explaining, "I have such strong feelings against Planned parenthood [sic] that I can't find words to be tell you what I think. It's wrong to kill a child and sell their parts. It may be law but it's bad law. To give my tax dollars to these vile people is wrong" (participant 488). Other participants tied the various arguments together to reach the opposite conclusion. Participant 785 wrote, "The comments by Representative Cummings are reasonable and accurate. When abortions are performed at Planned Parenthood agencies, that is within the law and, hopefully, will remain that way. I support a woman's right to choose."

In the vast majority of cases, participants who offered an opinion or commented on the tone of conversation maintained a civil tone. Only 9 percent of all of the comments were coded as uncivil (see table 5.3), and that incivility took two primary forms: name-calling and aspersions directed toward the individuals in the clips, and more general characterizations of politicians, reality television, or other groups. Many of these insults were left without any additional commentary—"That Representative is a dick" (participant 101) or "What a bitch!!!" (participant 252)—but others combined incivility with opinions about politics or policy more generally. Participant 438 wrote, "Self serving, do nothing congress. Putting their own opinions above all else and making the sika [*sic*] virus tied in with defunding planned parenthood. What a bunch of idiots that should not even be classified as human beings." Participant 3114 also used incivility to express his or her opinion about Planned Parenthood and abortion: "Planned parenthood murders babies and then sell the body parts. They are disgusting."

While incivility was less frequent in the comments than reflection on the quality or content of the conversation being held in the clip, the participation-quality hypothesis suggests that each of these elements varies systematically with individuals' conflict orientation and their exposure to incivility in the treatment clips. Before we investigate the effects of the interaction between conflict orientation and incivility, it is important to assess the treatment effects generally. Did exposure to incivility produce greater incivility in individuals' own comments, as social-learning theory would suggest? Does civility promote more engagement with the issues themselves, as measured through a willingness to offer an opinion, agreeing or disagreeing?

One-way ANOVAs demonstrate that the treatments have an effect on both the presence of incivility ($F(3, 1953) = 17.86, p = 0.001$) and the expression of an opinion in participants' comments ($F(3,1953) = 152.57, p = 0.001$).

Looking at the likelihood that comments will contain incivility, Bonferroni tests show that these differences are driven by the presence or absence of incivility in the clips shown. The uncivil *Master Chef* and Planned Parenthood clips both have a higher incidence of uncivil responses than do their civil counterparts; however, there is no difference between different types of programs using the same tone. In other words, people who watched an uncivil *Master Chef* clip were no more or less likely to use incivility than those who watched the uncivil political clip, but those in both conditions were more likely to use incivility than the participants who viewed civil *Master Chef* or CSPAN clips.

Although the type of program did not affect the expression of incivility, it did shape participants' likelihood of offering their own opinion on the issue. As figure 5.5 shows, participants were substantially more likely

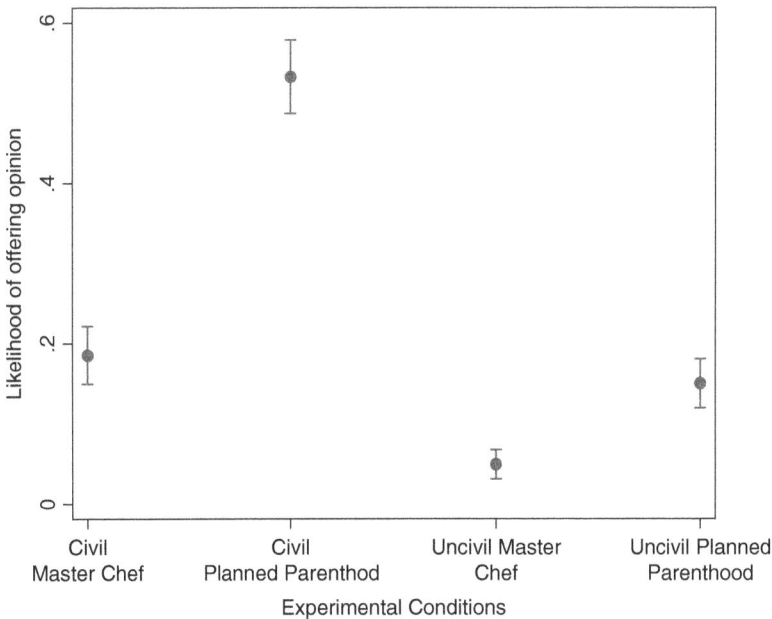

FIGURE 5.5 Incivility reduces participants' probability of stating an opinion.
Source: GfK.

to offer an opinion if they had watched the civil Planned Parenthood clip than if they had watched the uncivil clip about the same topic, and the same pattern holds for the *Master Chef* clips. As deliberative theorists would expect, civility created a space for more people to offer their own perspective on the issue. Regardless of the tone of the clip, participants were also more likely to offer opinions about politics than about food. They were about as likely to offer an opinion about Planned Parenthood in the uncivil condition as they were an opinion about the *Master Chef* competition in the civil condition.

It is clear that the presence or absence of incivility in the video clips has an impact on what people say in response. But how does conflict orientation come into play? The *participation-quality hypothesis* argues that conflict-approaching individuals who are exposed to incivility will be more likely to use incivility in their own online comments. To test this hypothesis, I estimated two models—one for the *Master Chef* treatments and one for the Planned Parenthood treatments—to explore the interaction between incivility and conflict orientation. Because logistic regression results and interactive effects are difficult to interpret from a standard table, the results are presented in graphical form. Figure 5.6 suggests that the primary driver of an individual's use of uncivil language is assignment to the uncivil treatment; conflict orientation has a statistically insignificant effect on the use of incivility in one's own comments. However, it is possible that this relationship, particularly with regard to the *Master Chef* treatments, is statistically insignificant because there are so few individuals who identify as strongly conflict-approaching. With so few individuals at the highest end of the scale, the confidence interval increases, obscuring any differences that may result from conflict orientation. The slope of the lines suggests that among those who saw the civil treatment, almost no one, regardless of conflict orientation, made an uncivil comment. Among those who were exposed to incivility, the most conflict-avoidant individuals had about a 10 percent likelihood of using uncivil language in their comments. The most conflict-approaching individuals, on the other hand, used uncivil language in approximately 20 percent of their comments. The same pattern does not appear when looking at the Planned Parenthood treatments.

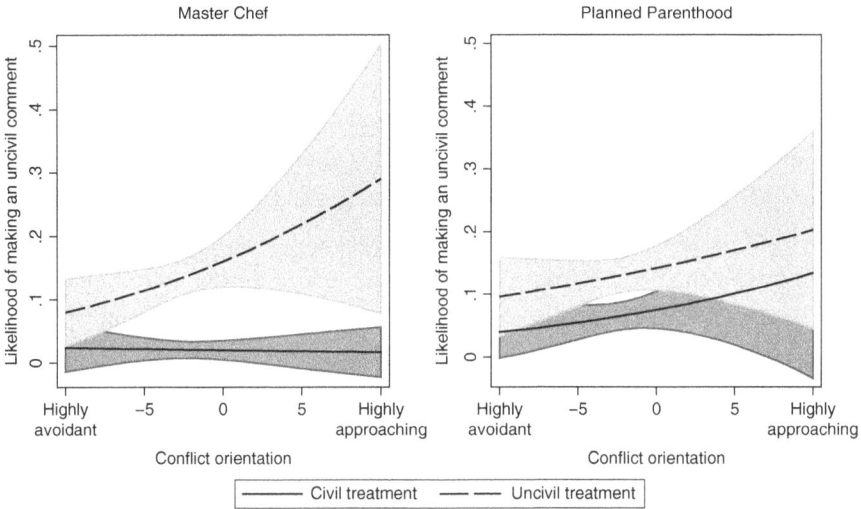

FIGURE 5.6 Presence of incivility is strongest predictor of participants' use of incivility.

Note: Figures display predicted probabilities based on two separate logistic regressions. The direct effect of the treatments is statistically significant; the interactive effect with conflict orientation is only significant for the Master Chef clips.

Source: GfK.

For participants who watched these clips, there is once again a statistically significant direct effect of the treatment: those who watched the uncivil clip use more incivility in their comments. If there is an effect of conflict orientation, it is statistically undetectable, but, based on figure 5.6, it appears to affect the civil and uncivil treatments similarly. The results do not support the hypothesis because there is no statistically significant effect of conflict orientation on participants' likelihood of using incivility, but they do suggest that further investigation of the relationship could benefit from oversampling of highly conflict-approaching individuals.

These findings provide slight support for my hypotheses: the conflict-approaching are using more incivility, particularly when exposed to incivility themselves. Incivility begets incivility; those who see it, particularly the conflict-approaching, turn around and use it in their own political commentary. This makes the conflict-approaching out to be the "bad guys"; they are engaging, but in a way that is detrimental to overall deliberative values. However, the conflict-approaching are also more likely to offer an opinion about political topics, regardless of whether they watch a civil or an uncivil video. As figure 5.7 shows, many participants felt strongly enough about Planned Parenthood and abortion-related issues to offer some type of opinion in their response to the video. In the civil condition, conflict orientation played a minimal role—the most conflict-averse and conflict-approaching all had about a 55 percent probability of articulating an opinion. In the uncivil treatment, however, the conflict-avoidant shied away from offering an opinion. The conflict-approaching, on the other hand, were just as likely to offer their opinion in the face of incivility as they were in the civil condition. While these findings highlight the importance of civil discourse for encouraging others to enter into the conversation, they also suggest that the conflict-approaching do not

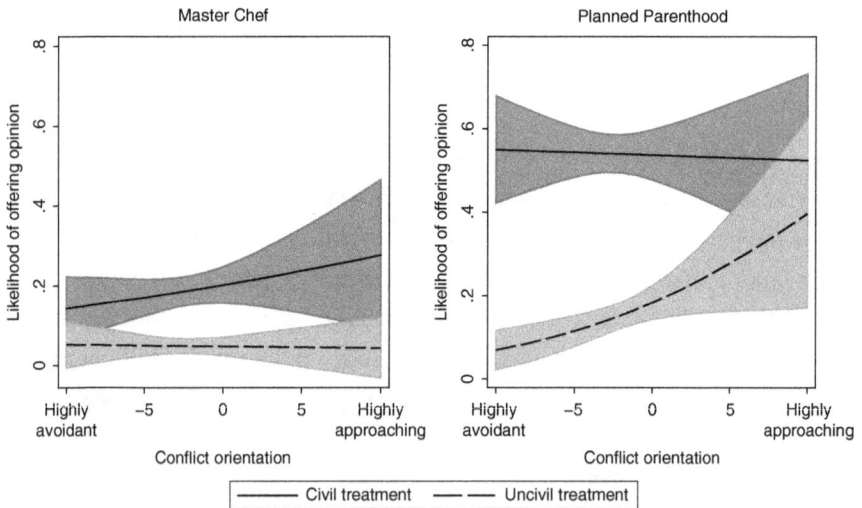

FIGURE 5.7 Conflict-approaching participants offer opinions regardless of treatment.
Source: GfK.

need civil conditions to engage; they can operate just as easily in the face of name-calling and belittling commentary.

* * *

Previous research has demonstrated that conflict orientation shapes individuals' political engagement. My research is consistent with this work. While the conflict-approaching are more likely than the conflict-avoidant to participate in high-conflict activities, such as commenting on a blog or persuading others to vote, there is no difference across conflict orientation in participation in midrange to low-conflict activities. When these findings are considered in light of variation in political interest, conflict orientation plays a greater role in the likelihood of participation for the most politically interested.

When these voices are heard, what do they say, and how do they say it? We model our political conversations on those we read, watch, or listen to, so it is no surprise that when our role models for how to talk about politics, cooking, or any other issue incorporate incivility into their conversations, we do too. The qualitative evidence from this chapter suggests that people do monitor the tone of conversations they watch on television, commenting when they find a particular exchange to be an egregious violation of norms or a surprising demonstration of civility and respect. Although the evidence does not paint a crystal-clear picture of the role of conflict orientation in shaping the quality of discourse, it at least suggests that the conflict-approaching are even more likely to use incivility when they see it on television than are their conflict-avoidant peers. At the same time, the conflict-approaching are more likely to offer their opinion on contentious issues, such as abortion or the role of Planned Parenthood, regardless of whether they watch a civil or an uncivil video clip. Their conflict-avoidant counterparts are silent in the face of incivility. Like time or public-speaking skills, a conflict-approaching orientation is a resource that helps certain citizens get involved in politics and express their ideas.

These results paint a picture of a political world in which the conflict-approaching are more likely to engage in certain types of behaviors and, once engaged, to articulate their opinions, even in ways that are not always civil. In the realm of political engagement, differences in behaviors across the conflict-orientation spectrum affect whose voices get heard and what those voices are saying. As I discuss in the next chapter, a political world in which the conflict-approaching are engaging in political discussion and communication while the conflict-avoidant stay silent could have implications for the quality of our democratic discourse and the ability to hear the other side.

6

A MORE DISRESPECTFUL DEMOCRACY?

I've been thinking a lot about civility, civic duty, and kindness, and how pervasive and powerful they are, how enduringly persuasive those qualities are in American life and how I see them all around me, day after day.

—C. J. CREGG, "THE LONG GOODBYE," *THE WEST WING* (2003)

OOK AT ANY survey about American politics today, and you will see that many Americans would disagree with fictional White House press secretary C. J. Cregg about the prevalence of civility, civic duty, and kindness in contemporary politics. After all, examples of rudeness and cruelty abound in today's political media: a recent news cycle included stories about singer Ed Sheeran leaving Twitter because of trolls' cruelty (O'Connor 2017) and the president's Twitter attack on CNN journalist Mika Brzezinski, in which he called her "crazy," "low I.Q.," and "bleeding from a face-lift" (McAfee 2017). Lest these examples lead you to believe that Twitter is the prime culprit in the rising ubiquity of incivility, just take a look at the comments on any YouTube video—the responses to Black Lives Matter rallies or campus lectures by Manhattan Institute fellow Heather Mac Donald or white nationalist Richard Spencer. Incivility is a part of contemporary American politics, and it is unlikely to disappear anytime soon.

Given this reality, effective democratic citizens could benefit from a coat of armor that protects them from the negative impact of incivility. As I have shown throughout this book, a conflict-approaching orientation is one type of armor. The inclination to approach conflict—to confront those with whom you disagree, to publically engage in arguments, and to be excited about the prospect of debate—mitigates some of our normative concerns about political incivility. When faced with incivility, people who are conflict-approaching feel more positive emotions. They are less likely to keep seeking out uncivil news. And while they are slightly more likely to use incivility in their own political conversations, they are also more likely to offer substantive opinions about the issues being discussed. In these ways, they are better able to cope with the reality of contemporary political conversation and make space for incivility to play a productive role in mass political behavior.

SUMMARY AND CONTRIBUTIONS

This book began by laying out incivility as a contested concept that can be defined in a variety of ways. Some scholars and citizens identify incivility in the content of a political message—in the stereotyping of a particular race or minority group or threats to democratic rights—while others conceive of it as a function of the tone of communication. It is this second understanding that I use throughout this book, operationalizing incivility as name-calling, finger-pointing, aggressive language, interruption, and insults. When this sort of nasty language is used in political media—whether on a talk show or on Twitter—scholars have shown it has a range of effects on political behavior. Incivility lowers trust in government, reduces perceptions of government legitimacy, and discourages open-minded deliberation (Mutz 2007, 2015; Gervais 2014). It also encourages participation and improves recall of candidates' issue positions (Brooks and Geer 2007; Kahn and Kenney 1999; Mutz 2015).

The primary argument of this book is that the effects of incivility depend on differences in how individuals react to conflict in their interpersonal conversations. Following Mondak's (2010) paradigm of heterogeneous treatment effects, the findings in this book overwhelmingly demonstrate that incivility negatively affects certain individuals more than others. The conflict-avoidant become weaker democratic citizens, associating politics with a range of negative emotions, searching for more uncivil news coverage, and engaging less in political activities. From a participatory standpoint, if the conflict-avoidant and conflict-approaching were otherwise similar—if the tendency to be one or the other were not correlated with socioeconomic or demographic traits—we might not worry about these distinctions. The conflict-approaching would hold the same preferences as the conflict-avoidant and would be able to express them to political leaders on behalf of everyone. However, this is not the case. The conflict-avoidant are also more likely to be less educated, members of minority groups, and women—groups that are traditionally underrepresented in politics (Brady, Verba, and Schlozman 1995; Schlozman, Verba, and Brady 2012). The interaction between incivility and conflict orientation has the potential to exacerbate political inequality.

Humans are naturally inclined to engage with certain stimuli and avoid others; it's how we know to run away from a king cobra but want to cuddle puppies. Many stimuli fall somewhere in between these two, and individual differences lead one person to avoid or approach a particular activity or creature more than another person would. Over the course of this book, I have demonstrated that these individual differences play out in our conflict orientation—some people are more likely to avoid conflict in their lives, while others embrace and thrive on it. While psychologists have argued that conflict orientation is a relatively entrenched component of one's personality, they have primarily focused on how it might be shaped by cultural and life-span factors. For example, as individuals age or become more educated, they may become more comfortable with and accepting of conflict (Birditt, Fingerman, and Almeida 2005; Eliasoph 1998). By examining longitudinal data on individuals' conflict orientations, even over a small increment of time, this book not only speaks to previous psychological findings but also demonstrates that changes in conflict orientation occur as small fluctuations around an initial stable point. An individual who is predisposed to be highly conflict-avoidant is not going to become highly conflict-approaching simply by growing older and becoming more educated.

Across six studies, I demonstrated that there is substantial variation in individuals' conflict orientation; even in a sample of 350 people, you can find some individuals who avoid conflict at all costs and some who take every opportunity to start an argument. This book marks one of the first analyses of conflict orientation using large-N, representative survey samples. The ability to look at the conflict orientation of a wide range of people over time offers insight not only into the interplay between conflict orientation and incivility in the political sphere, but also into the connection between conflict orientation and a broad range of psychological phenomena.

The empirical portion of the book offers evidence that conflict-approaching individuals are better able to handle the challenges presented by uncivil politics than their conflict-avoidant peers. In the third chapter, I focus on affective reactions to incivility across two different samples and three different pairs of video clips. While the specific emotional responses vary with the clips, the overarching pattern is clear: the conflict-avoidant are more likely to experience negative affect—disgust, anxiety, and anger—in the face of incivility. The conflict-approaching feel more positively, reporting greater amusement, entertainment, and enthusiasm. What is more, these reactions are not specific to politics; the patterns hold both when watching political clips about abortion or the U.S. budget deficit and when exposed to the judging process on Fox's *Master Chef*. From these results, we see the first indication that the conflict-approaching are not turned off by incivility. If anything, it draws them in and makes them more engaged than they were previously.

The divergent experiences of the conflict-avoidant and conflict-approaching are seen again in participants' media habits and decisions when searching for information. People choose to seek out political information, and they choose where and how they want to receive that information. These choices are most clearly a function of a person's interest in politics, but can also be shaped by an assessment of the likelihood that a given choice will expose one to incivility and conflict. When I categorize media platforms by their likelihood of incivility exposure, I find weak evidence that conflict orientation shapes preferences—both for how frequently individuals turn on the news and what sorts of platforms they turn to when they do. More specifically, network news and social media are preferred far more by the conflict-avoidant than the conflict-approaching. Norms of journalistic objectivity steer network news away from broadcasting uncivil political conversations, while the potential to maintain homogeneous networks on social media can act as a barrier to incivility as well.

Conflict orientation only slightly shapes overall media choice in surveys, but the experimental evidence in chapter 4 suggests that it affects the choices people make about consuming news in the wake of incivility. The conflict-approaching spend less time watching additional video clips, watch fewer uncivil clips, and watch fewer political clips than the conflict-avoidant. This may seem like a strike against the conflict-approaching; after all, we want citizens to pay attention and acquire political knowledge in order to be engaged democratic citizens. However, not all attention is normatively positive; when people are anxious, they seek out information about whatever is causing their heightened anxiety. In this case, the conflict-avoidant, who have already been shown to experience greater anxiety in the face of incivility, are seeking out political videos and uncivil videos because that content is causing them to feel anxious. The conflict-approaching, in contrast, are satisfied once they have viewed uncivil political content and are content to shift to other clips or to other activities entirely.

When we turn to the effects of incivility on the quantity and quality of political engagement, the conflict-approaching once again come out ahead. Like media platforms, political activities can be categorized based on their likelihood to expose an individual to incivility. Some of the most important activities, including voting, are low-conflict and offer minimal risk. Others, such as posting on social media, persuading others to vote, or protesting, open an individual up to uncivil political discourse, even if that discourse is not directed at them. Data from the Project Implicit study demonstrate that there is no difference between the conflict-approaching and conflict-avoidant in their likelihood of participating in low-conflict activities. When we increase the risk of exposure to conflict and incivility, however, the conflict-approaching become more likely than their conflict-avoidant counterparts to get involved.

This observational finding is buttressed by experimental evidence. The GfK study demonstrates that the conflict-approaching are more likely to share a story on social media than their conflict-avoidant counterparts, regardless of whether that story is civil or uncivil. The quality of conflict-approaching individuals' engagement with uncivil news is also more robust than that of their conflict-avoidant peers. While conflict-approaching individuals were more likely to use incivility in their comments about the uncivil congressional Planned Parenthood hearing and *Master Chef* judging, they were also more likely to offer opinions about the issues presented in each clip. While both the conflict-avoidant and conflict-approaching offered opinions about Planned Parenthood after watching the civil clip, the conflict-approaching were just as likely to offer comments when they watched the uncivil video. They were capable of discussing politics regardless of whether the elected officials on their screen were calm or shouting.

Given all of these results, the rise of incivility in political media—critical institutions that inform and motivate citizens—has transformed the nature of who gets involved by changing the resources needed to engage successfully with the style and structure of political discourse. Specifically, citizens now need to be able to regularly tolerate or even welcome incivility in the political sphere in order to participate comfortably in the broader democratic process. Citizens with a conflict-approaching orientation, who enjoy conflict, have the ability to navigate political media and certain types of political activities in a way their conflict-avoidant counterparts do not. Certain Americans are marginalized in this political environment not only on the basis of ascriptive or demographic characteristics such as race, gender, or income, but also because their psychological preferences are incongruent with the modern practice of political discourse.

These findings add to the continuing conversation about the role of civility and incivility in American politics. The tension between the characteristics of strong deliberative and participatory democracy has been well documented (e.g., Mutz 2006), and the evidence presented in this book only reinforces it. As I elaborate later in this chapter, writing this book leaves me skeptical that civil discourse is truly a panacea for America's political ills. Rising incivility raises some serious concerns for the state of our democracy, but a shift toward an extremely civil society does not necessarily solve the problems associated with incivility. I find that individuals who are turned off by incivility are not more engaged by civil presentation of policy issues or campaign information. Civility does not make the conflict-avoidant more entertained or amused, nor does it provide clear emotional benefits to the conflict-approaching. In other words, the findings detailed in this book highlight how challenging it can be to evaluate incivility's normative benefits and harms to the political system.

HOW WE STUDY INCIVILITY

The bulk of the research presented in this book relies on experiments. Experiments have been clearly identified as the gold standard in studying causal mechanisms (Druckman and Kam 2011; Spencer, Zanna, and Fong 2005), and those implemented in this book were designed specifically to maximize internal validity while maintaining a sense of ecological realism. However, there are several methodological choices I made that should be considered when designing future research on incivility and conflict orientation.

Experimentalists know to be careful about the extent to which they generalize their findings from nonrepresentative samples to the broader population. Therefore, it is important to recognize that the experiments presented in this book have some significant limitations when it comes to their applicability across different dimensions. For example, each treatment used in this book is visual; participants watched a video clip rather than reading a newspaper article or listening to an audio recording. Television, and cable television in particularly, is one of the most common venues for uncivil discourse (Berry and Sobieraj 2014), and specific attributes of the medium—the presence of visuals and, in particular, the use of close-up camera perspectives—make it more likely to convey violations of social norms for communication (Mutz 2015; Sydnor 2018). Therefore, while these treatments represent the most likely way in which participants would experience incivility in their daily lives, the relationship between televised incivility and conflict orientation might be different than the relationship between conflict orientation and incivility on social media or talk radio.

While the treatments were constant in their televised presentation, they varied in the types of issues discussed in an uncivil manner. The SSI study used clips that discussed two different economic issues, while MTurk Study 2 and GfK assessed individuals' responses to a highly salient social issue—abortion and funding of Planned Parenthood—as well as entertainment television in the form of *Master Chef*. While effect sizes vary across the different issues, the relationship between incivility, conflict orientation, and the outcomes of interest typically follows the same pattern regardless of the issue being presented. There are some caveats. For example, in chapter 3, I found that some emotional responses, such as anxiety, manifest the same way across video clips, but others change. Conflict orientation conditions feelings of anger and disgust when watching uncivil clips from *Master Chef* or about economic topics, but does not have an effect on individuals' reactions to an uncivil exchange about Planned Parenthood. Additional research may be able to tease out whether these differences are an artifact of the experiment or if the contentious nature of the issue itself matters. However, these findings increase my confidence that I have captured an enduring interaction between conflict orientation and televised incivility that occurs regardless of whether uncivil rhetoric is being used to describe more or less prominent issues.

As I acknowledged earlier, this book represents one of only a few attempts to document conflict orientation through several large-N surveys. With the exception of the Qualtrics Panels survey, each of the survey experiments presented here gives us a glimpse into individuals' feelings toward conflict at a single moment in time. However, implicit in my argument is a claim that political participation has changed as incivility has become a greater presence in political communication. Long-term panel data on conflict orientation would not only offer greater insight into my claim that this trait is in fact stable and exogenous to our political experience, but also allow scholars to track who is participating as incivility inevitably ebbs and flows over the next several decades.

THE FUTURE OF INCIVILITY RESEARCH

The six studies in this book offer a great deal of insight into the interplay between conflict orientation and incivility and its effects on political behavior. However, even after documenting the ways in which the conflict-approaching are better suited for today's confrontational and vitriolic political climate, I am left with further questions about the role of conflict orientation in and the impact of incivility on politics. These questions can motivate further research at the intersection of political psychology and political communication by those scholars interested in how individual differences shape our reactions to political incivility.

The first set of open questions focuses on conflict orientation. My findings demonstrate that when faced with incivility, the conflict-approaching are able to effectively engage in politics while the conflict-avoidant struggle with negative emotions, biased information processing, and less participation in political activities and conversation. One might expect, then, that in the absence of incivility, the conflict-avoidant would experience more positive outcomes. This does not seem to be the case; none of my results demonstrates that civility exercises a dramatic pull for the conflict-avoidant. Exposure to civility does not produce more positive emotional reactions nor less biased information search. While civility may encourage the conflict-avoidant to offer their own opinions about political events, it clearly does not draw people in as much as incivility does. So what does it take to engage the conflict-avoidant? Is there another approach to communicating about politics that could lead them to experience politics in a positive light, or are they as lost to political engagement as the least politically interested citizens? Future research could explore the extent to which different interventions produce greater participation or positive affect in the conflict-avoidant.

This book focuses exclusively on the implications of incivility for mass behavior. It argues that incivility has a place in political communication because of the positive effects it can have, whether by holding powerful individuals accountable or by encouraging citizens to become a part of the political process. It leaves open the questions of the effects of conflict orientation and incivility on political elites. Presumably, it takes a comfort with conflict to run for public office. If this is the case, the vast majority of our elected officials are likely to be at least somewhat conflict-approaching. What does this do to negotiation and compromise on an elite level? On the one hand, conflict-approaching Congress members might be better able to arrive at solutions even when faced with nastiness from the opposing party. On the other hand, we can imagine that these elected officials, more willing to use incivility in their own speech, would simply hunker down on opposing sides and produce policy gridlock. Thoughtful treatment of the effects of conflict orientation on politicians, journalists, and others could help political scientists understand how institutional constraints and personality interact to affect governance.

Similarly, while incivility might have some desirable consequences for mass behavior, it is unclear that it produces positive outcomes at the elite level. Incivility appears to rise as affective and substantive polarization increase (Jacobson 2013; Shea 2013; Shea and Sproveri 2012). Citizens, in turn, blame political incivility on the opposing party and double down on their own party, encouraging leaders to stand firm and avoid compromise (Wolf, Strachan, and Shea 2012). Incivility might encourage certain types of democratic expression and engagement, but if elites are perpetually engaged in policy gridlock and partisan sniping, that expression and that engagement are ineffective.

Beyond questions about the impact of incivility on the elite level, this book also opens additional avenues of research into the interactive effects of incivility and the communication environment. Incivility's effects may be platform dependent; incivility on Twitter may produce more anger or outrage than incivility in a comments section, for example. Beyond media effects, scholars can, of course, continue to explore how the strategy for measuring incivility or the characteristics of the speaker and receiver shape their responses to uncivil language. Gervais (2011, 2015) and Druckman et al. (2019) have cleared an initial path in this regard, focusing on differences between incivility from one's copartisan and incivility from a member of the other party. As one *Washington Post* analysis pointed out, "If Trump's petty and vindictive, he's petty and vindictive to people whom his base hates, and many of them are perfectly fine with that, at a minimum. It's not the sort of civility that people expect from Washington—but that's exactly what many of his supporters wanted. They wanted that incivility and embrace it" (Bump 2018). Partisanship affects our reactions to incivility, but what about the status of the speaker as an elected official? Her race or gender? And whether the listener shares her gender or ethnic identity? Investigating the interaction of uncivil communication and these individual-level characteristics will help researchers understand when and under what conditions incivility has positive and negative effects.

Finally, future research should explore the extent to which conflict orientation reinforces or breaks down existing political inequalities. As I showed in chapter 2, conflict orientation is tied to gender, age, race, and education. Differences in political participation can also be explained by each of these characteristics: women, younger people, minorities, and those with less education are less likely to participate in politics, particularly in resource-intensive activities such as protest or contacting one's member of Congress. If members of these groups are systematically less likely to engage in politics and are also more likely to be conflict-avoidant—a characteristic that I have shown also lowers the probability of participating—conflict orientation could be compounding already existing inequalities in the political sphere.

The studies used in this book offer few indications of this compound effect of conflict orientation and demographics. When I examined participants' likelihood of participation at the various levels of conflict orientation across demographic categories, the interaction, for the most part, was statistically insignificant.[1] However, one result in particular stands out and should be explored further. Conflict orientation interacts with race—specifically, whether an individual is African American or white—to create substantial disparities in the likelihood of attending a protest or demonstration. However, it does so by dramatically increasing the likelihood of African American participation while having minimal effect on whites. As figure 6.1 shows, extremely conflict-avoidant whites and blacks (those with CCS scores below –8) were equally likely to participate in demonstrations, around a 20 percent likelihood. But while highly conflict-approaching white participants hovered at a 25 percent probability of having participated in a protest or demonstration in the past year, the most conflict-approaching African Americans are more than three times more likely to report participation in a protest.[2] Rather than emphasize traditional divisions in participation, this result suggests that conflict orientation may facilitate a "closing of the gap," offering members of marginalized groups a resource that helps them participate in an activity that would otherwise be very difficult. It also helps explain the rise of groups like Black Lives Matter in an era rife with

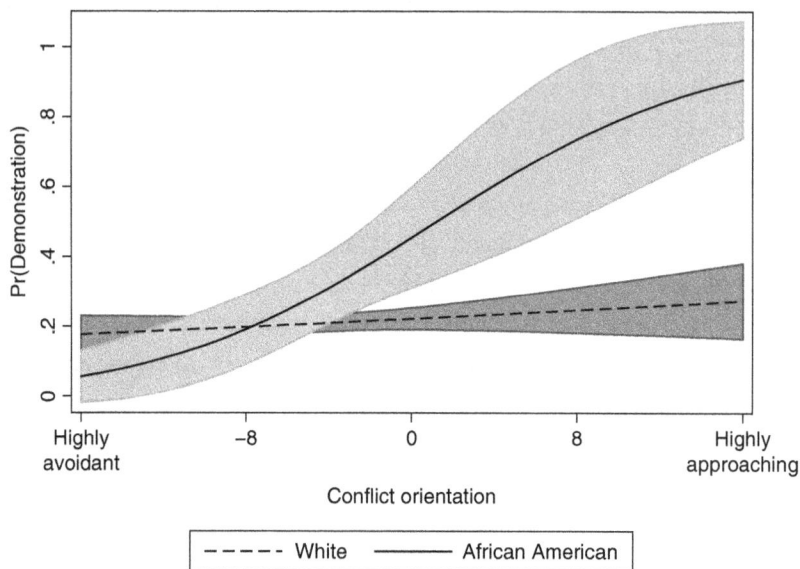

FIGURE 6.1 Conflict orientation and race shape protest behavior.

Note: Probabilities are reported from a logistic regression of conflict orientation and race on having attended a demonstration or protest in the past year. The regression controls for personality, gender, age, education, party identification, party strength and political interest.

Source: Project Implicit.

political incivility and suggests that there are other dimensions of the relationship between conflict orientation and incivility that would be valuable to explore.

(IN)CIVILITY AND DEMOCRATIC CITIZENSHIP

In June 2018, civility rose to the forefront of the national conversation after White House press secretary Sarah Huckabee Sanders was asked to leave a restaurant in Lexington, Virginia. The owner of the restaurant, Stephanie Wilkinson, said she had made the decision with the support of her staff, many of whom were gay or had immigrated to the United States and were therefore members of groups that had been targeted by recent Trump administration policies. The exchange did not violate standard conversational norms; Wilkinson noted that she was polite in her request that Sanders leave and that Sanders and her family were polite as they left the restaurant (Selk and Murray 2018).

The reaction from the online community was less genteel. While many people supported Wilkinson's decision, others, including the president, were swift to respond with vitriol. "The Red Hen Restaurant should focus more on cleaning its filthy canopies, doors and windows (badly needs a paint job) rather than refusing to serve a fine person like Sarah Huckabee Sanders," the president tweeted. "I always had a rule, if a restaurant is dirty on the outside, it is dirty on the inside!" Throughout this book, I have made the argument that incivility can be a good thing. For a set of Americans, it encourages positive emotions and greater participation. But to what extent does incivility have desirable consequences in the mass public and at the elite level? The incident at the Red Hen and its aftermath suggest that incivility provides several important democratic benefits while also raising concerns about our ability to communicate across identities and experiences.

For those who were upset with Wilkinson's decision, the act of asking Sanders to leave the restaurant was in itself uncivil. Never mind that all parties behaved decorously, the demand was seen as the first step down a road where dining establishments are segregated by party, where Americans are "divided by red plates & blue plates" (Axelrod 2018). I could spend pages discussing the arguments for whether asking Sanders to leave should or should not be considered uncivil, and how the labeling of the action as uncivil has its own set of consequences for our interpretations of the event and subsequent attitudes about it. But these comments raised an additional question about the role of incivility in a democracy: Are there moments when uncivil behavior and language are part and parcel of good democratic citizenship?

In the days following Sanders and Wilkinson's altercation, the *Washington Post* released an editorial decrying the lack of civility in the Trump era. The editorial team warned against incivility as a slippery slope to political violence, writing, "Those who are insisting that we are in a special moment justifying incivility should think for a moment how many Americans might find their own special moment. How hard is it to imagine, for example, people who strongly believe that abortion is murder deciding that judges or other officials who protect abortion rights should not be able to live peaceably with their families?" (Editorial Board 2018). Scholars who study the effects of uncivil or violent rhetoric find that violent rhetoric can affect individuals psychologically in much the same way that violent actions do (Barrett 2017; Teicher et al. 2010) and that violent rhetoric can lead to greater support for violent action (Kalmoe 2014). We should not lose sight of the fact that incivility, especially violent and hateful speech, can have harmful effects on individuals and communities.

But incivility can also be a necessary means by which we hold elected officials and powerful groups accountable. Sanders's supporters saw the request for her to leave the Red Hen as an uncivil act, a violation of social norms for dining establishments. Others, like *Vox* reporter Zack Beauchamp, saw Wilkinson's decision as a democratic moment in which a citizen "acted to punish a political official for a specific set of severe wrongs, not to harm an average customer whose political views she happened to disagree with" (Beauchamp 2018). Democratic republican government is premised on the idea that elected officials are responsible to citizens and that it is the citizens' job to punish those officials who fail to meet their standards. Language and behavior that break social norms are sometimes a necessary part of that punishment. It can also be a way for citizens to draw attention to examples of government's failure to support its citizens. In other words, uncivil rhetoric might serve as a slippery slope to greater violence, but it is also a vital tool in the citizen's democratic arsenal.

This debate over the role of incivility in democratic life makes the findings from this book more important than ever. Incivility is an important and intractable part of politics. A world of perpetually civil agreement seems anathema to pluralist society. A promising step, then, seems to be to think about how we can be good democratic citizens in spite of incivility. The conflict-approaching, while not paragons of democratic citizenship, nonetheless are capable of engaging in politics even when it gets nasty.

We cannot change everyone's conflict orientation, of course, but we might think about ways in which the conflict-avoidant could be encouraged to overcome their aversion. Perhaps this is simply a matter of framing engagement as a moral imperative. In an interview with the *Washington Post*, Wilkinson noted that she is "not a huge fan of confrontation . . . [but] this feels like the moment in our democracy when people have to make uncomfortable actions and decisions to uphold their morals" (Selk and Murray 2018). While her natural preference would have been to avoid conflict, she felt she had to overcome her anxiety because of a higher moral commitment.

Alternatively, encouraging citizens to behave as if they are conflict-approaching might be more about teaching relevant skills than trying to tap into the moral frames that propel them to act. Here, engaging in politics in the face of incivility is analogous to public speaking. Many people experience extreme anxiety when asked to give a public speech or to stand up in front of a room full of people. They are naturally averse to the experience, which leads to negative emotional responses and a desire to avoid having to participate in any activities that might require them to speak in front of an audience. However, through the education system, certain types of employment, church groups, and other organizations, many people are given tools for overcoming their public-speaking anxiety. Whether they consistently "imagine the audience in their underwear," practice a presentation for hours before delivering it, or simply stand up in front of people so frequently it becomes second nature, people learn how to deal with this experience that they would otherwise avoid. The same strategy—identifying ways of overcoming one's aversion to conflict—could help citizens persevere in the uncivil political landscape and even engage in uncivil behavior when necessary.

Incivility—name-calling, insults, obscenities, finger-pointing—should not be the default in politics. As Hua Hsu wrote in a 2014 piece for the *New Yorker*, "There should be nothing controversial about everyday kindness; civility as a kind of individual moral compass should remain a virtue" (Hsu 2014). Like C. J. in the comment that opened this chapter, Hsu argues that our personal baseline should be to treat each other with mutual respect, to seek to understand others' viewpoints, and to give people the benefit of the doubt. But Hsu takes the argument a step further: "But civility as a type of discourse—as a high road that nobody ever actually walks— is the opposite. It is bullshit" (Hsu 2014). America might have an "incivility problem," but interventions that focus only on civility as the high road miss the mark. Civility alone cannot solve our political problems. Instead, it is a starting place. When name-calling and vitriol are used to promote democratic discussion and broaden the political conversation, we must follow in the footsteps of the conflict-approaching, finding entertainment and motivation in incivility.

APPENDIX A

Additional Study Information

T O TEST THE claim that incivility interacts with conflict orientation to influence affective and behavioral reactions, I fielded a series of six surveys and survey experiments between March 2012 and August 2016, using five different online recruitment services: Qualtrics Panels, Survey Sampling International, GfK, Project Implicit (PI), and Amazon's Mechanical Turk. Mechanical Turk (MTurk) and PI both provide non-representative convenience samples of individuals who have registered to take studies or complete tasks, while Survey Sampling International and Qualtrics Panels use a quota system to achieve a more balanced but non-probability-based sample of individuals registered through their site. GfK uses probabilistic national sampling to recruit participants to its online surveys; if a selected individual does not have access to the Internet, the company works to make it available to them. Table A.1 displays a general summary of the sample size, procedure, and relevant empirical chapters for each of the six studies. This appendix includes relevant information from each study used in the book. In some cases, the study included additional experimental measures or survey questions that are not included here because they were not relevant to the analyses conducted as part of this project.

TABLE A.1 SUMMARY OF ALL STUDIES

#	SAMPLE SOURCE	N	DATE COLLECTED	DESCRIPTION	DV	RELEVANT CHAPTER
1	Qualtrics Panels (nationally representative)	500	July–August 2016	In this two-wave panel study, participants completed a fifteen-question version of the Conflict Communication Scale in July in conjunction with research not included in this book. Three weeks later, they were asked to fill out the CCS again, as well as a battery of psychological scales measuring conflict-resolution strategies and alternative measures of conflict orientation.	Conflict orientation	2
2	Survey Sampling International (nationally representative)	600	April 2014	As part of a larger omnibus survey, participants filled out one subsection of the CCS, viewed either a civil or an uncivil clip, and then answered questions about their emotional reactions to those clips and their recall of the issues discussed in the clips.	Emotional response	3
3	GfK (nationally representative)	3,000	July 2016	Participants completed the CCS, then were randomly assigned to watch either the Planned Parenthood hearings or a clip from the reality show *Master Chef.* After the video, they responded to questions about their emotional reactions and their willingness to share or respond to the video, and offered their own comments on what they watched.	Emotional response, political participation	3, 5

#	Project	N	Date	Description	Topics	
4	Project Implicit (online convenience)	1,800	March 2012	Respondents completed a Brief IAT (BIAT), then filled out the CCS and answered questions about the frequency of their media consumption and about political participation habits.	Media habits, political participation	4, 5
5	Mechanical Turk 1 (online convenience)	625	December 2012	Citizens filled out the CCS, reported their political participation and their media consumption. This study asked participants to rank their favorite programs in order of preference. As a distractor, they were given basic arithmetic problems to solve, then asked to read a *New York Times* story about a mentally ill criminal and a randomized treatment text. After the treatment, they responded to questions about it and filled out basic social and demographic information.	Media habits, political participation	4, 5
6	Mechanical Turk 2 (online convenience)	350	May 2016	Respondents filled out the CCS, were randomly assigned to see a civil or an uncivil political clip from CSPAN about hearings on Planned Parenthood, and were then asked if they wanted to learn more about any of five headlines that varied in topic (news vs. entertainment) and civility (civil vs. uncivil).	Media habits	4

The primary data for the empirical chapters in this book come from experiments in which the incivility of the media environment is manipulated. While details of each experiment are explained more fully in the relevant chapters, many of them had participants randomly assigned to view either a civil or an uncivil version of a news clip, series of online comments, or newspaper article. When possible, findings were replicated using different media clips and platforms. Additionally, throughout the book, I present the findings of these experiments graphically so as to best convey the relationships being discussed. The underlying statistical models and results can be found in Appendix B.

QUALTRICS PANELS, JULY–AUGUST 2016

The Qualtrics Panels survey was conducted in two waves in order to assess change in conflict orientation over a short period of time. Individuals who participated in the first wave were invited to participate in the second to facilitate within-subject assessment between wave 1, which was in the field in July 2016, and wave 2, which collected data three weeks later. Wave 1 also included an experimental manipulation that is not a part of the research.

WAVE 1: JULY 2016

Age. Please enter your current age.
Gender. Are you male or female?

☐ Male
☐ Female

Education. What is the highest level of school you have completed?

☐ No high school diploma
☐ High school graduate—high school diploma or equivalent (GED)

☐ Some college, no degree
☐ Associate degree
☐ Bachelor's degree
☐ Master's degree
☐ Professional degree

Race. Please check one or more categories to indicate what race(s) you consider yourself to be.

☐ White
☐ Black or African American
☐ American Indian or Alaska Native
☐ Asian
☐ Native Hawaiian or Pacific Islander
☐ Other

Ethnicity. This question is about Hispanic ethnicity. Are you of Spanish, Hispanic, or Latino descent? Please select only one of the following:

☐ No, I am not.
☐ Yes, Mexican, Mexican-American or Chicano
☐ Yes, Puerto Rican.
☐ Yes, Cuban.
☐ Yes, Central American.
☐ Yes, South American.
☐ Yes, Caribbean.
☐ Yes, other Spanish/Hispanic/Latino.

Conflict Communication Scale. Please indicate your level of agreement with the following statements [strongly disagree, disagree, neither agree nor disagree, agree, strongly agree]

☐ I enjoy challenging the opinions of others.
☐ I find conflicts exciting.

☐ I hate arguments.

☐ I feel upset after an argument.

☐ Arguments don't bother me.

☐ I feel more comfortable having an argument in person than over the phone.

☐ I dislike when others make eye contact with me during an argument.

☐ If I were upset with a friend, I would discuss it with someone else rather than the friend who upset me.

☐ When I have a conflict with someone, I try to resolve it by being extra nice to him or her.

☐ I always prefer to solve disputes through face-to-face discussion.

☐ After a dispute with a neighbor, I would feel uncomfortable seeing him or her again, even if the conflict had been resolved.

☐ I feel uncomfortable seeing others argue in public.

☐ I don't mind strangers arguing in my presence.

☐ It doesn't bother me to be in a situation where others are arguing.

☐ Getting emotional only makes conflicts worse.

☐ Everything should be out in the open in an argument, including emotions.

☐ It makes me uncomfortable watching other people express their emotions in front of me.

☐ I feel like running away when other people start showing their emotions in an argument.

☐ It shows strength to express emotions openly.

☐ Showing you feelings in a dispute is a sign of weakness.

Political interest. Some people seem to follow politics most of the time, while others aren't that interested. Would you say you follow what's going on in politics most of the time, some of the time, only now and then, or hardly at all? Please choose only one of the following.

☐ Most of the time

☐ Some of the time

☐ Only now and then

☐ Hardly at all

Party identification. Generally speaking, do you usually think of yourself as a Republican, a Democrat, an Independent, or what?

☐ Republican
☐ Democrat
☐ Independent
☐ Other

Party strength. [If Republican or Democrat selected] Would you consider yourself a strong Democrat/Republican or not very strong Democrat/Republican?

☐ Strong
☐ Not very strong

Party lean. [If Independent or other selected] Do you think of yourself as closer to the Republican or Democratic Party?

☐ Republican Party
☐ Democratic Party
☐ Neither party

Ideology. Here is a seven-point scale on which the political views that people might hold are arranged from extremely liberal to extremely conservative. Where would you put yourself on this scale?

☐ Extremely liberal
☐ Liberal
☐ Slightly liberal
☐ Moderate; middle of the road
☐ Slightly conservative
☐ Conservative
☐ Extremely conservative

Income. Which of the income groups listed below includes the total 2015 income before taxes of all members of your family living in your home? Please include salaries, wages, pensions, dividends, interest, and all other income.

☐ Under $15,000
☐ $15,000–$30,000
☐ $30,000–$45,000
☐ $45,000–$60,000
☐ $60,000–$75,000
☐ $75,000–$90,000
☐ Above $90,000

WAVE 2: AUGUST 2016

Conflict Communication Scale. Please indicate your level of agreement with the following statements [strongly disagree, disagree, neither agree nor disagree, agree, strongly agree]

☐ I enjoy challenging the opinions of others.
☐ I find conflicts exciting.
☐ I hate arguments.
☐ I feel upset after an argument.
☐ Arguments don't bother me.
☐ I feel more comfortable having an argument in person than over the phone.
☐ I dislike when others make eye contact with me during an argument.
☐ If I were upset with a friend, I would discuss it with someone else rather than the friend who upset me.
☐ When I have a conflict with someone, I try to resolve it by being extra nice to him or her.
☐ I always prefer to solve disputes through face-to-face discussion.
☐ After a dispute with a neighbor, I would feel uncomfortable seeing him or her again, even if the conflict had been resolved.

☐ I feel uncomfortable seeing others argue in public.

☐ I don't mind strangers arguing in my presence.

☐ It doesn't bother me to be in a situation where others are arguing.

☐ Getting emotional only makes conflicts worse.

☐ Everything should be out in the open in an argument, including emotions.

☐ It makes me uncomfortable watching other people express their emotions in front of me.

☐ I feel like running away when other people start showing their emotions in an argument.

☐ It shows strength to express emotions openly.

☐ Showing you feelings in a dispute is a sign of weakness.

Ten Item Personality Inventory. Here are a number of personality traits that may or may not apply to you. Please select the extent to which you agree or disagree with each statement. You should rate the extent to which the pair of traits applies to you, even if one characteristic applies more strongly than others. [strongly disagree, disagree, somewhat disagree, neither agree nor disagree, somewhat agree, agree, strongly agree]

☐ Extraverted, enthusiastic

☐ Critical, quarrelsome

☐ Dependable, self-disciplined

☐ Anxious, easily upset

☐ Open to new experiences, complex

☐ Reserved, quiet

☐ Sympathetic, warm

☐ Disorganized, careless

☐ Calm, emotionally stable

☐ Conventional, uncreative

Blake and Mouton's Managerial Grid. Below is a list of statements about leadership behavior. Read each one carefully, then, using the following scale, decide the extent to which it actually applies to you. For best results, answer as truthfully as possible. [Never, sometimes, about half the time, most of the time, always]

- ☐ I encourage my team to participate when it comes to decision-making time, and I try to implement their ideas and suggestions.
- ☐ I enjoy reading articles, books, and trade journals about my profession, and then implementing the new procedures I have learned.
- ☐ Nothing is more important than accomplishing a goal or task.
- ☐ I closely monitor the schedule to ensure a task or project will be completed in time.
- ☐ I enjoy coaching people on new tasks and procedures.
- ☐ The more challenging a task is, the more I enjoy it.
- ☐ I encourage my employees to be creative about their job.
- ☐ When seeing a complex task through to completion, I ensure that every detail is accounted for.
- ☐ I find it easy to carry out several complicated tasks at the same time.
- ☐ I enjoy reading articles, books, and journals about training, leadership and psychology, then putting what I have read into action.
- ☐ When correcting mistakes, I do not worry about jeopardizing relationships.
- ☐ I manage my time very efficiently.
- ☐ I enjoy explaining the intricacies and details of a complex task or project to my employees.
- ☐ Breaking large projects into small manageable tasks is second nature to me.
- ☐ Nothing is more important than building a great team.
- ☐ I enjoy analyzing problems.
- ☐ I honor other people's boundaries.
- ☐ Counseling my employees to improve their performance or behavior is second nature to me.

Thomas Kilmann instrument (conflict resolution). Consider situations in which you find your wishes differing from those of another person. How do you usually respond in such situations? The following screens contain 30 pairs of statements describing possible behavioral responses. For each pair, please select the statement that best characterizes your behavior. In many cases, neither statement may be very typical of your behavior; but please select the response you would be more likely to use.

- ☐ There are times when I let others take responsibility for solving the problem.
  Rather than negotiate the things on which we disagree, I try to stress those things on which we both agree.
- ☐ I try to find a compromise solution.
  I attempt to deal with all of his/her and my concerns.
- ☐ I am usually firm in pursuing my goals.
  I might try to soothe the other's feelings and preserve our relationship.
- ☐ I try to find a compromise solution.
  I sometimes sacrifice my own wishes for the wishes of the other person.
- ☐ I consistently seek the other's help in working out a solution.
  I try to do what is necessary to avoid useless tensions.
- ☐ I try to avoid creating unpleasantness for myself.
  I try to win my position.
- ☐ I try to postpone the issue until I have had some time to think it over.
  I give up some points in exchange for others.
- ☐ I am usually firm in pursuing my goals.
  I attempt to get all concerns and issues immediately out in the open.
- ☐ I feel that differences are not always worth worrying about.
  I make some effort to get my way.
- ☐ I am firm in pursuing my goals.
  I try to find a compromise solution.
- ☐ I attempt to get all concerns and issues immediately out in the open.
  I might try to soothe the other's feelings and preserve our relationship.
- ☐ I sometimes avoid taking positions that would create controversy.
  I will let the other person have some of his/her positions if he/she lets me have some of mine.
- ☐ I propose a middle ground.
  I press to get my points made.
- ☐ I tell the other person my ideas and ask for his/hers.
  I try to show the other person the logic and benefits of my position.

☐ I might try to soothe the other's feelings and preserve our relationship.
I try to do what is necessary to avoid tensions.

☐ I try not to hurt the other's feelings.
I try to convince the other person of the merits of my position.

☐ I am usually firm in pursuing my goals.
I try to do what is necessary to avoid useless tensions.

☐ If it makes other people happy, I might let them maintain their views.
I will let other people have some of their positions if they let me have some of mine.

☐ I attempt to get all concerns and issues immediately out in the open.
I try to postpone the issue until I have had some time to think it over.

☐ I attempt to immediately work through our differences.
I try to find a fair combination of gains and losses for both of us.

☐ In approaching negotiations, I try to be considerate of the other person's wishes.
I always lean toward a direct discussion of the problem.

☐ I try to find a position that is intermediate between his/hers and mine.
I assert my wishes.

☐ I am very often concerned with satisfying all our wishes.
There are times when I let others take responsibility for solving the problem.

☐ If the other's position seems very important to him/her, I would try to meet his/her wishes.
I try to get the other person to settle for a compromise.

☐ I try to show the other person the logic and benefits of my position.
In approaching negotiations, I try to be considerate of the other person's wishes.

☐ I propose a middle ground.
I feel that differences are not always worth worrying about.

☐ I sometimes avoid taking positions that would create controversy.
If it makes other people happy, I might let them maintain their views.

☐ I am usually firm in pursuing my goals.
I usually seek the other's help in working out a solution.

☐ I propose a middle ground.
  I feel that differences are not always worth worrying about.
☐ I try not to hurt the other's feelings.
  I always share the problem with the other person so that we can work it out.

Testa et al. conflict orientation. People choose to talk or not talk about politics for a variety of reasons. Please tell us which of the following statements apply to you (True/False):
  I am sometimes reluctant to talk about politics:

☐ (N1) Because I don't like arguments;
☐ (N2) Because it creates enemies;
☐ (N3) Because I worry about what people would think of me.

  When I talk about politics I do so:

☐ (P1) Because it is enjoyable or entertaining;
☐ (P2) Because I like to debate and argue about politics;
☐ (P3) Because I want to share my views and convince others.

Ulbig and Funk conflict orientation. Some people try to avoid getting into political discussions because they think that people can get into arguments and it can get unpleasant. Other people enjoy discussing politics even though it sometimes leads to arguments. What is your feeling on this—do you usually try to avoid political discussions, do you enjoy them, or are you somewhere in between?

☐ Try to avoid political discussions
☐ Enjoy political discussions.
☐ Somewhere in between.

SURVEY SAMPLING INTERNATIONAL

Gender. What best describes your gender?

- ☐ Male
- ☐ Female

Race & Ethnicity. What best describes your ethnicity?

- ☐ Caucasian
- ☐ Hispanic
- ☐ African American
- ☐ Asian
- ☐ Other
- ☐ Native American
- ☐ Pacific Islander

Age. What is your age?

- ☐ 18–24 years old
- ☐ 25–34 years old
- ☐ 35–44 years old
- ☐ 45–54 years old
- ☐ 55–64 years old
- ☐ 65–74 years old
- ☐ 75+ years old

Education. What best describes your educational background?

- ☐ Some high school
- ☐ Completed high school
- ☐ Completed some college
- ☐ College degree

☐ Master's degree
☐ Doctoral degree

Conflict Communication Scale. Please indicate your level of agreement with the following statements. [Strongly agree, agree, neutral, disagree, strongly disagree]

☐ I enjoy challenging the opinions of others.
☐ I find conflicts exciting.
☐ I hate arguments.
☐ Arguments don't bother me.
☐ I feel upset after an argument.

Please watch the news clip below and answer the questions on the following screens.
[see treatments at end of the questionnaire]

Manipulation check. To what extent was the clip you just watched . . . [not at all, slightly, moderately, very, extremely]

☐ Informative?
☐ Entertaining?
☐ Civil?
☐ Impolite?
☐ Expressive of multiple viewpoints?

Emotions. To what extent did the clip you just watched make you feel any of the following? [not at all, slightly, moderately, very, extremely]

☐ Angry
☐ Disgusted
☐ Anxious
☐ Interested
☐ Amused

Ideology. Here is a 7-point scale on which the political views that people might hold are arranged from extremely liberal to extremely conservative. Where would you put yourself on this scale?

☐ Extremely liberal
☐ Liberal
☐ Slightly liberal
☐ Moderate: middle of the road
☐ Slightly conservative
☐ Conservative
☐ Extremely conservative

Party identification. Generally speaking, do you usually think of yourself as a Republican, a Democrat, an Independent, or what?

☐ Republican
☐ Democrat
☐ Independent
☐ Other

Party strength. [If Democrat/Republican] Would you consider yourself a strong Republican/Democrat or a not very strong Republican/Democrat?

☐ Strong Republican/Democrat
☐ Not very strong Republican/Democrat

Party lean. [If independent/other] Do you think of yourself as closer to the Republican or Democratic Party?

☐ Republican Party
☐ Democratic Party
☐ Neither party

Income. Please provide an approximation of your annual income.

TRANSCRIPTS OF SSI TREATMENTS

Morning Joe (MSNBC): Uncivil

MIKA BRZEZINSKI: Here with us now, Republican Representative from Virginia and House Minority Whip, Congressman Eric Cantor.

LAWRENCE O'DONNELL: What I want to know Congressman Cantor . . .

JOE SCARBOROUGH: It's unconstitutional!

O'DONNELL: If you're opposed to these bonuses, have you finally found the tax increase that you like specifically targeted to these bonuses? If not, how would you get the money?

CANTOR: Listen, I am for whatever we can do right now to get that money back.

O'DONNELL: Congressman, you said that your idea . . .

CROSSTALK

. . . for getting that money back is to ask Tim Geithner how to do it.

CANTOR: He's the Secretary of the Treasury, he's the one that put the taxpayer dollars out there that allows the bonuses to go forward.

O'DONNELL: And you have confidence in his ability to get it back, that's what you've just said.

CANTOR: Well, well, listen, if he is the president's secretary, he ought to be responsible for his actions.

Morning Joe (MSNBC): Civil

MIKA BRZEZINSKI: Here with us now, Republican representative from Virginia and House Minority Whip, Congressman Eric Cantor.

MSNBC REPORTER: Congressman, the president yesterday said that he has full confidence in Secretary Geithner, do you?

CANTOR: Listen, I don't think you're going to find anybody on Capitol Hill that doesn't have some real concerns about what's going on at the treasury department. And I think Secretary Geithner owes his country an explanation as to first of all how he approved the second transfer of the TARP money without catching these bonuses.

The Dylan Ratigan Show (MSNBC): Uncivil

DYLAN RATIGAN: Can a leader address these issues, considering how dependent they are for funding for political campaigns from those who benefit from those tax loopholes that he would have . . . he or she would have to close?

KAREN FINNEY: Wait a second! Wait a second! It is Congress that holds the power of the purse—and I'm going to get back to Dylan's question—this president was willing to put on the table a big deal, and who couldn't get the votes? John Boehner.

RATIGAN: Ok. Ok, ok, what are you talking about, four trillion dollars?

FINNEY: Four trillion dollars. I'm saying . . .

RATIGAN: We owe 70 trillion dollars . . .

FINNEY: I understand that but . . .

RATIGAN: He goes to walk out a 4 trillion dollar solution that is basically just a way for the Democrats to avoid dealing with this until 2017!

The Dylan Ratigan Show (MSNBC): Civil

RATIGAN: Makes me wonder if there's any way out of this that doesn't acknowledge the root problems that are at the root of trade, taxes and banking that are removing trillions from our nation. Can a leader address these issues, considering how dependent they are for funding for political campaigns from those who benefit from those tax loopholes that he would have, he or she would have to close?

SUSAN DEL PERCIO (MSBC CONTRIBUTOR): Well right now you can't expect . . . it's not going to come from Congress. It's not going to come from an individual Congress . . . member of the House of Representatives or a U.S. Senator. Nor does anyone really expect it to. Who does it fall on? It falls on the executive, it falls on the president.

GFK

Conflict Orientation. Please indicate your level of agreement with the following statements. [Strongly agree, agree, neutral, disagree, strongly disagree]

☐ I enjoy challenging the opinions of others.
☐ I find conflicts exciting.
☐ I hate arguments.
☐ I feel upset after an argument.

Treatments. Each group watched one of four video clips. A free-text box was included underneath the video where participants could offer comments/questions/feedback per the instructions below. The text box was labeled "Add your comment:"

Instructions. Please watch the video below. After watching the clip, you are invited to ask questions or offer your own comments in the box below if you would like to do so.

[Prompt if no comment] We noticed you chose not to leave a comment on the video clip. Why did you decide not to leave a comment?

Share Story. The news organization also allows you to share the content you just watched with your social network on Facebook, Twitter, or other social networking sites. Would you be interested in sharing this story? [Yes/no]

[If yes] Please write below any commentary you would include in your shared post.
[If no] Why wouldn't you share the story?

Emotions. To what extent did the clip you just watched make you feel any of the following? [not at all, slightly, moderately, very, extremely]

☐ Angry
☐ Disgusted
☐ Anxious
☐ Amused
☐ Entertained
☐ Enthusiastic

Manipulation Check. To what extent was the clip you just watched . . . [not at all, slightly, moderately, very, extremely]

☐ Informative?
☐ Civil?
☐ Biased?

PROJECT IMPLICIT

Conflict Communication Scale:

(Strongly Agree, Agree, Neutral, Disagree, or Strongly Disagree)

Approach/Avoidance Scale

1. I enjoy challenging the opinions of others.
2. I find conflicts exciting.
3. I hate arguments.
4. Arguments don't bother me.
5. I feel upset after an argument.

Public/Private Behavior

1. I avoid arguing in public.
2. I feel uncomfortable seeing others argue in public.
3. It wouldn't bother me to have an argument in a restaurant.

Media Consumption. During a typical week, how many days do you watch, read, or listen to . . . [0–7 days]

☐ News on the Internet, not including sports?
☐ News on the radio, not including sports?
☐ News on network TV, not including sports?
☐ News in a printed newspaper, not including sports?
☐ News on cable TV, not including sports?

Political Participation. During the past year did you . . . (select all that apply)

☐ Attend local political meetings (such as school board or city council)
☐ Go to a political speech, march, rally, or demonstration
☐ Try to persuade someone to vote
☐ Put up a political sign (such as a lawn sign or bumper sticker)
☐ Work for a candidate or campaign
☐ Wear a campaign button or sticker
☐ Phone, email, write to, or visit a government official to express your views on a public issue
☐ Comment on political blogs or online forums (not surveys)
☐ Donate money to a candidate, campaign, or political organization

Vote. Did you vote in the last political election?

☐ Yes
☐ No

Ten Item Personality Inventory[1]. Here are a number of personality traits that may or may not apply to you. For each statement, indicate the extent to which you agree or disagree with that statement. You should rate the extent to which the pair of traits applies to you, even if one characteristic applies more strongly than the other. (Disagree strongly, disagree moderately, disagree a little, neither agree nor disagree, agree a little, agree moderately, agree strongly)

I see myself as:

1. Extraverted, enthusiastic
2. Critical, quarrelsome
3. Dependable, self-disciplined
4. Anxious, easily upset
5. Open to new experiences, complex
6. Reserved, quiet

7. Sympathetic, warm
8. Disorganized, careless
9. Calm, emotionally stable
10. Conventional, uncreative

Party identification. Generally speaking, do you usually think of yourself as a Republican, a Democrat, an Independent, or what? (Democrat/Republican /Independent/Other/No preference)

Party strength. [If answered Democrat or Republican] Would you call yourself a strong Republican/Democrat or a not very strong Republican/ Democrat?

Party lean. [If answered Independent, Other, or No preference] Do you think of yourself as closer to the Republican or Democratic Party? (Democrat/Republican)

Political interest. Some people don't pay much attention to politics. How about you? Would you say that you are:

☐ Not at all interested in politics
☐ Not very interested in politics
☐ Somewhat interested in politics
☐ Very interested in politics
☐ Extremely interested in politics

The following demographics are collected from all participants who visit the Project Implicit site:

Gender

☐ Male
☐ Female

Birth date (Month, Date, Year)
Education

- ☐ elementary school
- ☐ junior high
- ☐ some high school
- ☐ high school graduate
- ☐ some college
- ☐ associate's degree
- ☐ bachelor's degree
- ☐ some graduate school
- ☐ master's degree
- ☐ JD
- ☐ MD
- ☐ PhD
- ☐ other advanced degree
- ☐ MBA

Political ideology

- ☐ Strongly conservative
- ☐ Moderately conservative
- ☐ Slightly conservative
- ☐ Neutral/Moderate
- ☐ Slightly liberal
- ☐ Moderately liberal
- ☐ Strongly liberal

Religiosity

- ☐ Very religious
- ☐ Moderately religious
- ☐ Somewhat religious
- ☐ Not at all religious

Race

- ☐ American Indian/Alaska Native
- ☐ East Asian
- ☐ South Asian
- ☐ Native Hawaiian or other Pacific Islander
- ☐ Black or African American
- ☐ White
- ☐ More than one race—Black/White
- ☐ More than one race—Other
- ☐ Other or Unknown

Ethnicity

- ☐ Hispanic or Latino
- ☐ Not Hispanic or Latino
- ☐ Unknown

MECHANICAL TURK STUDY 1

Conflict Communication Scale.
(Strongly Agree, Agree, Neutral, Disagree, or Strongly Disagree)

Approach/Avoidance Scale

1. I enjoy challenging the opinions of others.
2. I find conflicts exciting.
3. I hate arguments.
4. Arguments don't bother me.
5. I feel upset after an argument.

Public/Private Behavior

1. I avoid arguing in public.
2. I feel uncomfortable seeing others argue in public.

3. It wouldn't bother me to have an argument in a restaurant.
4. I don't want anyone besides those involved to know about an argument I've had.
5. I would be embarrassed if neighbors heard me argue with a family member.

Confrontation

1. I feel more comfortable having an argument in person than over the phone
2. I prefer to express points of disagreement with others by speaking with them directly rather than by writing them notes.
3. When I have a conflict with someone I try to resolve it by being extra nice to him or her.
4. After a dispute with a neighbor, I would feel uncomfortable seeing him or her again, even if the conflict had been resolved.
5. I prefer to solve disputes through face-to-face discussion.

Ulbig and Funk's Conflict Avoidance. Some people try to avoid getting into political discussions because they think that people can get into arguments and it can get unpleasant. Other people enjoy discussing politics even though it sometimes leads to arguments. What is your feeling on this—do you usually try to avoid political discussions, do you enjoy them, or are you somewhere in between?

(Avoid discussions, Enjoy discussions, In between)

Political Behavior and Participation. During the past year did you . . . (check all that apply)

- ☐ Attend local political meetings (such as school board or city council)
- ☐ Go to a political speech, march, rally, or demonstration
- ☐ Try to persuade someone to vote
- ☐ Put up a political sign (such as a lawn sign or bumper sticker)
- ☐ Work for a candidate or campaign

☐ Wear a campaign button or sticker
☐ Phone, email, write to, or visit a government official to express your views on a public issue
☐ Comment on political blogs or online forums (not surveys)
☐ Donate money to a candidate, campaign, or political organization

Vote. Did you vote in the 2012 presidential election? (Yes/No)

Party identification. Generally speaking, do you usually think of yourself as a Republican, a Democrat, an Independent, or what? (Democrat/Republican/Independent/Other/No preference)

Party strength. [If answered Democrat or Republican] Would you call yourself a strong Republican/Democrat or a not very strong Republican/Democrat?

Party lean. [If answered Independent, Other, or No preference] Do you think of yourself as closer to the Republican or Democratic Party? (Democrat/Republican)

Political interest. Some people don't pay much attention to politics. How about you? Would you say that you are:

☐ Not at all interested in politics
☐ Not very interested in politics
☐ Somewhat interested in politics
☐ Very interested in politics
☐ Extremely interested in politics

Media Consumption. Which of the following is your main source of political news and information? (From NBC Poll, July 2012)

☐ Newspaper
☐ Network television

☐ Cable television
☐ Radio
☐ Social media like Facebook and Twitter
☐ Talking with others
☐ Don't really follow political news

Second media preference. And, which is your next major source of political news and information?

☐ Newspaper
☐ Network television
☐ Cable television
☐ Radio
☐ Social media like Facebook and Twitter
☐ Talking with others
☐ Don't really follow political news

Ideology. In general, do you think of yourself as . . .

☐ Extremely liberal
☐ Liberal
☐ Slightly liberal
☐ Moderate, middle of the road
☐ Slightly conservative
☐ Conservative

Gender. Are you male or female?

☐ Male
☐ Female

Age. Please enter your current age.

Education. What is the highest level of school you have completed?

☐ 9th grade
☐ 10th grade
☐ 11th grade
☐ 12th grade
☐ High school graduate—high school diploma or equivalent
☐ Some college, no degree
☐ Associate's degree
☐ Bachelor's degree
☐ Master's degree
☐ Professional or doctoral degree

Income. Which of the income groups listed below includes the total 2011 income before taxes of all members of your family living in your home?

☐ Under $15,000
☐ $15,000–$30,000
☐ $30,000–$45,000
☐ $45,000–$60,000
☐ $60,000–$75,000
☐ $75,000–$90,000
☐ Above $90,000

Ethnicity. This is about Hispanic ethnicity. Are you of Spanish, Hispanic, or Latino descent?

☐ No, I am not
☐ Yes, Mexican, Mexican-American, Chicano
☐ Yes, Puerto Rican
☐ Yes, Cuban
☐ Yes, Central American

☐ Yes, South American
☐ Yes, Caribbean
☐ Yes, Other Spanish/Hispanic/Latino

Race. Please check one or more categories below to indicate what **race(s)** you consider yourself to be.

☐ White
☐ Black or African American
☐ American Indian or Alaskan Native
☐ East Asian
☐ South Asian
☐ Native Hawaiian or Pacific Islander
☐ Other

MECHANICAL TURK STUDY 2

Conflict Orientation. Please indicate your level of agreement with the following statements. [Strongly agree, agree, neutral, disagree, strongly disagree]

☐ I enjoy challenging the opinions of others.
☐ I find conflicts exciting.
☐ I hate arguments.
☐ I feel upset after an argument.
☐ Arguments don't bother me.

Political Interest. Some people seem to follow politics most of the time, while others aren't that interested. Would you say you follow what's going on in politics most of the time, some of the time, only now and then, or hardly at all? Please choose only one of the following.

☐ most of the time
☐ some of the time

☐ only now and then
☐ hardly at all

Political Efficacy. Please indicate your level of agreement with the following statements. Please choose the appropriate response for each item. [Strongly agree, agree, neutral, disagree, strongly disagree]

- People like me don't have any say about what the government does.
- I don't think public officials care much about what people like me think.
- Sometimes politics and government seem so complicated that a person like me can't really understand what's going on.

Party ID. Generally speaking, do you usually think of yourself as a Republican, a Democrat, an Independent, or what?

- Republican
- Democrat
- Independent
- Other

Party strength. [If Democrat/Republican] Would you consider yourself a strong Republican/Democrat or a not very strong Republican/Democrat?

☐ Strong Republican/Democrat
☐ Not very strong Republican/Democrat

Party lean. [If independent/other] Do you think of yourself as closer to the Republican or Democratic Party?

☐ Republican Party
☐ Democratic Party
☐ Neither party

Media preferences. Imagine you had a choice among the four television shows listed below. Please rank these shows on the basis of how much you would like to watch them, with your most preferred show at the top and your least-preferred show at the bottom.

- *The O'Reilly Factor* with Bill O'Reilly on the FOX News Channel
- *The Last Word with Lawrence O'Donnell* on the MSNBC News Channel
- *Pet Star* on the Animal Planet network
- *For Rent* on the HGTV network

Random Assignment to treatment here. There are five treatments:

1. Forced consumption: political news, civil
2. Forced consumption: political news, uncivil
3. Forced consumption: entertainment, civil
4. Forced consumption: entertainment, uncivil
5. Choice of article from the four listed above

Manipulation Check. To what extent was the clip you just watched . . . [not at all, slightly, moderately, very, extremely]

- ☐ Informative?
- ☐ Entertaining?
- ☐ Civil?

Emotional reaction. To what extent did the article you just read make you feel any of the following?

- ☐ angry
- ☐ disgusted
- ☐ anxious
- ☐ enthusiastic
- ☐ amused

Perceptions of politics as civil/uncivil. Generally speaking, to what extent do you see politics today as civil?

- Mostly civil
- Somewhat civil
- Somewhat uncivil
- Mostly uncivil

Information Search. We would now like to give you the option to read some other stories about politics and entertainment. To access the story, please click the button beside the headline, followed by the arrow at the bottom of the screen. When you have read the story, you will be asked a few additional questions and then brought back to this screen. When you no longer wish to read any additional stories, please select the option labelled "I am finished," followed by the arrow button.

Participants could choose from the following video clips:

- *The Amazing Race*: "Contestants reflect on their success plate spinning"
- *Survivor*: "Sierra accuses teammates of lying, double-crossing her"
- CNN: "GOP activists feud over Trump's potential damage to the party"
- CNN: "Poll: Americans want a hearing for next justice"

After watching all the clips that interest them, participants once again asked manipulation check, emotional reaction questions

Ideology. Here is a seven-point scale on which the political views that people might hold are arranged from extremely liberal to extremely conservative. Where would you put yourself on this scale?

- ☐ extremely liberal
- ☐ liberal
- ☐ slightly liberal
- ☐ moderate: middle of the road

☐ slightly conservative
☐ conservative
☐ extremely conservative

Almost done! Now we'd like to ask you some basic demographic information.

Age. Please enter your current age.
   [short free response]

Gender. Are you male or female?

☐ male
☐ female

Education. What is the highest level of school you have completed?

☐ no high school diploma
☐ high school graduate-high school diploma or equivalent (GED)
☐ some college, no degree
☐ associate degree
☐ bachelor's degree
☐ master's degree
☐ professional degree

Income. Which of the income groups listed below includes the total 2015 income before taxes of all members of your family living in your home? Please include salaries, wages, pensions, dividends, interest and all other income.

☐ Under $15,000
☐ $15,000–$30,000
☐ $30,000–$45,000
☐ $45,000–$60,000
☐ $60,000–$75,000

☐ $75,000–$90,000

☐ Above $90,000

Race. Please check one or more categories to indicate what race(s) you consider yourself to be.

☐ White
☐ Black or African-American
☐ American Indian or Alaska Native
☐ East Asian
☐ South Asian
☐ Native Hawaiian or Pacific Islander

Ethnicity. This question is about Hispanic ethnicity. Are you of Spanish, Hispanic, or Latino descent?

Please choose only one of the following:

☐ No, I am not.
☐ Yes, Mexican, Mexican-American or Chicano.
☐ Yes, Puerto Rican.
☐ Yes, Cuban.
☐ Yes, Central American.
☐ Yes, South American.
☐ Yes, Caribbean.
☐ Yes, other Spanish/Hispanic/Latino

APPENDIX B

Statistical Models and Results

CHAPTER 2

TABLE B.1 CONFLICT ORIENTATION IS TIED
TO OTHER PSYCHOLOGICAL TRAITS

	QUALTRICS PANEL, AUGUST 2016
Extraversion	0.27*
Agreeableness	−0.07
Conscientiousness	0.09
Emotional stability	0.18*
Openness	0.25*

*$p < 0.05$

TABLE B.2 THE INTERACTION BETWEEN CONFLICT ORIENTATION AND INCIVILITY INFLUENCES EMOTIONAL RESPONSES

	ANXIOUS	DISGUSTED	ANGRY	AMUSED	ENTER-TAINED	ENTHUSI-ASTIC
Conflict orientation	0.01	0.005	0.004	0.03*	0.03*	0.03**
	(0.012)	(0.016)	(0.14)	(0.011)	(0.012)	(0.010)
Treatments						
Master Chef civil	0.03	−0.11	−0.07	0.20**	0.28**	−0.15**
	(0.062)	(0.081)	(0.073)	(0.059)	(0.061)	(0.053)
Master Chef uncivil	0.21**	0.50**	0.33**	0.27**	0.32**	−0.20**
	(0.062)	(0.082)	(0.074)	(0.060)	(0.062)	(0.054)
Planned Parenthood uncivil	0.32**	1.04**	0.83**	0.22**	−0.03	−0.24**
	(0.063)	(0.082)	(0.074)	(0.060)	0.062)	(0.054)
C.O. x Treatments						
Master Chef civil	−0.01	0.01	0.01	−0.003	−0.04*	−0.01
	(0.016)	(0.021)	(0.019)	(0.015)	(0.016)	(0.014)
Master Chef uncivil	−0.05**	−0.10**	−0.05**	0.014	0.02	−0.004
	(0.017)	(0.22)	(0.020)	(0.016)	(0.016)	(0.014)
Planned Parenthood uncivil	−0.05**	−0.02	0.004	0.04*	0.03	0.005
	(0.017)	(0.022)	(0.019)	(0.016)	(0.016)	(0.014)
Seven-point party ID	0.02	0.01	0.02	−0.006	−0.01	0.02
	(0.011)	(0.014)	(0.013)	(0.010)	(0.010)	(0.009)
Ideology	0.0004	0.03	0.02	0.01	−0.007	−0.005
	0.013)	(0.017)	(0.016)	(0.013)	(0.013)	(0.011)
Female	0.08*	−0.03	0.03	−0.10**	−0.02	0.01
	(0.035)	(0.046)	(0.042)	(0.034)	(0.035)	(0.030)
Education	0.03	0.02	−0.007	−0.06**	−0.04*	−0.04**
	(0.018)	(0.024)	(0.021)	(0.017)	(0.018)	(0.015)
Race/Ethnicity						
Black	−0.22**	−0.29**	−0.31**	0.05	0.23**	0.09
	(0.064)	(0.083)	(0.075)	(0.061)	(0.063)	(0.054)
Other	0.32**	−0.07	−0.13	0.36**	0.41**	0.42**
	(0.089)	(0.116)	(0.105)	(0.085)	(0.087)	(0.076)
Hispanic	0.08	−0.12	0.03	0.03	0.13*	0.04
	(0.058)	(0.076)	(0.069)	(0.056)	(0.057)	(0.050)
Multiracial (2+)	−0.05	−0.09	−0.13	−0.03	0.04	−0.03
	(0.092)	(0.120)	(0.108)	(0.087)	(0.090)	(0.078)
Constant	1.07**	1.42**	1.32**	1.67**	1.64**	1.58**
	(0.12)	(0.16)	(0.14)	(0.12)	(0.12)	(0.104)
R^2	0.06	0.16	0.11	0.04	0.07	0.04
N	3,048	3,048	3,048	3,048	3,048	3,048

Source: GfK.
Note: Cell entries are OLS regression coefficients with standard errors in parentheses.
*$p < 0.05$, **$p < 0.01$

CHAPTER 4

TABLE B.3 BIVARIATE REGRESSION OF CONFLICT ORIENTATION ON MEDIA CONSUMPTION: PROJECT IMPLICIT

	AVERAGE WEEKLY USE	NEWSPAPER	NETWORK TV	CABLE TV	RADIO	INTERNET
Conflict orientation	0.03**	0.03*	0.01	0.01	0.04**	0.05**
	(0.009)	(0.012)	(0.013)	(0.012)	(0.013)	(0.012)
Constant	3.18**	2.04**	3.26**	2.59**	3.02**	4.99**
	(0.069)	(0.093)	(0.106)	(0.096)	(0.102)	(0.094)
R^2	0.010	0.004	0.001	0.001	0.008	0.018
N	1094	1094	1093	1093	1094	1094

Note: Cell entries are OLS regression coefficients with standard errors in parentheses.

$^*p < 0.05, ^{**}p < 0.01$

TABLE B.4 BIVARIATE REGRESSION OF CONFLICT ORIENTATION ON MEDIA CONSUMPTION: MECHANICAL TURK STUDY 1

	NEWSPAPER	NETWORK TV	CABLE TV	RADIO	INTERNET	SOCIAL MEDIA
Conflict Orientation	0.007	−0.04**	0.01	0.01	0.01	−0.02
	(0.009)	(0.012)	(0.010)	(0.017)	(0.008)	(0.020)
Constant	−1.24**	−2.15**	−1.59**	−2.79**	−0.69**	−3.13**
	(0.091)	(0.130)	(0.100)	(0.160)	(0.080)	(0.194)
χ^2	0.49	0.004	0.33	0.53	0.23	0.42
N	886	886	886	886	886	886

Note: Cell entries are logistic regression coefficients with standard errors in parentheses.

$^*p < 0.05, ^{**}p < 0.01$

TABLE B.5 REGRESSION OF FREQUENCY OF MEDIA EXPOSURE ON THE INTERACTION BETWEEN CONFLICT ORIENTATION AND POLITICAL INTEREST

	AVERAGE WEEKLY USE	NEWSPAPER	NETWORK TV	CABLE TV	RADIO	INTERNET
Conflict orientation	−0.02	0.03	−0.01	−0.012	−0.052	−0.041
	(0.029)	(0.044)	(0.049)	(0.26)	(1.10)	(1.00)
Interest						
Not very	0.42	−0.17	0.17	0.214	0.451	1.452
	(0.333)	(0.500)	(0.559)	(0.42)	(0.84)	(3.12)**
Somewhat	1.28*	0.55	1.18*	0.757	1.691	2.230
	(0.282)	(0.421)	(0.473)	(1.78)	(3.72)**	(5.67)**
Very	2.18*	1.26*	2.03*	1.664	2.454	3.505
	(0.281)	(0.42)	(0.471)	(3.92)**	(5.41)**	(8.94)**
Extremely	2.89	1.93*	2.62*	2.678	3.085	4.124
	(0.278)	(0.42)	(0.466)	(6.37)**	(6.87)**	(10.63)**
CCS–Interest Interaction						
Not very	0.003	−0.04	0.003	0.015	0.007	0.035
	(0.037)	(0.056)	(0.063)	(0.26)	(0.11)	(0.68)
Somewhat	0.03	−0.04	0.02	−0.009	0.102	0.088
	(0.033)	(0.049)	(0.055)	(0.19)	(1.93)	(1.92)
Very	0.0008	−0.02	−0.04	−0.016	0.028	0.052
	(0.033)	(0.050)	(0.056)	(0.32)	(0.52)	(1.11)
Extremely	−0.001	−0.06	−0.03	−0.024	0.072	0.035
	(0.033)	(0.049)	(0.055)	(0.49)	(1.35)	(0.76)
Constant	1.34*	1.00*	1.60*	1.123	0.918	2.072
	(0.256)	(0.384)	(0.431)	(2.89)**	(2.21)*	(5.78)**
R^2	0.27	0.09	0.12	0.14	0.12	0.24
N	1087	1087	1086	1,086	1,087	1,087

Source: Project Implicit.

Note: Cell entries are OLS regression coefficients with standard errors in parentheses.

*$p < 0.05$, **$p < 0.01$

TABLE B.6 EFFECTS OF CONFLICT ORIENTATION AND INCIVILITY ON INFORMATION SEARCH

	(1) NUMBER OF ARTICLES	(2) TIME ON ARTICLES	(3) PROPORTION UNCIVIL	(3) PROPORTION POLITICAL
Conflict orientation	−0.0675***	−4.486***	−0.0106**	−0.00298
	(0.0187)	(1.377)	(0.00431)	(0.00488)
Uncivil treatment	0.356***	13.03	0.0820***	0.0764**
	(0.133)	(9.778)	(0.0306)	(0.0347)
Uncivil treatment ×	0.0754***	3.810**	0.0157***	0.0107*
Conflict orientation	(0.0240)	(1.772)	(0.00554)	(0.00628)
Prefer news	−0.0735	2.088	0.0205	0.101***
	(0.114)	(8.438)	(0.0264)	(0.0299)
Political efficacy	0.0186	0.436	0.00509	−0.00103
	(0.0234)	(1.729)	(0.00541)	(0.00613)
Political interest	0.192***	15.23***	0.0411**	0.0829***
	(0.0738)	(5.444)	(0.0170)	(0.0193)
Democrat	−0.180	−19.39*	−0.0700**	−0.0319
	(0.149)	(10.96)	(0.0343)	(0.0389)
Independent	−0.230	−16.18	−0.0389	−0.00428
	(0.169)	(12.48)	(0.0390)	(0.0442)
Strong party	−0.129	−6.436	−0.0288	−0.0110
	(0.140)	(10.31)	(0.0323)	(0.0366)
Female	−0.152	−3.589	−0.0352	−0.0520*
	(0.118)	(8.734)	(0.0273)	(0.0310)
Reported anger	0.00820	−2.707	−0.0109	0.00820
	(0.0733)	(5.409)	(0.0169)	(0.0192)
Reported disgust	0.00207	1.513	0.0150	−0.00913
	(0.0684)	(5.043)	(0.0158)	(0.0179)
Reported anxiety	0.0300	1.107	−0.00145	−0.00789
	(0.0620)	(4.571)	(0.0143)	(0.0162)
Reported enthusiasm	−0.114	−5.332	−0.0154	−0.0188
	(0.0744)	(5.489)	(0.0172)	(0.0195)
Reported amusement	0.153**	7.743*	0.0290**	−0.000535
	(0.0635)	(4.686)	(0.0147)	(0.0166)
Constant	1.674***	45.03**	0.111*	0.0469
	(0.247)	(18.24)	(0.0571)	(0.0647)
Observations	299	299	299	299
R^2	0.107	0.088	0.106	0.165

Source: Mechanical Turk Study 2.
Note: Cell entries are OLS regression coefficients with standard errors in parentheses.
*$p < 0.1$, **$p < 0.05$, ***$p < 0.01$

TABLE B.7 ANXIETY FAILS TO MEDIATE THE CONFLICT ORIENTATION–INCIVILITY INTERACTION

	(1)	(2)	(3)	(4)
	ARTICLES READ	TIME SPENT ON ARTICLES	PROPORTION UNCIVIL	PROPORTION POLITICAL
Conflict orientation	0.0209	0.249	0.00772**	0.0112**
	(0.0165)	(1.196)	(0.00379)	(0.00450)
Uncivil treatment	−0.273**	−8.846	−0.0642**	−0.0697**
	(0.127)	(9.161)	(0.0289)	(0.0343)
Uncivil treatment × Conflict orientation	−0.077***	−3.696**	−0.015***	−0.0116*
	(0.0240)	(1.738)	(0.00549)	(0.00652)
Anxiety	0.0246	−0.337	−0.00240	−0.00651
	(0.0556)	(4.022)	(0.0127)	(0.0151)
Constant	2.139***	74.53***	0.229***	0.300***
	(0.0906)	(6.555)	(0.0207)	(0.0246)
Observations	304	304	301	301
R^2	0.042	0.025	0.029	0.030

Source: Mechanical Turk Study 2.

Note: Cell entries are OLS regression coefficients with standard errors in parentheses.

$^{*}p < 0.1, ^{**}p < 0.05, ^{***}p < 0.01$

TABLE B.8 ANGER FAILS TO MEDIATE THE CONFLICT
ORIENTATION–INCIVILITY INTERACTION

	(1) ARTICLES READ	(2) TIME SPENT ON ARTICLES	(3) PROPORTION UNCIVIL	(4) PROPORTION POLITICAL
Conflict orientation	0.0206	0.292	0.00787**	0.0112**
	(0.0165)	(1.195)	(0.00379)	(0.00450)
Uncivil treatment	−0.263**	−7.133	−0.0588**	−0.0732**
	(0.129)	(9.357)	(0.0295)	(0.0351)
Uncivil treatment ×	−0.078***	−3.819**	−0.015***	−0.0113*
Conflict orientation	(0.0241)	(1.742)	(0.00550)	(0.00654)
Anger	0.00024	−2.612	−0.00914	0.000958
	(0.0509)	(3.679)	(0.0116)	(0.0138)
Constant	2.151***	75.81***	0.233***	0.297***
	(0.0911)	(6.586)	(0.0209)	(0.0248)
Observations	304	304	301	301
R^2	0.041	0.026	0.031	0.030

Source: Mechanical Turk Study 2.

Note: Cell entries are OLS regression coefficients with standard errors in parentheses.

$^*p < 0.1$, $^{**}p < 0.05$, $^{***}p < 0.01$

TABLE B.9 DISGUST FAILS TO MEDIATE THE CONFLICT
ORIENTATION–INCIVILITY INTERACTION

	(1) ARTICLES READ	(2) TIME SPENT ON ARTICLES	(3) PROPORTION UNCIVIL	(4) PROPORTION POLITICAL
Conflict orientation	0.0203	0.251	0.00764**	0.0112**
	(0.0166)	(1.197)	(0.00379)	(0.00451)
Uncivil treatment	−0.274**	−9.059	−0.0694**	−0.0746**
	(0.131)	(9.478)	(0.0299)	(0.0355)
Uncivil treatment ×	−0.077***	−3.679**	−0.0143**	−0.0112*
Conflict orientation	(0.0243)	(1.758)	(0.00555)	(0.00659)
Anger	0.0134	0.0792	0.00497	0.00252
	(0.0498)	(3.599)	(0.0113)	(0.0135)
Constant	2.144***	74.33***	0.226***	0.296***
	(0.0904)	(6.538)	(0.0207)	(0.0246)
Observations	304	304	301	301
R^2	0.041	0.025	0.030	0.030

Source: Mechanical Turk Study 2.

Note: Cell entries are OLS regression coefficients with standard errors in parentheses.

*$p < 0.1$, **$p < 0.05$, ***$p < 0.01$

TABLE B.10 ENTHUSIASM FAILS TO MEDIATE THE CONFLICT
ORIENTATION–INCIVILITY INTERACTION

	(1) ARTICLES READ	(2) TIME SPENT ON ARTICLES	(3) PROPORTION UNCIVIL	(4) PROPORTION POLITICAL
Conflict orientation	0.0214	0.301	0.00787**	0.0114**
	(0.0165)	(1.195)	(0.00379)	(0.00450)
Uncivil treatment	−0.260**	−8.865	−0.0650**	−0.0722**
	(0.124)	(8.983)	(0.0283)	(0.0337)
Uncivil treatment ×	−0.0752**	−3.540**	−0.014***	−0.0109*
Conflict orientation	(0.0241)	(1.742)	(0.00550)	(0.00654)
Anger	−0.0581	−3.602	−0.0106	−0.0113
	(0.0657)	(4.752)	(0.0150)	(0.0178)
Constant	2.180***	76.22***	0.234***	0.303***
	(0.0929)	(6.723)	(0.0213)	(0.0253)
Observations	304	304	301	301
R^2	0.043	0.026	0.031	0.031

Source: Mechanical Turk Study 2.

Note: Cell entries are OLS regression coefficients with standard errors in parentheses.

$^*p < 0.1, ^{**}p < 0.05, ^{***}p < 0.01$

TABLE B.11 AMUSEMENT FAILS TO MEDIATE THE CONFLICT ORIENTATION–INCIVILITY INTERACTION

	(1) ARTICLES READ	(2) TIME SPENT ON ARTICLES	(3) PROPORTION UNCIVIL	(4) PROPORTION POLITICAL
Conflict orientation	0.0190	0.160	0.00729*	0.0116**
	(0.0166)	(1.198)	(0.00380)	(0.00452)
Uncivil treatment	−0.288**	−10.43	−0.0718**	−0.0673*
	(0.126)	(9.136)	(0.0288)	(0.0342)
Uncivil treatment × Conflict orientation	−0.080***	−3.845**	−0.015***	−0.0108*
	(0.0241)	(1.741)	(0.00549)	(0.00653)
Amusement	0.0608	3.455	0.0158	−0.0125
	(0.0562)	(4.065)	(0.0128)	(0.0153)
Constant	2.113***	72.25***	0.219***	0.305***
	(0.0932)	(6.744)	(0.0213)	(0.0253)
Observations	304	304	301	301
R^2	0.045	0.027	0.034	0.032

Source: Mechanical Turk Study 2.

Note: Cell entries are OLS regression coefficients with standard errors in parentheses.

$^*p < 0.1$, $^{**}p < 0.05$, $^{***}p < 0.01$

TABLE B.12 THE IMPACT OF CONFLICT ORIENTATION
AND INCIVILITY ON GENERAL MOOD

	(1) POSITIVE MOOD	(2) NEGATIVE MOOD
Conflict orientation	0.0144*	0.00709
	(0.00789)	(0.00697)
Uncivil treatment	−0.00940	0.295***
	(0.0583)	(0.0515)
Uncivil treatment × Conflict orientation	0.0202* (0.0116)	−0.0138 (0.0102)
Constant	0.601***	0.553***
	(0.0396)	(0.0350)
Observations	342	342
R²	0.061	0.130

Source: Mechanical Turk Study 2.

Note: Cell entries are OLS regression coefficients with standard errors in parentheses.

*p < 0.1, **p < 0.05, ***p < 0.01

TABLE B.13 THE MEDIATING EFFECT OF POSITIVE MOOD ON THE CONFLICT ORIENTATION-INCIVILITY INTERACTION

	(1) INITIAL EFFECT ON INFO SEARCH	(2) MEDIATED EFFECT ON INFO SEARCH	(3) INITIAL EFFECT ON TIME SEARCHING	(4) MEDIATED EFFECT ON TIME SEARCHING	(5) INITIAL EFFECT ON PROPORTION UNCIVIL	(6) MEDIATED EFFECT ON PROPORTION UNCIVIL	(7) INITIAL EFFECT ON PROPORTION POLITICAL	(8) MEDIATED EFFECT ON PROPORTION POLITICAL
Conflict orientation	0.00661	0.0103	−0.193	−0.103	0.00774**	0.00726*	0.0112**	0.0113**
	(0.0181)	(0.0181)	(1.130)	(1.136)	(0.00378)	(0.00379)	(0.00449)	(0.00452)
Uncivil treatment	−0.0277	−0.0301	−0.744	−0.802	−0.653**	−0.668**	−0.0725**	−0.0722**
	(0.134)	(0.133)	(8.349)	(8.354)	(0.0283)	(0.0283)	(0.0336)	(0.0337)
Uncivil treatment × Conflict orientation	−0.074***	−0.068**	−3.52**	−3.396**	−0.0147**	−0.016***	−0.0114*	−0.0112*
	(0.0265)	(0.0265)	(1.655)	(1.664)	(0.00546)	(0.00548)	(0.00649)	(0.00653)
Positive mood	—	−0.258**	—	−6.229	—	0.0370	—	−0.00773
		(0.124)		(7.798)		(0.0260)		(0.0310)
Constant	1.779***	1.934***	61.52***	65.26***	0.228***	0.209***	0.297***	0.301***
	(0.0909)	(0.117)	(5.674)	(7.362)	(0.0198)	(0.0240)	(0.0235)	(0.0286)
Observations	342	342	342	342	301	301	301	301
R²	0.039	0.051	0.030	0.032	0.029	0.036	0.030	0.030

Source: Mechanical Turk Study 2.

Note: Cell entries are OLS regression coefficients with standard errors in parentheses.

*$p < 0.1$, **$p < 0.05$, ***$p < 0.01$

CHAPTER 5

TABLE B.14 BIVARIATE REGRESSION OF POLITICAL PARTICIPATION ON CONFLICT ORIENTATION (PROJECT IMPLICIT)

	ATTEND MEETINGS	DONATE MONEY	ATTEND A PROTEST	PERSUADE OTHERS	POST A SIGN	WORK FOR CANDIDATE	WEAR A BUTTON	CALL YOUR REPRESENTATIVE	COMMENT ON BLOGS	VOTE
Conflict orientation	0.037	0.015	0.065	0.056	0.026	0.042	0.028	0.043	0.067	0.001
	$(3.21)^{**}$	(1.31)	$(5.63)^{**}$	$(5.61)^{**}$	$(2.14)^{*}$	$(2.44)^{*}$	$(2.36)^{*}$	$(4.28)^{**}$	$(6.32)^{**}$	(0.10)
Constant	−1.100	−1.220	−0.988	0.082	−1.361	−2.287	−1.270	−0.359	−0.527	0.888
	$(12.64)^{**}$	$(13.47)^{**}$	$(11.69)^{**}$	(1.05)	$(14.55)^{**}$	$(17.96)^{**}$	$(13.94)^{**}$	$(4.61)^{**}$	$(6.65)^{**}$	$(10.52)^{**}$
N	1,095	1,095	1,095	1,095	1,095	1,095	1,095	1,095	1,095	1,094

Source: Project Implicit.

Note: Cell entries are logistic regression coefficients with standard errors in parentheses.

$^{*}p < 0.05$, $^{**}p < 0.01$

TABLE B.15 BIVARIATE REGRESSION OF POLITICAL PARTICIPATION ON CONFLICT ORIENTATION (MECHANICAL TURK STUDY 1)

	VOTE	ATTEND MEETINGS	ATTEND A PROTEST	PERSUADE OTHERS	POST A SIGN	WORK FOR CANDIDATE	WEAR A BUTTON	CALL REPRE- SENTATIVE	COMMENT ON BLOGS	DONATE MONEY
Conflict Orienation	−0.006	0.044	0.047	0.028	0.020	0.043	0.035	0.022	0.031	0.031
	(0.53)	(3.51)**	(3.73)**	(3.49)**	(1.78)	(2.52)*	(3.17)**	(2.33)*	(3.57)**	(2.70)**
Constant	1.933	−2.128	−2.098	−0.342	−1.784	−2.870	−1.728	−1.318	−0.792	−1.892
	(17.04)**	(17.98)**	(17.93)**	(4.43)**	(16.84)**	(17.86)**	(16.78)**	(14.42)**	(9.75)**	(17.34)**
N	883	886	886	886	886	886	886	886	886	886

Source: Mechanical Turk Study 1.

Note: Cell entries are logistic regression coefficients with standard errors in parentheses.

$^* p < 0.05, ^{**} p < 0.01$

TABLE B.16 EFFECTS OF CONFLICT ORIENTATION ON PARTICIPATION, CONTROLLING FOR DEMOGRAPHICS (PROJECT IMPLICIT)

	(1) ATTEND MEETINGS	(2) ATTEND PROTEST	(3) DONATE MONEY	(4) PERSUADE OTHERS	(5) POST A SIGN	(6) WORK FOR CANDIDATE	(7) WEAR A BUTTON	(8) CALL A REP-RESENTATIVE	(9) COMMENT ON BLOGS	(10) VOTE
Conflict orientation	0.0105	0.0339**	-0.00429	0.0238*	0.0108	0.0159	0.00713	0.0314**	0.0385***	-0.0176
	(0.0153)	(0.0158)	(0.0162)	(0.0142)	(0.0163)	(0.0230)	(0.0160)	(0.0139)	(0.0146)	(0.0184)
Extraversion	0.0339	0.0444	0.00758	0.0188	0.0495*	0.104**	0.0585**	-0.0231	0.0206	0.0240
	(0.0266)	(0.0278)	(0.0281)	(0.0244)	(0.0284)	(0.0418)	(0.0279)	(0.0239)	(0.0253)	(0.0312)
Agreeableness	-0.0416	-0.0312	-0.00897	0.00601	-0.00575	-0.0576	0.0305	-0.00768	-0.0129	0.00760
	(0.0400)	(0.0415)	(0.0417)	(0.0369)	(0.0425)	(0.0607)	(0.0422)	(0.0359)	(0.0379)	(0.0480)
Conscientiousness	-0.0454	-0.0575*	0.0361	0.0101	-0.0408	-0.0292	-0.0645**	-0.0385	-0.102***	0.0706*
	(0.0311)	(0.0320)	(0.0332)	(0.0290)	(0.0332)	(0.0471)	(0.0322)	(0.0282)	(0.0296)	(0.0377)
Emotional Stability	0.0365	0.0464	0.0389	0.0409	0.0574*	0.0568	0.0252	0.000193	-0.0249	0.0426
	(0.0321)	(0.0336)	(0.0343)	(0.0295)	(0.0345)	(0.0493)	(0.0334)	(0.0287)	(0.0304)	(0.0367)
Openness	0.107**	0.0949**	0.0959**	0.0277	-0.0156	0.0298	0.0332	0.0540	0.0114	0.0273
	(0.0419)	(0.0432)	(0.0438)	(0.0362)	(0.0427)	(0.0645)	(0.0428)	(0.0356)	(0.0377)	(0.0454)
Political interest	0.591***	0.847***	0.601***	0.939***	0.652***	0.559***	0.591***	0.745***	0.889***	0.668***
	(0.0937)	(0.103)	(0.102)	(0.0879)	(0.103)	(0.153)	(0.0986)	(0.0843)	(0.0925)	(0.0993)
Party strength	-0.306	0.145	0.115	0.291	0.458**	0.00633	0.225	-0.219	0.966	0.357
	(0.220)	(0.222)	(0.217)	(0.188)	(0.225)	(0.334)	(0.220)	(0.191)	(0.203)	(0.251)

(continued)

TABLE B.16 (Continued)

	(1) ATTEND MEETINGS	(2) ATTEND PROTEST	(3) DONATE MONEY	(4) PERSUADE OTHERS	(5) POST A SIGN	(6) WORK FOR CANDIDATE	(7) WEAR A BUTTON	(8) CALL A REPRESENTATIVE	(9) COMMENT ON BLOGS	(10) VOTE
Democrat	-0.0351	0.393*	0.859***	0.338*	0.198	0.166	0.450**	0.416**	-0.337	0.528**
	(0.211)	(0.220)	(0.220)	(0.179)	(0.226)	(0.335)	(0.218)	(0.180)	(0.196)	(0.219)
Age	0.0117*	-0.0137**	0.0316***	0.000164	0.00904	0.0269***	-0.000757	0.0180***	0.00527	0.143***
	(0.00611)	(0.00663)	(0.00627)	(0.00570)	(0.00640)	(0.00897)	(0.00651)	(0.00555)	(0.00577)	(0.0130)
Hispanic	-0.726*	0.146	0.411	0.188	-0.323	-1.132	0.274	-0.369	0.202	-0.372
	(0.378)	(0.316)	(0.318)	(0.274)	(0.360)	(0.745)	(0.308)	(0.283)	(0.289)	(0.323)
Black	0.365	0.201	-0.0522	0.206	-0.590*	0.196	-0.107	-0.481*	-0.151	0.301
	(0.271)	(0.283)	(0.290)	(0.268)	(0.334)	(0.397)	(0.298)	(0.267)	(0.281)	(0.388)
Female	0.351*	0.337*	-0.0569	0.146	0.325*	0.205	0.709***	0.649***	0.0507	-0.0556
	(0.186)	(0.191)	(0.191)	(0.169)	(0.195)	(0.276)	(0.200)	(0.170)	(0.172)	(0.224)
Constant	-4.152***	-4.546***	-5.751***	-3.975***	-4.599***	-5.945***	-4.448***	-4.223***	-3.921***	-6.264***
	(0.421)	(0.460)	(0.488)	(0.376)	(0.460)	(0.699)	(0.446)	(0.379)	(0.396)	(0.541)
Observations	998	998	998	998	998	998	998	998	998	997

Source: Project Implicit.

Note: Cell entries are logistic regression coefficients with standard errors in parentheses.

* $p < 0.1$, ** $p < 0.05$, *** $p < 0.01$

TABLE B.17 EFFECTS OF CONFLICT ORIENTATION ON PARTICIPATION, CONTROLLING FOR DEMOGRAPHICS (MECHANICAL TURK STUDY 1)

	(1) ATTEND MEETINGS	(2) ATTEND PROTEST	(3) DONATE MONEY	(4) PERSUADE OTHERS	(5) POST A SIGN	(6) WORK FOR A CANDIDATE	(7) WEAR A BUTTON	(8) CALL A REPRESENTATIVE	(9) COMMENT ON BLOGS	(10) VOTE
Conflict orientation	0.0346*	0.0448***	0.0100	0.0336***	0.0203	0.00369	0.0262*	0.0268**	0.0136	-0.0255
	(0.0178)	(0.0165)	(0.0153)	(0.0121)	(0.0143)	(0.0222)	(0.0143)	(0.0132)	(0.0119)	(0.0189)
Democrat	0.501	0.117	1.119	-0.605	0.858	1.275	0.186	0.514	-1.183**	0.486
	(0.786)	(0.793)	(0.764)	(0.519)	(0.665)	(0.994)	(0.650)	(0.644)	(0.551)	(0.755)
Strong partisan	-0.0738	0.525	0.386	0.646	0.803	-0.397	1.432***	-0.270	0.578	-0.186
	(0.635)	(0.676)	(0.634)	(0.425)	(0.536)	(0.832)	(0.546)	(0.534)	(0.450)	(0.609)
Ideology	0.207	-0.0788	0.144	-0.138	0.229*	0.274	0.0653	0.00332	-0.333***	-0.0997
	(0.138)	(0.138)	(0.131)	(0.0900)	(0.123)	(0.169)	(0.123)	(0.107)	(0.0963)	(0.134)
Political interest	0.571***	0.579***	0.709***	0.752***	0.263*	0.677***	0.381*	0.656***	0.728***	1.140***
	(0.194)	(0.183)	(0.169)	(0.124)	(0.150)	(0.233)	(0.152)	(0.142)	(0.127)	(0.214)
Education	0.373*	0.398**	0.332**	0.128	-0.00140	0.675***	0.118	0.127	-0.0984	0.131
	(0.195)	(0.182)	(0.166)	(0.117)	(0.147)	(0.256)	(0.152)	(0.137)	(0.120)	(0.170)
Black	0.0276	0.386	-0.0662	-0.321	-0.164	-0.290	-0.437	-0.760	0.142	-1.138**

(continued)

TABLE B.17 (Continued)

	(1) ATTEND MEETINGS	(2) ATTEND PROTEST	(3) DONATE MONEY	(4) PERSUADE OTHERS	(5) POST A SIGN	(6) WORK FOR A CANDIDATE	(7) WEAR A BUTTON	(8) CALL A REPRESENTATIVE	(9) COMMENT ON BLOGS	(10) VOTE
	(0.653)	(0.546)	(0.523)	(0.402)	(0.505)	(0.790)	(0.550)	(0.533)	(0.403)	(0.559)
Income	-0.141	-0.109	-0.000494	0.0231	0.0688	-0.156	0.106	-0.0374	-0.0229	0.196**
	(0.0945)	(0.0869)	(0.0788)	(0.0575)	(0.0740)	(0.117)	(0.0742)	(0.0667)	(0.0592)	(0.0977)
Female	-0.0914	-0.191	0.471*	1.110***	0.839***	0.212	0.672**	0.590**	0.646	0.976***
	(0.343)	(0.318)	(0.286)	(0.215)	(0.269)	(0.405)	(0.272)	(0.243)	(0.215)	(0.368)
Age	-0.0179	-0.0218	-0.00977	-0.0173*	-0.00403	-0.0424**	-0.0649***	0.0229*	-0.00296	-0.00291
	(0.0145)	(0.0137)	(0.0117)	(0.00873)	(0.0108)	(0.0196)	(0.0139)	(0.00925)	(0.00888)	(0.0146)
Constant	-3.395***	-3.697***	-4.579***	-1.931***	-3.242***	-4.677***	-1.981***	-3.755***	-1.528***	-0.563
	(0.809)	(0.780)	(0.742)	(0.477)	(0.641)	(1.088)	(0.656)	(0.587)	(0.485)	(0.691)
Observations	533	533	533	533	533	533	533	533	533	532

Source: Mechanical Turk Study 1.

Note: Cell entries are logistic regression coefficients with standard errors in parentheses.

$^{*}p < 0.1$, $^{**}p < 0.05$, $^{***}p < 0.01$

TABLE B.18 EFFECTS OF CONFLICT ORIENTATION AND INCIVILITY ON WILLINGNESS TO SHARE VIDEO CLIP

	INTEREST IN SHARING STORY
Uncivil clip	0.36*
	(0.176)
Conflict orientation	0.11*
	(0.038)
Incivility × Conflict orientation	−0.002
	(0.051)
Party ID: Democrat	0.34
	(0.254)
Party ID: Independent	0.46
	(0.265)
Party strength	0.66*
	(0.212)
Ideology	−0.02
	(0.059)
Female	0.09
	(0.160)
Age	−0.007
	(0.0047)
Education: High school	0.18
	(0.288)
Education: Some college	−0.30
	(0.299)
Education: Bachelor's degree +	−0.34
	(0.310)
Income	−0.04*
	(0.018)
White	−0.82*
	(0.188)
Hispanic	−0.21
	(0.248)
Constant	−1.73*
	(0.471)
Pseudo R^2	0.06
N	3017

Source: GfK.

Note: Cell entries are logistic regression coefficients with standard errors in parentheses.

*$p < 0.05$

TABLE B.19 PARTICIPATORY EFFECTS OF THE INTERACTION BETWEEN CONFLICT ORIENTATION AND RACE (PROJECT IMPLICIT)

	(1) COMMENT ON BLOGS	(2) ATTEND A PROTEST	(3) PERSUADE OTHERS	(4) CALL A REP-RESENTATIVE
Conflict orientation	0.0407***	0.0210	0.0234	0.0279*
	(0.0151)	(0.0164)	(0.0146)	(0.0142)
Extraversion	0.0206	0.0426	0.0188	−0.0236
	(0.0253)	(0.0279)	(0.0244)	(0.0239)
Agreeableness	−0.0139	−0.0268	0.00611	−0.00605
	(0.0380)	(0.0417)	(0.0369)	(0.0359)
Conscientiousness	−0.102***	−0.0603*	0.0101	−0.0384
	(0.0296)	(0.0324)	(0.0290)	(0.0282)
Emotional stability	−0.0250	0.0493	0.0409	0.000475
	(0.0305)	(0.0338)	(0.0295)	(0.0288)
Openness	0.0109	0.103**	0.0279	0.0551
	(0.0378)	(0.0438)	(0.0362)	(0.0356)
Political interest	0.890***	0.858***	0.939***	0.746***
	(0.0926)	(0.104)	(0.0879)	(0.0843)
Party strength	0.0918	0.171	0.291	−0.215
	(0.203)	(0.224)	(0.188)	(0.191)
Democrat	−0.0302	0.380*	0.338*	0.412**
	(0.197)	(0.221)	(0.179)	(0.181)
Age	0.00540	−0.0148**	0.000136	0.0178***
	(0.00578)	(0.00667)	(0.00571)	(0.00555)
Hispanic	0.201	0.160	0.189	−0.365
	(0.289)	(0.315)	(0.274)	(0.282)
Black	−0.291	0.859**	0.235	−0.260
	(0.353)	(0.377)	(0.368)	(0.335)
Female	0.0520	0.320*	0.145	0.647***
	(0.172)	(0.192)	(0.169)	(0.170)
Black × Conflict orientation	−0.0315	0.165***	0.00544	0.0499
	(0.0482)	(0.0583)	(0.0478)	(0.0461)
Constant	−3.917***	−4.629***	−3.977***	−4.242***
	(0.397)	(0.464)	(0.376)	(0.380)
Observations	998	998	998	998

Source: Project Implicit.

Note: Cell entries represent logistic regression coefficients with standard errors in parentheses.

*p < 0.1, **p < 0.05, ***p < 0.01

TABLE B.20 PARTICIPATORY EFFECTS OF THE INTERACTION
BETWEEN CONFLICT ORIENTATION AND RACE
(MECHANICAL TURK STUDY 1)

	(1) COMMENT ON BLOGS	(2) ATTEND PROTEST	(3) PERSUADE OTHERS	(4) CALL A REP-RESENTATIVE
Conflict orientation	0.0141	0.0452***	0.0288**	0.0251*
	(0.0121)	(0.0168)	(0.0123)	(0.0134)
Democrat	−1.187**	0.113	−0.563	0.525
	(0.551)	(0.794)	(0.521)	(0.643)
Strong partisan	0.583	0.527	0.600	−0.282
	(0.451)	(0.676)	(0.427)	(0.534)
Ideology	−0.335***	−0.0801	−0.125	0.00736
	(0.0966)	(0.138)	(0.0909)	(0.107)
Political interest	0.727***	0.579***	0.767***	0.661***
	(0.127)	(0.183)	(0.125)	(0.142)
Education	−0.0979	0.399**	0.125	0.124
	(0.120)	(0.183)	(0.117)	(0.137)
Black	0.0415	0.316	0.905	−0.317
	(0.610)	(0.751)	(0.738)	(0.743)
Black x Conflict orientation	−0.0129	−0.0113	0.156*	0.0647
	(0.0583)	(0.0813)	(0.0819)	(0.0846)
Income	−0.0223	−0.108	0.0202	−0.0399
	(0.0593)	(0.0869)	(0.0577)	(0.0668)
Female	0.0629	−0.192	1.132***	0.591**
	(0.216)	(0.318)	(0.215)	(0.242)
Age	−0.00302	−0.0219	−0.0174**	0.0232**
	(0.00889)	(0.0138)	(0.00876)	(0.00925)
Constant	−1.528***	−3.699***	−1.939***	−3.753***
	(0.485)	(0.780)	(0.480)	(0.587)
Observations	533	533	533	533

Source: Mechanical Turk Study 1.

Note: Cell entries are logistic regression coefficients with standard errors in parentheses.

*$p < 0.1$, **$p < 0.05$, ***$p < 0.01$

TABLE B.21 PARTICIPATORY EFFECTS OF THE INTERACTION BETWEEN CONFLICT ORIENTATION AND GENDER (PROJECT IMPLICIT)

	(1) COMMENT ON BLOGS	(2) PROTEST	(3) PERSUADE OTHERS	(4) CALL WA REP
Conflict orientation	0.0538**	0.0441*	4.25e-05	0.0377*
	(0.0216)	(0.0235)	(0.0209)	(0.0208)
Extraversion	0.0208	0.0444	0.0183	−0.0231
	(0.0253)	(0.0278)	(0.0245)	(0.0239)
Agreeableness	−0.0120	−0.0307	0.00500	−0.00751
	(0.0379)	(0.0415)	(0.0370)	(0.0359)
Conscientiousness	−0.102***	−0.0569*	0.00951	−0.0384
	(0.0296)	(0.0320)	(0.0291)	(0.0282)
Emotional stability	−0.0276	0.0451	0.0450	−0.000775
	(0.0306)	(0.0337)	(0.0297)	(0.0288)
Openness	0.0135	0.0968**	0.0253	0.0548
	(0.0379)	(0.0434)	(0.0362)	(0.0357)
Interest	0.891***	0.847***	0.940***	0.746***
	(0.0925)	(0.103)	(0.0882)	(0.0843)
Party strength	0.0992	0.145	0.287	−0.218
	(0.203)	(0.222)	(0.189)	(0.191)
Democrat	−0.0382	0.393*	0.344*	0.414**
	(0.197)	(0.220)	(0.179)	(0.181)
Age	0.00551	−0.0136**	−0.000149	0.0181***
	(0.00578)	(0.00663)	(0.00570)	(0.00556)
Hispanic	0.197	0.142	0.194	−0.370
	(0.290)	(0.316)	(0.274)	(0.283)
Black	−0.143	0.206	0.187	−0.478*
	(0.282)	(0.284)	(0.267)	(0.267)
Female	−0.0422	0.286	0.306	0.611***
	(0.197)	(0.210)	(0.199)	(0.194)
Female × Conflict orientation	−0.0259	−0.0170	0.0394	−0.0103
	(0.0266)	(0.0289)	(0.0257)	(0.0252)
Constant	−3.904***	−4.542***	−4.025***	−4.216***
	(0.396)	(0.460)	(0.379)	(0.380)
Observations	998	998	998	998

Source: Project Implicit.

Note: Cell entries are logistic regression coefficients with standard errors in parentheses.

*$p < 0.1$, **$p<0.05$, ***$p < 0.01$

TABLE B.22 PARTICIPATORY EFFECTS OF THE INTERACTION BETWEEN CONFLICT ORIENTATION AND GENDER (MECHANICAL TURK STUDY 1)

	(1)	(2)	(3)	(4)
	COMMENT ON BLOGS	PROTEST	PERSUADE OTHERS	CALL REP
Conflict orientation	0.0310*	0.0598***	0.0259	0.0528***
	(0.0161)	(0.0218)	(0.0158)	(0.0188)
Democrat	−1.181**	0.151	−0.611	0.556
	(0.552)	(0.798)	(0.520)	(0.648)
Strong partisan	0.577	0.511	0.648	−0.292
	(0.451)	(0.680)	(0.426)	(0.537)
Ideology	−0.340***	−0.0810	−0.137	−1.20e−05
	(0.0965)	(0.138)	(0.0902)	(0.107)
Political interest	0.734***	0.579***	0.752***	0.667***
	(0.128)	(0.183)	(0.124)	(0.142)
Education	−0.0995	0.399**	0.126	0.131
	(0.120)	(0.183)	(0.117)	(0.136)
Black	0.124	0.370	−0.309	−0.794
	(0.403)	(0.544)	(0.403)	(0.536)
Income	−0.0166	−0.103	0.0215	−0.0293
	(0.0596)	(0.0876)	(0.0576)	(0.0670)
Female	−0.107	−0.284	1.202***	0.420
	(0.242)	(0.337)	(0.249)	(0.262)
Age	−0.00244	−0.0205	−0.0174**	0.0237**
	(0.00887)	(0.0137)	(0.00877)	(0.00922)
Female × Conflict orientation	−0.0382	−0.0355	0.0182	−0.0513**
	(0.0234)	(0.0332)	(0.0244)	(0.0260)
Constant	−1.546***	−3.778***	−1.926***	−3.847***
	(0.486)	(0.783)	(0.478)	(0.592)
Observations	533	533	533	533

Source: Mechanical Turk Study 1.

Note: Cell entries are logistic regression coefficients with standard errors in parentheses.

*$p < 0.1$, **$p < 0.05$, ***$p < 0.01$

NOTES

1. INTEGRATING THE POLITICAL AND THE PSYCHOLOGICAL

1. Flaming is an uninhibited (and frequently aggressive) reaction to a real or perceived aggressive comment; trolling, another frequently cited uncivil online behavior, is defined as the use of deception, baiting, or sometimes aggressive behavior to provoke others (Hmielowski, Hutchens, and Cicchirillo 2014).

2. This is not to say that media-effects and political-communication research is ignoring interactive effects; many scholars have investigated the complicated relationship between humans and their media environment. See, for example, Zhu and Boroson (1997); Cacciatore, Scheufele, and Iyengar (2016).

3. This does not have to be the case, however. The *Diane Rehm Show* on NPR, for example, frequently offered many different viewpoints but did so in a civil manner. This example would fall closer to "high school debate" in figure 1.1 than to the top right quadrant.

4. A caveat is necessary here. In their articulation of politeness, Brown and Levinson note that "certain kinds of acts intrinsically threaten face" and are therefore impolite. These acts include the "raising of dangerously emotional or divisive topics, e.g. politics, race, religion, women's liberation" (1987, 65, 67). Under this definition, all political conversation is considered impolite; if the two terms were truly equivalent, all political discussion would be uncivil and there would be no way to manipulate political incivility.

5. A total of 61 percent of participants attributed the decline in civility to both radio and television news. Other media-related causes included blogs (42 percent), Glenn Beck (40 percent), late night talk shows like Stewart and Leno (38 percent), and Rachel Maddow (25 percent). It is worth noting that six of the twelve options were media-related, even if they were selected by the researchers rather than provided by the respondents.

2. THE POLITICAL PSYCHOLOGY OF CONFLICT COMMUNICATION

1. Descriptions of each study are available in appendix A.
2. The full scale shows high reliability, discriminant and convergent validity, and minimal influence of social desirability (Goldstein 1999). To assess each of these scale characteristics, Goldstein asked 350 student participants to complete a 150-item version of the CCS, from which the 75-item scale was ultimately developed. Participants were also randomly assigned to complete either the Marlowe-Crowne Social Desirability Scale, the Conflict Resolution Inventory, the Self-Disclosure Scale, or the Personality Research Form (Crowne and Marlowe 1960; Jackson 1974; Jourard 1979; McFall and Lillesand 1971). The Conflict Resolution Inventory and the Self-Disclosure Scale serve as independent measures of a similar trait for purposes of convergent validity. The Personality Research Form, an assessment of willingness to persevere on difficult tasks, was used as a measure of discriminant validity. Both the CCS subscales and individual items correlated minimally with the Marlowe-Crowne scale, demonstrating minimal social desirability bias. The subscales of the CCS correlated with the Conflict Resolution Inventory, Self-Disclosure Scale, and Personality Research Form in the expected directions, demonstrating convergent and divergent validity. Thirty of the students in the initial sample were also asked to take the 150-item CCS again three and a half weeks after the first administration. Looking just at the 75 items ultimately used in the scale, the five subscales all demonstrated test-retest correlations greater than 0.80, and each correlation was significant at $p<0.001$. Each of the 75 items also showed strong scale reliability, with item variance greater than 1.5 and Cronbach's alphas greater than 0.80 for each subscale.
3. Appendix A offers a full discussion of the scale, including distributions of conflict orientation across all seven studies.

3. TO LAUGH OR CRY? EMOTIONAL RESPONSES TO INCIVILITY

1. I will not outline any of these specific theories here, but see McDermott (2004) for a good explanation of five theories of emotion as they relate specifically to decision-making and have implications for political science.
2. In a pretest, three hundred Mechanical Turk participants were randomly assigned to watch one of six videos—a civil or uncivil clip from *Morning Joe*, *The Dylan Ratigan Show*, or *Hannity*. They were then asked, "To what extent was the clip you just watched uncivil?" They could respond on a scale from 1 to 5, with 1 indicating "not at all uncivil" and 5 representing "extremely uncivil." *Morning Joe* and *The Dylan Ratigan Show* were found to be statistically indistinguishable in both the civil and uncivil conditions. The uncivil clips used to build the treatments in this paper were evaluated as follows: $M_{MorningJoe} = 2.89$, $M_{Ratigan} = 2.98$, $p < 0.69$. Both the civil and uncivil clips from *Hannity*

were seen as more uncivil than their MSNBC counterparts and were therefore excluded from the treatment set.

3. *Morning Joe* has been on MSNBC since 2007. It currently airs from 6 to 9 a.m. EST. *The Dylan Ratigan Show* aired weekdays on MSNBC from 4 to 5 p.m. EST from January 2010 to June 2012. The show focused on debate and discussion related to politics, the economy, and business. I selected *Dylan Ratigan* over better-known MSNBC shows because of his focus on the economy and in a desire to minimize partisan bias in responding to the news clip.

4. Statistical significance calculated from a two-sample, two-tailed t-test.

5. The scale contained four of the five statements used in the first experiment. The fifth, "Arguments don't bother me," was dropped to keep the TESS-funded survey on the shorter side, thereby increasing the number of participants that could be collected. This statement was chosen because it showed the weakest correlation with the other measures in a series of pairwise correlation evaluations.

6. Full regression results are available in appendix B, table B.2.

4. CHOOSING OUTRAGE: SELECTIVE EXPOSURE AND INFORMATION SEARCH

1. The transcripts used in this content analysis were pulled from a LexisNexis search of coverage of the Arizona immigration law (SB 1070) and the congressional debate over health-care reform (specifically, passage of the Affordable Care Act) from March 1 to April 30, 2010. The initial search of television coverage of these two issues resulted in more than two thousand articles, and we randomly sampled from this population to produce a set of 666 program transcripts, 267 on health care and 399 on immigration. Within each of these transcripts, we coded any segment—a section of the program typically beginning with a return from commercial break and ending with the host shifting to a new topic or cutting to commercial again—that dealt directly with immigration or health care. The full coding scheme is available in appendix A. Many thanks to Edward Smith for his assistance with the coding and data collection for this project.

2. $\overline{x_{CNN}} = 1.7$, $\overline{x_{NBC}} = 1.5$, $\overline{x_{ABC}} = 1.2$. In a one-way ANOVA, there was no statistically significant difference between the number of incidents found on MSNBC and Fox or the number of incidents found on NBC and CNN, but there was a difference between MSNBC, Fox, and the other three outlets.

3. Participants were then asked a follow-up question that asked them to list their top three specific programs used for gathering political information. Unfortunately, the range of programs offered makes data analysis difficult; only a dozen programs were reported by enough participants to draw reliable statistical conclusions.

4. This is unsurprising, given that this is a nonprobability sample; these participants are also selecting to participate in online surveys.

5. Full tables of regression results for both the bivariate and multivariate models are presented in appendix B, tables B.3–B.6. I do not report the results of the multivariate models

here beyond the interaction between media consumption and political interest, but there are few statistically significant results to be discussed from those models.

6. Returning to the set of concerns about media-exposure measures, some scholars argue that these frequency measures of media are really measuring political interest instead of capturing any effects the media might have on an individual's political ideas.

7. For simplicity, this regression does not contain controls for the other demographic characteristics. I did not conduct the same analysis on media preferences in the Mechanical Turk 1 study because of concerns about the limitations imposed by sample size that already led many of the relationships to be statistically insignificant.

8. There are also some counterintuitive findings concerning political interest. Participants who are not at all interested in politics and are extremely conflict-approaching use newspapers much more frequently than their conflict-avoidant peers. More investigation needs to be done into why this group is likely to turn to newspapers and if they are looking at the online versions or investing in paper subscriptions.

9. Ideally, the treatments would vary in their level of civility but not in how informative they were seen to be. However, participants found the civil clip to be both more civil and more informative ($\overline{x} = 1.3$, sd $= 0.98$) than the uncivil clip ($\overline{x}_{civil} = 0.76$, sd $= 0.87$, $p < 0.01$; $\overline{x}_{informative} = 0.88$, sd $= 0.97$, $p < 0.01$). Based on these assessments, there is a possibility that participants were responding to how informative they believed the treatment to be, rather than to its level of incivility.

10. All mediation models are available in appendix B.

5. MIMICRY AND TEMPER TANTRUMS: POLITICAL DISCUSSION AND ENGAGEMENT

1. Data for the Project Implicit study were collected in March 2012, and people were asked if they had voted "in the last presidential election." Mechanical Turk Study 1 combines data collected in December 2012 and June 2013; those participants were asked if they had voted "in the 2012 presidential election."

2. Because both sets of studies measure participation in the same way, I present only one set of results here unless there are major differences between studies in the outcomes of interest. The analyses for the Mechanical Turk Study 1 are in appendix B.

3. In addition to this interaction between conflict orientation and political interest, I also explored the effects of conflict orientation across race and gender. The results of these interactions were almost all statistically nonsignificant and, for those that did demonstrate statistical significance, were not robust across samples. The results of these analyses are available in appendix B.

4. Upon reading the content of the comments, it becomes clear that some people typed "comments" that essentially said "no comment" or "I don't have anything to say." These comments are captured in this 63 percent.

5. In July 2015, Planned Parenthood came under fire from abortion opponents after a video was posted online that depicted a doctor from Planned Parenthood having a conversation with two off-camera individuals who were posing as buyers of tissue from aborted fetuses. Activists claimed the video was evidence that the organization was selling fetal tissue, while Planned Parenthood maintained that fetal remains were only donated to scientific research, and only after the consent of the patients (Calmes 2015).

6. A MORE DISRESPECTFUL DEMOCRACY?

1. I ran interactions of conflict orientation and race (described here) as well as gender. None of the interactions of conflict orientation and gender is statistically significant, but the graphical results are displayed in appendix B.
2. This finding does not replicate in the MTurk Study 1 sample. It is highly probable that the samples do not really contain an adequate number of participants who are African American to test the interactive relationship with appropriate statistical power.

APPENDIX 1. ADDITIONAL STUDY INFORMATION

1. TIPI scale scoring ("R" denotes reverse-scored items): Extraversion—1, 6R; Agreeableness—2R, 7; Conscientiousness—3, 8R; Emotional Stability—4R, 9; Openness to Experience—5, 10R.

REFERENCES

Albertson, Bethany, and Shana Kushner Gadarian. 2015. *Anxious Politics: Democratic Citizenship in a Threatening World.* New York: Cambridge University Press.

"Allegheny Survey: 2016 Presidential Campaign Reveals Chilling Trend Lines for Civility in U.S. Politics." 2016. Allegheny College News Center, October 17, 2016. http://sites.allegheny.edu /news/2016/10/17/allegheny-survey-2016-presidential-campaign-reveals-chilling-trend -lines-for-civility-in-u-s-politics/.

Almond, Gabriel and Sidney Verba. 1963. *The Civic Culture: Political Attitudes and Democracy in Five Nations.* Thousand Oaks, CA: Sage.

Anderson, Ashley A., Dominique Brossard, Dietram A. Scheufele, Michael A. Xenos, and Peter Ladwig. 2014. "The 'Nasty Effect': Online Incivility and Risk Perceptions of Emerging Technologies." *Journal of Computer-Mediated Communication* 19(3): 373–387.

Arceneaux, Kevin, and Martin Johnson. 2007. "Channel Surfing: Does Choice Reduce Videomalaise?" Paper presented at the Midwest Political Science Association Annual Meeting, Chicago.

——. 2013. *Changing Minds or Changing Channels?* Chicago: University of Chicago Press.

Arceneaux, Kevin, Martin Johnson, and John Cryderman. 2013. "Communication, Persuasion, and the Conditioning Value of Selective Exposure: Like Minds May Unite and Divide but They Mostly Tune Out." *Political Communication* 30: 213–231.

Arceneaux, Kevin, Martin Johnson, and Chad Murphy. 2012. "Polarized Political Communication, Oppositional Media Hostility, and Selective Exposure." *Journal of Politics* 74(1): 174–186.

Arnold, Magna B. 1960. *Emotion and Personality.* Vol. 1, *Psychological Aspects.* New York: Columbia University Press.

Axelrod, David. Twitter Post. June 24, 2018, 12:09 PM. https://twitter.com/davidaxelrod/status /1010917905586970625?lang=en

Bandura, Albert. 1977. *Social Learning Theory.* Englewood Cliffs, NJ: Prentice-Hall.

——. 2002. "Social Cognitive Theory of Mass Communication." In *Media Effects: Advances in Theory and Research*, 2nd ed., ed. Jennings Bryant and Dolf Zillmann, 121–153. Mahwah, NJ: Erlbaum.

Baron, Rueben M., and David A. Kenny. 1986. "The Moderator-Mediator Variable Distinction in Social Psychological Research: Conceptual, Strategic, and Statistical Considerations." *Journal of Personality and Social Psychology* 51(6): 1173–1182.

Barrett, Lisa Feldman. 2017. "When Is Speech Violence?" *New York Times*, July 14, 2017. https://www.nytimes.com/2017/07/14/opinion/sunday/when-is-speech-violence.html.

Beauchamp, Zack. 2018. "Sarah Sanders and the Failure of 'Civility.' " *Vox* June 25, 2018. https://www.vox.com/policy-and-politics/2018/6/25/17499036/sarah-sanders-red-hen-restaurant-civility.

Bennett, Stephen Earl. 2002. "Predicting Americans' Exposure to Political Talk Radio in 1996, 1998, and 2000." *Harvard International Journal of Press/Politics* 7: 9–22.

Berry, Jeffrey M., and Sarah Sobieraj. 2014. *The Outrage Industry: Political Opinion Media and the New Incivility.* Oxford: Oxford University Press.

Birditt, Kira S., Karen L. Fingerman, and David M. Almeida. 2005. "Age Differences in Exposure and Reactions to Interpersonal Tensions: A Daily Diary Study." *Psychology and Aging* 20(2): 330–340.

Blake, Robert R., and Jane S. Mouton. 1964. *The Managerial Grid.* Houston, TX: Gulf.

Blanchard-Fields, Fredda, and Carolyn Cooper. 2004. "Social Cognition and Social Relationships." In *Growing Together: Personal Relationships Across the Life Span*, ed. Frieder R. Lang and Karen L. Fingerman, 268–289. Cambridge: Cambridge University Press.

Borah, Porismita. 2014. "Does It Matter Where You Read the News Story? Interaction of Incivility and News Frames in the Political Blogosphere." *Communication Research* 41(6): 809–827. https://doi.org/10.1177/0093650212449353.

Brader, Ted. 2005. "Striking a Responsive Chord: How Political Ads Motivate and Persuade Voters by Appealing to Emotions." *American Journal of Political Science* 49(2): 388–405.

Brader, Ted. 2006. *Campaigning for Hearts and Minds: How Emotional Appeals in Political Ads Work.* Chicago: University of Chicago Press.

Brady, Henry E., Sidney Verba, and Kay Lehman Schlozman. 1995. "Beyond SES: A Resource Model of Political Participation." *American Political Science Review* 89(2): 271–294.

Breland, Ali. 2017. "FCC Flooded with Net Neutrality Comments After John Oliver Plea." *The Hill*, May 9, 2017. http://thehill.com/policy/technology/332499-fcc-flooded-with-comments-on-net-neutrality-after-john-oliver-plea.

Bresnahan, Mary Jiang, William A. Donohue, Sachiyo M. Shearman, and Xiaowen Guan. 2009. "Research Note: Two Measures of Conflict Orientation." *Conflict Resolution Quarterly* 26(3): 365–379. https://doi.org/10.1002/crq.238.

Brooks, Deborah Jordan, and John G. Geer. 2007. "Beyond Negativity: The Effects of Incivility on the Electorate." *American Journal of Political Science* 51(1): 1–16. https://doi.org/10.1111/j.1540-5907.2007.00233.x.

Brown, Penelope, and Stephen C. Levinson. 1987. *Politeness: Some Universals in Language Usage.* Cambridge: Cambridge University Press.

Bump, Philip. 2018. "The Irony of Washignton's 'Civility' Debate: Trump Already Proved that Incivility Works." *Washington Post*, June 25, 2018. http://washingtonpost.com/news/politics /wp/2018/06/25/the-irony-of-d-c-s-civility-debate-trump-already-proved-that-incivility -works/.

Burnham, Walter Dean. 1970. *Critical Elections and the Mainsprings of American Politics*. New York: Norton.

Cacciatore, Michael A., Dietram A. Scheufele, and Shanto Iyengar. 2016. "The End of Framing As We Know It . . . and the Future of Media Effects." *Mass Communication and Society* 19(1): 7–23.

Cacioppo, John T., Joseph R. Priester, and Gary G. Berntson. 1993. "Rudimentary Determinants of Attitudes. II: Arm Flexion and Extension Have Differential Effects on Attitudes." *Journal of Personality and Social Psychology* 65(1): 5–17.

Calmes, Jackie. 2015. "Video Accuses Planned Parenthood of Crime." *New York Times* July 15, 2015. https://www.nytimes.com/2015/07/15/us/video-accuses-planned-parenthood-of-crime.html.

Campbell, Angus, Philip E. Converse, Warren E. Miller, and Donald E. Stokes. 1980. *The American Voter*. Abridged edition. Chicago: University of Chicago Press.

Cantril, Hadley. 1942. "Professor Quiz: A Gratifications Study." In *Radio Research 1941*, ed. Paul F. Lazarsfeld and Frank N. Stanton, 34–45. New York: Duell, Sloan and Pearce.

Carstensen, Laura L., Derek M. Isaacowitz, and Susan Turk Charles. 1999. "Taking Time Seriously: A Theory of Socioemotional Selectivity." *American Psychologist* 54(3): 165–181. https://doi.org/10.1037/0003-066X.54.3.165.

Carter, Stephen L. 1998. *Civility: Manners, Morals and the Etiquette of Democracy*. New York: Basic Books.

Carver, Charles S. 2004. "Negative Affects Deriving from the Behavioral Approach System." *Emotion* 4: 3–22.

Carver, Charles S., and Michael R. Scheier. 1990. "Origins and Functions of Positive and Negative Affect: A Control-Process View." *Psychological Review* 97(1): 19–35. https://doi.org /10.1037/0033-295X.97.1.19.

Cassino, Dan, and Milton Lodge. 2007. "The Primacy of Affect in Political Evaluations." In *The Affect Effect: Dynamics of Emotion in Political Thinking and Behavior*, ed. W. Russell Neuman, George E. Marcus, Ann N. Crigler, and Michael MacKuen, 101–123. Chicago: University of Chicago Press.

Chafe, William H. 1980. *Civilities and Civil Rights: Greensboro, North Carolina, and the Black Struggle for Freedom*. New York: Oxford University Press.

Chen, Gina. 2017. *Nasty Talk: Online Incivility and Public Debate*. New York: Palgrave Macmillan.

Chen, Gina Masullo, Paromita Pain, Victora Y. Chen, Madlin Mekelburg, Nina Springer, and Franziska Troger. 2018. "'You Really Have to Have a Thick Skin': A Cross-Cultural Perspective on How Online Harassment Influences Female Journalists." *Journalism*, online April 7, 2018. https://doi.org/10.1177/1464884918768500.

Clayton, Cornell W. 2012. "Op-Ed: Incivility Crisis of Politics Is Just a Symptom of Division." *Seattle Times*, October 27, 2012. http://seattletimes.com/html/opinion/2019534569_cornell-claytonopedxml.html.

Coe, Kevin, Kate Kenski, and Stephen A. Rains. 2014. "Online and Uncivil? Patterns and Determinants of Incivility in Newspaper Website Comments." *Journal of Communication* 64(4): 658–679. https://doi.org/10.1111/jcom.12104.

Conover, Pamela Johnston, Donald D. Searing, and Ivor M. Crewe. 2002. "The Deliberative Potential of Political Discussion." *British Journal of Political Science* 32(1): 21–62. https://doi.org /10.1017/S0007123402000029.

Converse, Philip E. 1964. "The Nature and Origins of Belief Systems in Mass Publics." In *Ideology and Discontent*, ed. David E. Apter. New York: Free Press.

Crowne, Douglas P., and David Marlowe. 1960. "A New Scale of Social Desirability Independent of Psychopathy." *Journal of Consulting Psychology* 24(4): 349–359.

Culpeper, Jonathan. 2011. *Impoliteness: Using Language to Cause Offence*. New York: Cambridge University Press.

Dahl, Robert A. 1967. *Pluralist Democracy in the United States*. Chicago: Rand McNally.

Delli Carpini, Michael X. and Scott Keeter. 1996. *What Americans Know About Politics and Why It Matters*. New Haven, CT: Yale University Press.

Deutsch, Morton. 1985. *Distributive Justice: A Social-Psychological Perspective*. New Haven, CT: Yale University Press.

Dilliplane, Susanna, Seth K. Goldman, and Diana C. Mutz. 2013. "Televised Exposure to Politics: New Measures for a Fragmented Media Environment." *American Journal of Political Science* 57(1): 236–248. https://doi.org/10.1111/j.1540-5907.2012.00600.x.

Disbrow, Lynn M. and Caorlyn M. Prentice. 2009. "Perceptions of Civility." *American Communication Journal* 11(3): 1–14.

Downs, Anthony. 1957. *An Economic Theory of Democracy*. New York: Harper.

Druckman, James N., Donald P. Green, James H. Kuklinski, and Arthur Lupia. 2011. "Experiments: An Introduction to Core Concepts." In *Cambridge Handbook of Experimental Political Science*, ed. James N. Druckman, Donald P. Green, James H. Kuklinski, and Arthur Lupia, 15–26. Cambridge: Cambridge University Press.

Druckman, James N., S. R. Gubitz, Matthew S. Levandusky, and Ashley M. Lloyd. 2019. "How Incivility on Partisan Media (De)Polarizes the Electorate," *Journal of Politics* 81(1): 291–295.

Druckman, James N., and Cindy D. Kam. 2011. "Students as Experimental Participants." In *Cambridge Handbook of Experimental Political Science*, ed James N. Druckman, Donald P. Green, James H. Kukliinski, and Arthur Lupia, 41–57. Cambridge: Cambridge University Press.

Druckman, James N., and Rose McDermott. 2008. "Emotion and the Framing of Risky Choice." *Political Behavior* 30(3): 297–321.

Duggan, Maeve, and Aaron Smith. 2016. "The Political Environment on Social Media." Pew Research Center, October 25, 2016. http://www.pewinternet.org/2016/10/25/the-political -environment-on-social-media/.

Editorial Board. 2018. "Let the Trump Team Eat in Peace" *Washington Post* June 24, 2018. https://www .washingtonpost.com/opinions/let-the-trump-team-eat-in-peace/2018/06/24/46882e16 -779a-11e8-80be-6d32e182a3bc_story.html?utm_term=.9aa81741e879.

Eliasoph, Nina. 1998. *Avoiding Politics: How Americans Produce Apathy in Everyday Life.* Cambridge: Cambridge University Press.

Elliot, Andrew J. 2006. "The Hierarchical Model of Approach-Avoidance Motivation." *Motivation and Emotion* 30(2): 111–116. https://doi.org/10.1007/s11031-006-9028-7.

Elliot, Andrew J., Andreas B. Eder, and Eddie Harmon-Jones. 2013. "Approach-Avoidance Motivation and Emotion: Convergence and Divergence." *Emotion Review* 5: 308–311.

Emery, Michael C., Edwin Emery, and Nancy L. Roberts. 2000. *The Press and America: An Interpretive History of the Mass Media.* New York: Pearson.

Enelow, James M., and Melvin J. Hinich. 1984. *The Spatial Theory of Voting: An Introduction.* New York: Cambridge University Press.

Federal Communications Commission. 1949. *Editorializing by Broadcast Licensees* (Report No. 8516). June 8, 1949. https://www.fcc.gov/document/editorializing-broadcast-licensees.

Feinberg, Joel. 1988. *The Moral Limits of the Criminal Law.* Vol. 2, *Offense to Others.* New York: Oxford University Press.

Feldman, Stanley, and Leonie Huddy. 2005. "Racial Resentment and White Opposition to Race-Conscious Programs: Principles or Prejudice?" *American Journal of Political Science* 49(1): 168–183. https://doi.org/10.1111/j.0092-5853.2005.00117.x.

Ferree, Myra Marx, William A. Gamson, Jurgen Gerhards, and Dieter Rucht. 2002. "Four Models of the Public Sphere in Modern Democracies." *Theory and Society* 31: 289–324.

Forgette, Richard and Jonathan S. Morris. 2006. "High-Conflict Television News and Public Opinion." *Political Research Quarterly* 59(3): 447–456.

Fowler, James. 2006. "Altruism and Turnout." *Journal of Politics* 68(3): 674–683.

Fredrickson, Barbara L. 2002. "Positive Emotions." In *Handbook of Positive Psychology,* ed. C. R. Snyder and Shane J. Lopez, 120–134. New York: Oxford University Press.

Frijda, Nico H. 1986. *The Emotions.* New York: Cambridge University Press.

Gastil, John. 2008. *Political Communication and Deliberation.* Thousand Oaks, CA: Sage.

Geer, John G. 2012. "The News Media and the Rise of Negativity in Presidential Campaigns." *PS: Political Science and Politics* 45(3): 422–427.

Geer, John, and Richard R. Lau. 2006. "Filling in the Blanks: A New Method for Estimating Campaign Effects." *British Journal of Political Science* 36(2): 269–290.

Gerber, Alan S., Gregory A. Huber, David Doherty, and Conor M. Dowling. 2012. "Disagreement and the Avoidance of Political Discussion: Aggregate Relationships and Differences Across Personality Traits." *American Journal of Political Science* 56(4): 849–874.

Gerber, Alan S., Gregory A. Huber, David Doherty, Conor M. Dowling, and Shang E. Ha. 2010. "Personality and Political Attitudes: Relationships Across Issue Domains and Political Contexts." *American Political Science Review* 104(1): 111–133.

Gervais, Bryan T. 2011. "The Effects of Incivility in News Media on Political Deliberation: The Mimicry of Uncivil Language in Political Opinions." Paper presented at the Midwest Political Science Association, Chicago.

——. 2014. "Following the News? Reception of Uncivil Partisan Media and the Use of Incivility in Political Expression." *Political Communication* 31(4): 564–583.

———. 2015. "Incivility Online: Affective and Behavioral Reactions to Uncivil Political Posts in a Web-Based Experiment." *Journal of Information Technology & Politics* 12(2): 167–185.

Goldstein, Susan. 1999. "Construction and Validation of a Conflict Communication Scale." *Journal of Applied Social Psychology* 29(9): 1803–1832.

Gosling, Samuel D., Peter J. Rentfrow, and William B. Swann, Jr. 2003. "A Very Brief Measure of the Big Five Personality Domains." *Journal of Research in Personality* 37: 504–528.

Graber, Doris A. 2001. *Processing Politics: Learning from Television in the Internet Age.* Chicago: University of Chicago Press.

Graziano, William G., Lauri A. Jensen-Campbell, and Elizabeth C. Hair. 1996. "Perceiving Interpersonal Conflict and Reacting to It: The Case for Agreeableness." *Journal of Personality and Social Psychology* 70(4): 820–835.

Grim, Ryan. 2009. "Joe Wilson Apologizes for Shouting 'You Lie!' at Obama." *Huffington Post,* November 9, 2009. http://www.huffingtonpost.com/2009/09/09/joe-wilson-apologizes-for _n_281541.html.

Grinberg, Emannuella. 2011. "Etiquette 101: Talking Politics Over Thanksgiving Dinner." *CNN,* November 22, 2011. http://www.cnn.com/2011/11/22/living/thanksgiving-political-etiquette /index.html.

Gross, Kimberly. 2008. "Framing Persuasive Appeals: Episodic and Thematic Framing, Emotional Response, and Policy Opinion." *Political Psychology* 29(2): 169–192.

Gudykunst, William B., and Stella Ting-Toomey. 1988. *Culture and Interpersonal Communication.* Newbury Park, CA: Sage.

Gutmann, Amy, and Dennis F. Thompson. 1996. *Democracy and Disagreement.* Cambridge, MA: Harvard University Press.

Hamilton, Alexander. 1800. "Letter from Alexander Hamilton, Concerning the Public Conduct and Character of John Adams, Esq. President of the United States" October 24, 1800. Founders Online. https://founders.archives.gov/documents/Hamilton/01-25-02-0110-0002.

Han, Soo-Hye, and LeAnn M. Brazeal. 2015. "Playing Nice: Modeling Civility in Online Political Discussions." *Communication Research Reports* 32(1): 20–28. https://doi.org/10.1080 /08824096.2014.989971.

Harmon-Jones, Eddie. 2003. "Anger and the Behavioral Approach System." *Personality and Individual Differences* 35(5): 995–1005.

Harmon-Jones, Eddie, Cindy Harmon-Jones, and Tom F. Price. 2013. "What Is Approach Motivation?" *Emotion Review* 5(3): 291–295.

Hayes, Andrew F., Dietram A. Scheufele, and Michael E. Huge. 2006. "Nonparticipation as Self-Censorship: Publicly Observable Political Activity in a Polarized Opinion Climate." *Political Behavior* 28(3): 259–283. https://doi.org/10.1007/s11109-006-9008-3.

Herbst, Susan. 2010. *Rude Democracy: Civility and Incivility in American Politics.* Philadelphia: Temple University Press.

Hetherington, Marc J., and Jonathan D. Weiler. 2009. *Authoritarianism and Polarization in American Politics.* New York: Cambridge University Press.

Himelboim, Itai, Stephen McCreery, and Marc Smith. 2013. "Birds of a Feather Tweet Together: Integrating Network and Content Analyses to Examine Cross-Ideology Exposure on

Twitter." *Journal of Computer-Mediated Communication* 18(2): 40–60. https://doi.org/10.1111/jcc4.12001.

Hmielowski, Jay D., Myiah J. Hutchens, and Vincent J. Cicchirillo. 2014. "Living in an Age of Online Incivility: Examining the Conditional Indirect Effects of Online Discussion on Political Flaming." *Information, Communication & Society* 17(10): 1196–1211.

"Holder and Cunningham Blow Up: 'Farrah Fawcett Wannabe!' 'Get Your Finger Out of My Face!'" 2013. *Fox News*, September 19, 2013. https://www.youtube.com/watch?v=uYgIYb9w_bc.

Horberg, Elizabeth J., Christopher Oveis, Dacher Keltner, and Adam B. Cohen. 2009. "Disgust and the Moralization of Purity." *Journal of Personality and Social Psychology* 97(6): 963–976.

Hsu, Hua. 2014. "The Civility Wars." *The New Yorker*, December 1, 2014. https://www.newyorker.com/culture/cultural-comment/civility-wars.

Huckfeldt, Robert R., and John Sprague. 1995. *Citizens, Politics and Social Communication: Information and Influence in an Election Campaign*. Cambridge: Cambridge University Press.

Huddy, Leonie, Stanley Feldman, and Erin Cassese. 2007. "On the Distinct Political Effects of Anxiety and Anger." In *The Affect Effect: Dynamics of Emotion in Political Thinking and Behavior*, ed. W. Russell Neuman, George E. Marcus, Ann N. Crigler, and Michael MacKuen, 202–230. Chicago: University of Chicago Press.

Hwang, Hyunseo, Youngju Kim, and Catherine U. Huh. 2014. "Seeing Is Believing: Effects of Uncivil Online Debate on Political Polarization and Expectations of Deliberation." *Journal of Broadcasting & Electronic Media* 58(4): 621–633.

Iyengar, Shanto, and Kyu S. Hahn. 2009. "Red Media, Blue Media: Evidence of Ideological Selectivity in Media Use. *Journal of Communication* 59(1): 19–39. https://doi.org/10.1111/j.1460-2466.2008.01402.x.

Jacobson, Gary C. 2013. "Presidents, Partisans and Polarized Politics." In *Can We Talk? The Rise of Rude, Nasty, Stubborn Politics*, ed. Daniel M. Shea and Morris P. Fiorina, 99–120. Upper Saddle River, NJ: Pearson.

Jackson, Douglas N. 1974. *Personality Research Form*. Port Huron, MI: Research Psychologists Press.

James, William. 1884. What Is an Emotion? *Mind* 9(34): 188–205.

Jamieson, Kathleen Hall, and Joseph N. Cappella. 2008. *Echo Chamber*. New York: Oxford University Press.

Jamieson, Kathleen Hall, and Bruce W. Hardy. 2012. "What Is Civil Engaged Argument and Why Does Aspiring to It Matter?" *PS: Political Science and Politics* 45(3): 412–415.

Jankowski, Richard. 2015. *Altruism and Self-Interest in Democracies: Individual Participation in Government*. New York: Palgrave Macmillan.

Jasper, James M. 1998. "The Emotions of Protest: Affective and Reactive Emotions In and Around Social Movements." *Sociological Forum* 13(3): 397–424.

"Joe vs Howard Pasta Challenge." 2013. *Masterchef US*. https://www.youtube.com/watch?v=AE72JczodEo.

Jost, John T., Jack Glaser, Arie W. Kruglanski, and Frank J. Sulloway. 2003. "Political Conservatism as Motivated Social Cognition." *Psychological Bulletin* 129(3): 339–375. https://doi.org/10.1037/0033-2909.129.3.339.

Jourard, Sidney. 1979. *Self-Disclosure: An Experimental Analysis of the Transparent Self.* Huntington, NY: Robert E. Krieger.

Kahn, Kim Fridkin, and Patrick J. Kenney. 1999. "Do Negative Campaigns Mobilize or Suppress Turnout? Clarifying the Relationship Between Negativity and Participation." *American Political Science Review* 93(4): 877. https://doi.org/10.2307/2586118.

Kalmoe, Nathan P. 2014. "Fueling the Fire: Violent Metaphors, Trait Aggression, and Support for Political Violence." *Political Communication* 31(4): 545–563.

Karl, Jonathan, and Gregory Simmons. 2010. "Uncivil War: Death of Decorum in Washington?" *ABC News*, August 12, 2010. http://abcnews.go.com/Politics/death-decorum-washington /story?id=11376406.

Katz, Elihu, Michael Gurevitch, and Hadassah Haas. 1973. "On the Use of Mass Media for Important Things." *American Sociological Review* 38: 164–181.

Key, V. O. 1955. "A Theory of Critical Elections." *Journal of Politics* 17(1): 3–18.

Kiesler, Sara, Jane Siegel and Timothy W. McGuire. 1984. "Social Psychological Aspects of Computer-Mediated Communication. *American Psychologist* 39(10): 1123–1134.

Kilmann, Ralph H., and Kenneth W. Thomas. 1977. "Developing a Forced-Choice Measure of Conflict-Handling Behavior: The 'MODE' Instrument." *Educational and Psychological Measurement* 37: 309–325.

Kim, Yonghwan, Shih-Hsien Hsu, and Homero Gil de Zúñiga. 2013. "Influence of Social Media Use on Discussion Network Heterogeneity and Civic Engagement: The Moderating Role of Personality Traits." *Journal of Communication* 63(3): 498–516. https://doi.org/10.1111/jcom.12034.

Kinder, Donald R., and Lynn M. Sanders. 1996. *Divided by Color.* Chicago: University of Chicago Press.

Knobloch, Silvia. 2003. "Mood Adjustment Via Mass Communication." *Journal of Communication* 53(2): 233–250. https://doi.org/10.1111/j.1460-2466.2003.tb02588.x.

Knobloch-Westerwick, Silvia. 2006. "Mood Management Theory, Evidence and Advancements." In *Psychology of Entertainment*, ed. Jennings Bryant and Peter Vorderer, 239–254. New York: Erlbaum.

Ladd, Jonathan M. 2011. *Why Americans Hate the Media and How It Matters.* Princeton, NJ: Princeton University Press.

Lasswell, Harold. 1936. *Politics: Who Gets What, When, and How.* New York: McGraw-Hill.

Lau, Richard R., and David P. Redlawsk. 2006. *How Voters Decide: Information Processing During Election Campaigns.* Cambridge: Cambridge University Press.

Lazarus, Richard S. 1994. *Emotion and Adaptation.* Reprint edition. New York: Oxford University Press.

Lee, Jasmine C., and Kevin Quealy. 2019. "The 567 People, Places and Things Donald Trump Has Insulted on Twitter: A Complete List." *New York Times*, February 20, 2019. https://www .nytimes.com/interactive/2016/01/28/upshot/donald-trump-twitter-insults.html.

Leong, Frederick T. L., Nicole S. Wagner, and Shiraz Piroshaw Tata. 1995. "Racial and Ethnic Variations in Help-Seeking Attitudes." In *Handbook of Multicultural Counseling*, ed. Joseph G. Ponterotto, J. Manuel Casas, Lisa A. Suzuki, and Charlene M. Alexander, 415–438. Thousand Oaks, CA: Sage.

Lepper, Mark R. 1994. " 'Hot' Versus 'Cold' Cognition: An Abelsonian Voyage. In *Beliefs, Reasoning, and Decision Making: Psychol-logic in Honor of Bob Abelson*, ed. Roger C. Schank and Ellen Langer, 237–275. Hillsdale, NJ: Lawrence Erlbaum.

Lerner, Jennifer S., and Larissa Z. Tiedens. 2006. "Portrait of the Angry Decision Maker: How Appraisal Tendencies Shape Anger's Influence on Cognition." *Journal of Behavioral Decision Making* 19(2): 115–137. https://doi.org/10.1002/bdm.515.

Lewin, Kurt. 1935. *A Dynamic Theory of Personality*. New York: McGraw-Hill.

Lupia, Arthur. 1994. "Shortcuts Versus Encyclopedias: Information and Voting Behavior in California Insurance Reform Elections." *American Political Science Review* 88(1): 63–76. https://doi.org/10.2307/2944882.

Lupia, Arthur and Mathew D. McCubbins. 1998. *The Democratic Dilemma: Can Citizens Learn What They Need to Know?* Cambridge: Cambridge University Press.

MacKuen, Michael, George E. Marcus, W. Russell Neuman, and Luke Keele. 2007. "The Third Way: The Theory of Affective Intelligence and American Democracy." In *The Affect Effect: Dynamics of Emotion in Political Thinking and Behavior*, ed. W. Russell Neuman, George E. Marcus, Ann N. Crigler, and Michael MacKuen, 124–151. Chicago: University of Chicago Press.

Maisel, L. Sandy. 2012. "The Negative Consequences of Uncivil Political Discourse." *PS: Political Science and Politics* 45(3): 405–411.

Marcus, George E., W. Russell Neuman, and Michael MacKuen. 2000. *Affective Intelligence and Political Judgment*. Chicago: University of Chicago Press.

Matthews, Dylan. 2011. "Everything You Need to Know About the Fairness Doctrine in One Post." *Washington Post*, August 23, 2011. http://www.washingtonpost.com/blogs/wonkblog /post/everything-you-need-to-know-about-the-fairness-doctrine-in-one-post/2011/08/23 /gIQAN8CXZJ_blog.html.

McAfee, Tierney. 2017. "Mika Brzezinski Reveals True Story Behind President Trump's 'Face-Lift' Tweet: He Begged for the Name of My Doctor." *People*, June 30, 2017. http://people .com/politics/mika-brzezinski-president-trump-face-lift-tweet-doctor/.

McCrae, Robert R., and Paul T. Costa, Jr. 2008. "The Five-Factor Theory of Personality." In *Handbook of Personality: Theory and Research*, 3rd ed., ed. Oliver P. John, Richard W. Robins, and Lawrence A. Pervin, 159–180. New York: Guilford Press.

McDermott, Rose. 2004. "The Feeling of Rationality: The Meaning of Neuroscientific Advances for Political Science." *Perspectives on Politics* 2(4): 691–706.

McDonald, Soraya Nadia. 2014. "John Oliver's Net Neutrality Rant May Have Caused FCC Site Crash." *Washington Post*, June 4, 2014. https://www.washingtonpost.com/news /morning-mix/wp/2014/06/04/john-olivers-net-neutrality-rant-may-have-caused-fcc-site -crash/?utm_term=.30df95479e51.

McFall, Richard M., and Diane B. Lillesand. 1971. "Behavioral Rehearsal with Modeling and Coaching in Assertion Training." *Journal of Abnormal Psychology* 77: 313–323.

Mill, John Stuart. (1859) 1989. *"On Liberty" and Other Writings*. ed. Stefan Collini. Cambridge: Cambridge University Press.

Milbrath, Lester W. 1965. *Political Participation: How and Why Do People Get Involved in Politics?* Chicago: Rand McNally.

Minich, Anthony Lee, Albee Therese O. Mendoza, and Emily Cheshire Brown. 2018. "Effect of Incivility on Attitudes and Information Seeking." *North American Journal of Psychology* 20(1): 195–210.

Mondak, Jeffery J. 2010. *Personality and the Foundations of Political Behavior.* New York: Cambridge University Press.

Mondak, Jeffery J., and Karen D. Halperin. 2008. A Framework for the Study of Personality and Political Behaviour. *British Journal of Political Science* 38(2): 335–362. https://doi.org/10.1017 /S0007123408000173.

Mondak, Jeffery J., Matthew V. Hibbing, Damarys Canache, Mitchell A. Seligson, and Mary R. Anderson. 2010. "Personality and Civic Engagement: An Integrative Framework for the Study of Trait Effects on Political Behavior." *American Political Science Review* 104(1): 85–110.

Muddiman, Ashley, and Natalie Jomini Stroud. 2016. *10 Things We Learned by Analyzing 9 Million Comments from the New York Times.* University of Texas at Austin, Center for Media Engagement. https://mediaengagement.org/research/10-things-we-learned-by-analyzing -9-million-comments-from-the-new-york-times/.

Mutz, Diana C. 2006. *Hearing the Other Side.* Cambridge: Cambridge University Press.

——. 2007. "Effects of 'In-Your-Face' Television Discourse on Perceptions of a Legitimate Opposition." *American Political Science Review,* 101(4): 621–645.

——. 2015. *In-Your-Face Politics: The Consequences of Uncivil Media.* Princeton, NJ: Princeton University Press.

Mutz, Diana C., and Paul S. Martin. 2001. "Facilitating Communication Across Lines of Political Difference: The Role of Mass Media." *American Political Science Review* 95(1): 97–114.

Mutz, Diana C., and Byron Reeves. 2005. "The New Videomalaise: Effects of Televised Incivility on Political Trust." *American Political Science Review* 99(1): 1–15.

Neuberg, Steven L., Douglas T. Kenrick, and Mark Schaller. 2011. "Human Threat Management Systems: Self-Protection and Disease Avoidance." *Neuroscience & Biobehavioral Reviews* 35(4): 1042–1051. https://doi.org/10.1016/j.neubiorev.2010.08.011.

Ng, Elaine W. J., and Benjamin H. Detenber. 2006. "The Impact of Synchronicity and Civility in Online Political Discussions on Perceptions and Intentions to Participate." *Journal of Computer-Mediated Communication* 10(3). http://onlinelibrary.wiley.com/doi/10.1111 /j.1083-6101.2005.tb00252.x/full.

O'Connor, Roisin. 2017. "Ed Sheeran Quits Twitter Over Comments That 'Ruin His Day.' " *Independent,* July 4, 2017. http://www.independent.co.uk/arts-entertainment/music/news /ed-sheeran-quits-twitter-trolls-comments-instagram-glastonbury-loop-pedal-performance -watch-a7822201.html.

Oz, Mustafa, Pei Zheng, and Gina Masullo Chen. 2017. "Twitter Versus Facebook: Comparing Incivility, Impoliteness, and Deliberative Attributes. *New Media & Society* 20(9): 3400–3419.

Page, Benjamin I., and Robert Y. Shapiro. 1992. *The Rational Public: Fifty Years of Trends in Americans' Policy Preferences.* Chicago: University of Chicago Press.

Papacharissi, Zizi. 2004. "Democracy Online: Civility, Politeness, and the Democratic Potential of Online Political Discussion Groups." *New Media and Society* 6(2): 259–283.

Papacharissi, Zizi. 2007. "An Exploratory Study of Reality Appeal: Uses and Gratifications of Reality TV Shows." *Journal of Broadcasting and Electronic Media* 51(2): 355–370.

Parsons, Bryan M. 2010. "Social Networks and the Affective Impact of Political Disagreement." *Political Behavior* 32: 181–204.

Patterson, Thomas E. 2011. *Out of Order.* New York: Vintage.

Phillips, Tim, and Philip Smith. 2004. "Emotional and Behavioral Responses to Everyday Incivility: Challenging the Fear/Avoidance Paradigm." *Journal of Sociology* 40: 378–399.

Pizarro, David, Yoel Inbar, and Chelsea Helion. 2011. "On Disgust and Moral Judgment." *Emotion Review* 3(3): 267–268.

Press, Andrea L., and Elizabeth R. Cole. 1999. *Speaking of Abortion: Television and Authority in the Lives of Women.* Chicago: University of Chicago Press.

Price, Vincent. 1993. "The Impact of Varying Reference Periods in Survey Questions About Media Use." *Journalism & Mass Communication Quarterly* 70(3): 615–627. https://doi.org /10.1177/107769909307000312.

Price, Vincent, Lilach Nir, and Joseph N. Cappella. 2006. "Normative and Informational Influences in Online Political Discussions." *Communication Theory* 16(1): 47–74.

Prior, Markus. 2007. *Post-Broadcast Democracy: How Media Choice Increases Inequality in Political Involvement and Polarizes Elections.* Cambridge: Cambridge University Press.

Proctor, Ben H. 2007. *William Randolph Hearst: The Later Years, 1911–1951.* Oxford: Oxford University Press.

Reeves, Byron, and Clifford Nass. 1996. *The Media Equation: How People Treat Computers, Television, and New Media Like Real People and Places.* Stanford, CA: CSLI Publications.

Roseman, Ira J. 1984. "Cognitive Determinants of Emotion: A Structural Theory." *Review of Personality & Social Psychology* 5: 11–36. http://doi.apa.org/psycinfo/1986-17263-001.

——. 2008. "Motivations and Emotivations: Approach, Avoidance and Other Tendencies in Motivated and Emotional Behavior." In the *Handbook of Approach and Avoidance Motivation*, ed. Andrew J. Elliot, 343–366. New York: Psychology Press.

Rosenstone, Steven J., and John Mark Hansen. 2002. *Mobilization, Participation, and Democracy in America.* New York: Longman.

Rozin, Paul, Jonathan Haidt, and Clark R. McCauley. 2008. "Disgust." In *Handbook of Emotions*, 3rd ed., ed. Michael Lewis, Jeannette M. Haviland-Jones, and Lisa Feldman Barrett, 757–776. New York: Guilford Press.

Rubin, Alan M. 1994. "Media Uses and Effects: A Uses and Gratifications Perspective." In *Media Effects: Advances in Theory and Research*, ed. Jennings Bryant and Dolf Zillman, 417–436. Hillsdale, NJ: Lawrence Erlbaum.

Ruggiero, Thomas E. 2000. "Uses and Gratifications Theory in the 21st Century." *Mass Communication and Society* 3(1):3–37.

Russell, Pascale Sophie, and Roger Giner-Sorolla. 2011. "Moral Anger, but Not Moral Disgust, Responds to Intentionality." *Emotion* 11(2): 233–240. https://doi.org/10.1037/a0022598.

Santana, Arthur D. 2014. "Virtuous or Vitriolic: The Effects of Anonymity on Civility in Online Newspaper Reader Comment Boards." *Journalism Practice* 8(1): 18–33. https://doi .org/10.1080/17512786.2013.813194.

Scherer, Klaus R. 1999. "Appraisal Theory." In *Handbook of Cognition and Emotion*, ed. Tim Dalgleish and Mick J. Power, 637–663. Chichester, UK: Wiley.

Schlozman, Kay Lerman, Nancy Burns, and Sidney Verba. 1999. " 'What Happened at Work Today?': A Multistage Model of Gender, Employment, and Political Participation." *Journal of Politics* 61(1): 29–53. https://doi.org/10.2307/2647774.

Schlozman, Kay Lerman, Sidney Verba, and Henry E. Brady. 2012. *The Unheavenly Chorus: Unequal Political Voice and the Broken Promise of American Democracy*. Princeton, NJ: Princeton University Press.

Schudson, Michael. 1981. *Discovering the News: A Social History of American Newspapers*. New York: Basic Books.

Schwarz, Norman, and Daphna Oyserman. 2001. "Asking Questions About Behavior: Cognition, Communication, and Questionnaire Construction." *American Journal of Evaluation* 22(2): 127–160. https://doi.org/10.1177/109821400102200202.

Seligman, D. (1960). "The New Masses." In *America in the Sixties: The Economy and the Society*, ed. Editors of *Fortune*, 118. New York: Harper Torchbooks.

Selk, Avi, and Sarah Murray. 2018. "The Owner of the Red Hen Explains Why She Asked Sarah Huckabee Sanders to Leave." *Washington Post*, June 25, 2018. https://www.washingtonpost.com/news/local/wp/2018/06/23/why-a-small-town-restaurant-owner-asked-sarah-huckabee-sanders-to-leave-and-would-do-it-again/.

Selyukh, Alina. 2016. "Postelection, Overwhelmed Facebook Users Unfriend, Cut Back." *NPR*, November 20, 2016. http://www.npr.org/sections/alltechconsidered/2016/11/20/502567858/post-election-overwhelmed-facebook-users-unfriend-cut-back.

Shea, Daniel M. 2013. "Our Tribal Nature and the Rise of Nasty Politics." In *Can We Talk? The Rise of Rude, Nasty, Stubborn Politics*, ed. Daniel M. Shea and Morris P. Fiorina, 82–98. Upper Saddle River, NJ: Pearson.

Shea, Daniel M., and Alex Sproveri. 2012. "The Rise and Fall of Nasty Politics in America." *PS: Political Science and Politics* 45(3): 416–421.

Shea, Daniel M., and Barbara Steadman. 2010. *Nastiness, Name-Calling and Negativity: The Allegheny College Survey of Civility and Compromise in American Politics*. Allegheny, PA: Allegheny College. Retrieved from https://sitesmedia.s3.amazonaws.com/civility/files/2010/04/AlleghenyCollegeCivilityReport2010.pdf.

Shearer, Elisa, and Jeffrey Gottfried. 2017. "News Use Across Social Media Platforms 2017." Pew Research Center, September 7, 2017. http://www.journalism.org/2017/09/07/news-use-across-social-media-platforms-2017/.

Sherman, David K., Traci Mann, and John A. Updegraff. 2006. "Approach/Avoidance Motivation, Message Framing, and Health Behavior: Understanding the Congruency Effect." *Motivation and Emotion* 30(2): 165–169.

Sobeiraj, Sarah, and Jeffrey M. Berry. 2011. "From Incivility to Outrage: Political Discourse in Blogs, Talk Radio, and Cable News." *Political Communication* 28(1): 19–41.

Spencer, Steven J., Mark P. Zanna, and Geoffrey T. Fong. 2005. "Establishing a Causal Chain: Why Experiments are Often More Effective than Mediational Analyses in Examining Psychological Phenomena. *Journal of Personality and Social Psychology* 89(6): 845–851.

Stanton, Brandon. 2018. "About." *Humans of New York.* https://www.humansofnewyork.com /about.

Stenner, Karen. 2005. *The Authoritarian Dynamic.* Cambridge: Cambridge University Press.

Stroud, Natalie Jomini. 2011. *Niche News: The Politics of News Choice.* Oxford: Oxford University Press.

Stroud, Natalie Jomini, Joshua M. Scacco, Ashley Muddiman, and Alexander L. Curry. 2015. "Changing Deliberative Norms on News Organizations' Facebook Sites." *Journal of Computer-Mediated Communication* 20(2): 188–203. https://doi.org/10.1111/jcc4.12104.

Suler, John. 2004. "The Online Disinhibition Effect." *CyberPsychology & Behavior* 7(3): 321–326. https://doi.org/10.1089/1094931041291295.

Sundquist, James L. 1983. *Dynamics of the Party System: Alignment and Realignment of Political Parties in the United States.* Washington, DC: Brookings Institution Press.

Sunstein, Cass R. 2009. *Going to Extremes: How Like Minds Unite and Divide.* Oxford: Oxford University Press.

Sydnor, Emily. 2018. "Platforms for Incivility: Examining Perceptions Across Media." *Political Communication* 35(1): 97–116. https://doi.org/10.1080/10584609.2017.1355857.

——. 2019. "Signaling Incivility: The Role of Speaker, Substance and Tone." In *A Crisis of Civility? Political Discourse and Its Discontents,* ed. Robert G. Boatright, Timothy J. Shaffer, Sarah Sobieraj, and Dannagal Goldthwaite Young, 61–80. New York: Routledge.

Tannen, Deborah. 1998. *The Argument Culture: Stopping America's War of Words.* New York: Ballantine Books.

Taylor, Jessica. 2017. "Americans Say Civility Has Worsened Under Trump; Trust in Institutions Down." *NPR,* July 3, 2017. http://www.npr.org/2017/07/03/535044005/americans-say-civility -has-worsened-under-trump-trust-in-institutions-down.

Testa, Paul F., Matthew V. Hibbing, and Melinda Ritchie. 2014. "Orientations Toward Conflict and the Conditional Effects of Political Disagreement." *Journal of Politics* 76(3): 770–785. https://doi.org/10.1017/S0022381614000255.

Teicher, Martin H., Jacqueline A. Samson, Yi-Shin Sheu, Ann Polcari, Cynthia E. McGreenery. 2010. "Hurtful Words: Exposure to Peer Verbal Aggression is Associated With Elevated Psychiatric Symptom Scores and Corpus Callosum Abnormalities." *The American Journal of Psychiatry.* 167(12): 1464.

Thorson, Kjerstin, Emily Vraga, and Brian Ekdale. 2010. "Credibility in Context: How Uncivil Online Commentary Affects News Credibility." *Mass Communication and Society* 13(3): 289–313. https://doi.org/10.1080/15205430903225571.

Trimble, Joseph E., C. M. Fleming, F. Beauvais, and P. Jumper-Thurman. 1996. "Essential Cultural and Social Strategies for Counseling Native American Indians." In *Counseling Across Cultures,* 4th ed., ed. Paul B. Pedersen, Juris G. Draguns, Walter J. Lonner, and Joseph E. Trimble, 177–209. Thousand Oaks, CA: Sage.

Ulbig, Stacy G., and Carolyn L. Funk. 1999. "Conflict Avoidance and Political Participation." *Political Behavior* 21(3): 265–282.

Verba, Sidney, Nancy Burns, and Kay Lerman Schlozman. 1997. "Knowing and Caring About Politics: Gender and Political Engagement." *Journal of Politics* 59(4): 1051–1072. https://doi .org/10.2307/2998592.

Verba, Sidney, Kay Lerman Schlozman, and Henry E. Brady. 1995. *Voice and Equality: Civic Voluntarism in American Politics*. Cambridge, MA: Harvard University Press.

Verba, Sidney and Norman H. Nie. 1972. *Participation in America: Political Democracy and Social Equality*. New York: Harper and Row.

Washington, George. 1988. *George Washington's Rules of Civility and Decent Behaviour in Company and Conversation*. Carlisle, MA: Applewood. https://www.applewoodbooks.com/George -Washingtons-Rules-of-Civility-and-Decent-Behaviour-P1407.aspx.

Weber Shandwick, KRC Research, and Powell Tate. 2013. *Civility in America 2013*. https://www .webershandwick.com/wp-content/uploads/2018/04/Civility_in_America_2013_Exec _Summary.pdf.

——. 2018. *Civility in America 2018*. https://www.webershandwick.com/wp-content/uploads /2018/06/Civility-in-America-VII-FINAL.pdf.

Weyr, Tara Nicole [Director]. 2017. "The Woman Behind the Clothes." *The Bold Type*. ABC, July 18, 2017.

Wolf, Michael R., J. Cherie Strachan, and Daniel M. Shea. 2012. "Incivility and Standing Firm: A Second Layer of Partisan Division." *PS: Political Science and Politics* 45(3): 428–434.

York, Chance. 2013. "Cultivating Political Incivility: Cable News, Network News, and Public Perceptions. *Electronic News* 7(3): 107–125.

Zajonc, Robert B. 1998. "Emotion." In *The Handbook of Social Psychology*, 4th ed., ed. Daniel T. Gilbert, Susan T. Fiske, and Gardner Lindzey, 591–632. New York: McGraw-Hill.

Zerilli, Linda M. G. 2014. "Against Civility: A Feminist Perspective." In *Civility, Legality, and Justice in America*, ed. Austin Sarat, 107–131. Cambridge: Cambridge University Press.

Zhu, Jian-Hua, with William Boroson. 1997. "Susceptibility to Agenda Setting: A Cross-Sectional and Longitudinal Analysis of Individual Differences." In *Communication and Democracy: Exploring the Intellectual Frontiers in Agenda-Setting Theory*, ed. Maxwell McCombs, Donald L. Shaw, and David Weaver, 69–84. Mahwah, NJ: Erlbaum.

INDEX

Page numbers in *italics* indicate figures or tables.

on reactions, 131–139, *135*, *137–138*; summary of, 157, *158–159*. *See also specific studies*
substantive disagreement, 11–12
surveys. *See specific surveys*
Survey Sampling International (SSI) study, 147–148; CCS in, 58, 171–172; conflict orientation in, 59, *60*; data from, 157, *158–159*; emotions in, 60–67, *61*, *63–64*, *66*; incivility in, 67–69, *70–71*; OLS regression in, 62–64, *63–64*; survey questions for, 170–172; transcripts of, 173–174

technology, 1
television: cable, *10*, 10–11, 19, 75; civil discourse on, 147; debates on, 21–22; radio and, 18–19; reality, 98–105, *99*, *101–103*, *105*. *See also* media
Ten-Item Personality Inventory (TIPI), 37–38, *38*, 165, 177–178
Thomas Kilmann instrument, 166–169
TIPI. *See* Ten-Item Personality Inventory
tolerance, 146
tone, of incivility, 14–16, *16*, 21
transcripts, 173–174, 217n1
treatments. *See* studies
trolls (online), 141
Trump, Donald J., 73, 150; political media and, 5–6; tweets by, 2

tune-in hypothesis, 75–76, 89–90, *91–93*, 93–94, *95*, 96–97
Twitter: Facebook and, 80, 116; as media, 142; outrage on, 150–151; politics on, 73–74; in society, 1–2; trolls on, 141

United States. *See* America

values, 13
Verba, Sidney, 111
violent rhetoric, 153–154
virtual reality (VR), 1
vitriol, 5–6
voting, 177, 182; engagement and, 149–150; participation in, 112–117, *114*; political science on, 38, 40; protests and, 120, *121*, 122; psychology of, 11, 71–72, 118–119
VR. *See* virtual reality

Washington, George, 12–13
Weber Shandwick, 6
West Wing, The (TV show), 141
Wilkinson, Stephanie, 152–154
willingness, *209*
Wilson, Joe, 15–17
word choice, 14–15

YouTube, 141

GPSR Authorized Representative: Easy Access System Europe, Mustamäe tee
50, 10621 Tallinn, Estonia, gpsr.requests@easproject.com

www.ingramcontent.com/pod-product-compliance
Lightning Source LLC
Chambersburg PA
CBHW032128020426
42334CB00016B/1086